OCEANS OF THE WORLD

☆

THE PACIFIC OCEAN

THE PACIFIC
OCEAN

BY FELIX RIESENBERG

ILLUSTRATED BY STEPHEN J. VOORHIES

Essay Index Reprint Series

BOOKS FOR LIBRARIES PRESS

FREEPORT, NEW YORK

Publisher's Note

At Felix Riesenberg's untimely death he
had not put the finishing touches on *The
Pacific Ocean*. We wish to acknowledge to
Russell Owen our appreciation of his whole-
hearted cooperation in doing editorial work
on the manuscript and in seeing it through
the press.

INTERNATIONAL STANDARD BOOK NUMBER:
0-8369-2125-9

LIBRARY OF CONGRESS CATALOG CARD NUMBER:
79-128300

PRINTED IN THE UNITED STATES OF AMERICA

To

EARL B. WILSON

Contents

Maps

THE PACIFIC OCEAN

The Unknown Ocean

THE Pacific is the greatest physical unit on earth. From pole to pole, from shore to shore, the Pacific Ocean, even within the arbitrary limitations of the frigid zones, is larger than all the dry lands of the earth put together. It comprises more than a third of the surface of the world and is almost twice as large as the great Atlantic, three times the size of the Indian Ocean, which in itself is larger than the continent of Asia. And this huge sea, strangely enough, was the lost ocean of our earliest recorded history. It was unknown to Europeans up to the Columbian era—only yesterday on the clock face of recorded events. Ancient Egypt is of the minute before now when compared with the dim past of the Pacific.

How the Pacific was formed is one of the mysteries of our earth's evolution. We can guess at what caused the Atlantic. There is, of course, the myth of the lost Atlantis, the continent that sank and left us with thousands of miles of water between the Americas and Europe and Africa. But

Wegener, a famous German geologist, produced the theory that in the beginning there was one huge land mass, of which the Americas and Europe and Asia were but parts. The cooling crust of the earth, he assumed, broke, and North and South America moved to the westward. If you look at the map of the Atlantic you can see that the general outlines of the continents would almost fit together if they were pushed. It is an interesting theory, over which geographers still dispute. Wegener lost his life in Greenland trying to substantiate it, and the observations taken there over a long period of time seem to indicate that Greenland is still moving west, as he predicted it must be. So there is a reasonable hypothesis to account for the Atlantic.

But what caused the Pacific? Nobody knows! It has been suggested that when the earth was in a formative period a vast mass of matter was whirled off by centrifugal force or some inner explosion to form the moon, our dead satellite. More mystical theorists have tried to find a counterpart of Atlantis in the lost continent of Mu, which they place in the middle of the Pacific. There is this much correspondence in the subsurface geography of the Pacific and the Atlantic; both have volcanic ridges through their centers. The basin of the Pacific, surrounded by volcanic peaks, scoured deep by great submarine ravines, tells of some final subsidence of its hemisphere. In the cooling process, with the formation of moisture, came the ocean, the present water cover.

The effect of the ice age, whether the first or one of many, has marked the rocks of the continents. What this accumulation of frozen moisture meant to the oceans, particularly the Pacific, is unknown. Geologists have estimated that the melting of the ice caps added a uniform 260 foot rise to the oceans when most of the waters were restored to the seas. Shallow shore lines, basking in the sun for ages, full of growing life forms, were inundated by the tide of returning waters. The rains, the storms, the lashing hurricanes of those times must have been magnificent beyond all power of description. With the coming back of the waters, the lunar tides gained in their floods, in what we might call the grand spring tides of the earth. Wave fronts of tremendous height and speeds rode across the widest of our oceans, irresistible chargers, sweeping all before them.

The Pacific, or any other ocean of today, differs no whit in appearance from the primitive sea. The aspect of the water world remains unchanged. This majestic permanence of the ocean is reassuring. As Byron wrote:

> Roll on, thou deep and dark-blue Ocean, roll!
> Ten thousand fleets sweep over thee in vain;
> Man marks the earth with ruin, his control
> Stops with the shore . . .

The enduring old sea makes the most ancient pyramids seem like puny milestones set up only a few day's journey backward into time. The age of the sea is nowhere so clearly stated as by Joseph Conrad.

"It seems to me," he wrote, "that no man born and truthful to himself could declare that he ever saw the sea looking young as the earth looks young in spring. But some of us, regarding the ocean with understanding and affection, have seen it looking old, as if the immemorial ages had been stirred up from the undisturbed bottom of ooze. For it is a gale of wind that makes the sea look old."

Conrad, out of bitter wisdom, set down a further deeply moving truth.

"If you would know the age of the earth, look upon the sea in a storm. The grayness of the whole immense surface, the wind furrows upon the faces of the waves, the great masses of foam, tossed about and waving, like matted white locks, give to the sea in a gale an appearance of hoary age, lustreless, dull, without gleams, as though it had been created before life itself."

And that is our Pacific, the vastest body of water under the sun, its origin remote and mysterious, its discovery a matter so recent that even now there are islets on which it is not certain that man ever stood. Its distances are so great that those who have crossed it have spent weeks without sighting land or ship, although they have gone through groups of islands and crossed ship lanes. It is Neptune's playground, if there is ever any place that that hoary old rascal would seek to hide, away from the prying eyes of modern skeptics.

One can only guess at its early navigators. The strange statues on Easter Island, the origin of which have puzzled investigators for years, the migrations of the Polynesians, the legends of the Far East, all indicate that the Pacific must have been crossed many centuries before Columbus. But by whom and how we do not know. There is the story of the Chinese sailor Hee Li, whose name is strangely significant in modern pronunciation, who was driven off the coast of China in the year 200 B.C. until he reached the distant land of Fu Sang and explored the coast for 100 miles. He is supposed to have entered the great bay of Hong Tee, said to be San Francisco Bay. But we rather think Hee Li.

The first intimation Europeans had of the Pacific came from Marco Polo, who hinted at a great sea east of Zipangu, or Japan, which he visited. But his account is somewhat confusing, for, although he says Zipangu lies in the Sea of Chin, which contains 7,440 islands and which sounds very much like the Pacific, there are also about that many islands in the Philippine group, bordering on the Sea of Chin, or the China Sea. But Polo could hardly have visited Japan without learning of a great ocean to the east, for the Japanese were hardy sailors.

There is no doubt, however, as to the Polynesian (including in that general designation all the racial groups in the South Seas) invasion of the Pacific long before a white man ever saw it. There were great migrations among the islands of the South Seas, and perhaps the first people who came to the islands were driven from Asia. Of their navigational skill there is no doubt.

On De Bougainville's voyage a native, Antourou, pointed at night to the bright star in Orion's shoulder, saying that if their course were guided by it they would in two days come to a fertile island where he had friends. When they paid no attention to him, he tried to take the wheel and put it over.

He might have underestimated the time, for it is probable that the Polynesian canoes sailed faster than the white man's ships. They were extraordinary craft, the ones used for long voyages being double, and anywhere from sixty to eighty feet long. The war canoes of Tahiti held 100 men. In these vessels the Polynesians made long voyages. Dr. Peter Buck, whose mother was a Maori and who has made the most thorough investigation of the South Sea Islanders' migrations, believes that some of the islanders, before the thirteenth century, made a 4,000 mile journey from the Marquesas to Peru and brought back the sweet potato, which has been widely distributed among the South Sea Islands. The potato was there when the white man arrived, and the nearest place it could have come from in those days was Peru.

Their navigation was largely by means of the trade winds and the stars, although they also made use of what is known as a kite chart, a frame held together with strings of fine fiber and marked with shells at the intersections to represent islands or reefs. These fascinating representations, oriented to the stars or the sun, show courses (directions), give data on prevailing winds at various seasons, current drifts, and distances between the islands. Every group of islands had its kite chart. Captain Winkler, of the Imperial German Navy, made a study of these navigation aids in an attempt to gain some knowledge of how they were used. The Polynesians used sea anchors to lie to in a storm and light anchors with which to gauge currents, instruments about as efficient as those used by the United States government expedition that explored the Pacific in the middle of the last century. They carried provisions for four or five weeks, cooked meat wrapped in leaves and water. And their craft were fast, so fast that it is not impossible that a large proa, manned by the old daring Polynesian sailors, would give any commodore, in an American Cup yacht, a run for his money.

So it is not astonishing that a race that could adapt itself to the ocean in so masterly a way should have crossed the Pacific from island group to island group. They probably came from Asia by way of Micronesia, with the center of the spreading, Tahiti, in the Society Islands. These islands were probably settled in 500 A.D., 1,200 years before Captain Cook's famous voyages. The Rarotongans count back to their ancestor, Tangiia, who was the last of the ancients to arrive on their islands, twenty-six generations back. Counting twenty-five years to a generation, Tangiia must have arrived about 1250 A.D. A more doubtful count of generations goes back ninety-two, to Tu-te-gangi-marama, who dwelt in a land believed by historians to have been India. This would put his journey 2,500 years ago, in 450 B.C. But Dr. Buck thinks such a prodigious feat of memory is somewhat doubtful.

Since there are no written records, what went on through the centuries to the time of recent historical discoveries must remain a mystery. But the old Magellanic navigators and the more recent voyagers found a people happy and free, and had they known it, the European stream was meeting the Pacific stream of the same old Asian stock, if some theories of the anthropologists hold true. Climate had modified them, but many of them were extremely intelligent and had features of such beauty that the early navigators could not help commenting on it.

This was the ocean and these the unknown and ancient people upon whom our European pioneers stumbled after Balboa stood on a mountain peak and saw the eastern sea.

Balboa Discovers the Pacific

A YEAR before the discovery of Florida, Vasco Núñez de Balboa, native of Xeres, Spain, a soldier of fortune who had sailed in the wake of the last Columbian voyages with those who sought fortune in the Indies, had become involved in debt. Process servers and marshals hounded him. His reputation as a fiery and adroit swordsman kept most of them at a distance, but in 1511 Balboa had himself headed up in a cask marked "Victuals for Voyage" and was hoisted aboard a caravel bound from Hispaniola to the mainland of New Spain.

When out of sight of land, Captain Hernandez de Encisco, master of the caravel, was confronted by the intrepid Balboa, tall, muscular, and fingering his famous sword, which he had taken with him into the cask. At once the adventurer found favor when he boldly declared to the ship's company that a venerable priest had assured him, "Don Núñez Balboa. God has reserved you for great things!"

So the world's most illustrious stowaway landed in Darien.

Balboa, intrepid, enterprising and ambitious, acquired authority over a vast tract of the country. He reformed the wretched remains of Santa Maria de Antigua, founded two years before by Ojeda. The settlers elected him their governor. Balboa married the beautiful young daughter of the powerful Cacique of Coyba, leading the cacique's warriors against the armies of neighboring native princes. On one of these expeditions, when 4,000 ounces of gold had been taken as booty, together with many golden vessels, Balboa divided it by weight, one fifth for King Ferdinand, one fifth for himself, and the rest share and share alike among his Spanish followers.

When a dispute arose as to the fairness of this division, one of the captured Indians, a prince from whom the treasure had been taken, spoke in disdain. "Why should you quarrel over such a trifle? If gold is so precious that you abandon your homes for it and invade the peaceful lands of others, I will tell you of a region where you may gratify your desires to the utmost."

Pointing westward across the cloud topped ridges, he continued, "Beyond those lofty mountains lies a mighty sea, greater than any your ships have yet sailed. It is navigated by people who have vessels almost as large as yours, and, like them, furnished with sails and oars. The streams that flow from yonder mountains into the great sea abound in gold. The people on its borders eat and drink from golden vessels. Gold is as common there as iron among you Spaniards."

News of the great sea and its ships and kings interested Balboa, but the story of its abundant gold fired him. He asked whether it would be difficult to reach this sea and its treasures.

"The task," the Indian warned him, "is most arduous and fraught with dangers. Powerful caciques will oppose you with all their forces. Cannibals will attack you and will devour those whom they kill. To accomplish this enterprise, Don Balboa, you will require a thousand armed men, like those you have with you. The caciques of the great sea have long been my enemies, if you wish I will accompany you at the head of my warriors."

This was the first word received by Europeans of a sea lying to the westward of the Indies of Columbus. Till then they had supposed themselves somewhere on the eastern edge of Asia, the land of the Grand Khan, on the outskirts of the Indies.

Balboa saw before him the prospect of immeasurable wealth and of a glorious discovery. He rewarded the Indian prince by baptizing him, calling him Jesus, thereby saving his soul and enlisting his help. Balboa marched back to the Mosquito Coast on the Gulf of Darien and prepared to undertake the great enterprise.

He sent gold to Hispaniola for men and provisions, but the ship of his emissary was cast away on Jamaica. He wrote Don Diego Columbus, Governor of Santo Domingo, telling of gold and of the existence of a vast new ocean to the westward and asking for 1,000 men with whom to carry on this new discovery. He then forwarded 15,000 crowns in gold to be transmitted to Ferdinand as his royal fifth of treasures already taken. Many of Balboa's followers sent home sums for their creditors in Spain. But, even though money talks, Balboa had fallen into disgrace with King Ferdinand, and only a brilliant achievement, a bold stroke, could return him to the royal favor. He would wait no longer. Choosing 190 of his most resolute men, with a body of native warriors and a pack of bloodhounds, Balboa started on the sixty mile march across the isthmus, and on Sept. 1, 1513, the expedition moved inland from Santa Maria de Antigua.

After the expedition had abandoned a stream that carried them in nine canoes and a small brigantine to the end of navigation at Coyba, the march was through tropical jungle. The steep mountains were thick with tangled forests; the low grounds were covered with swamps giving off toxic exhalations. Torrents raged down deep ravines, often forcing the marchers to retrace their steps. Hostile tribesmen clung to their flanks, attacking at night.

In a battle with a cacique named Quaragua, 600 Indians were slain. Balboa's men, in chain mail, charged them with swords and lances, and, as the wounded natives fell, they were torn by bloodhounds. Never had the Indians of the isthmus encountered such ferocious war makers. With the greatest geographical prize of all time lying close before him and the lure of vast treasures driving him on, with ambition and greed and desire for glory flying around in his feverish head, Balboa pushed through the ghastly region, dropping his men as they were wounded. Before them was the cool blue promise of the toppling hills. Many died of raging fevers. As the survivors gained altitude, the colder air revived them. Still only sixty-seven men remained to make the final ascent. Most of these were Spaniards, the natives having been killed or having deserted the leadership of the intrepid don.

Balboa made camp before the final climb, and all but the bloodhounds slept. On Sept. 26, at daybreak, the small party emerged from their forest camp, scaling the last of the higher slopes until only the bald summit remained.

The leader ordered them to halt. He himself, weary as he was, mounted to the topmost peak. As his sight fell upon the magnificent ocean, golden in the rays of the ascending sun, Balboa called his men, fell upon his knees and returned thanks to God. When they gathered about him, peering out into the morning west, the sun almost overhead by that time, they shaded their eyes, exclaiming their astonishment and joy. Vasco addressed those few survivors of the jungle, the dogs about them.

"Behold, my friends, the glorious sight we have so ardently longed for. Let us pray."

They knelt and gave thanks, making the sign of the cross.

"God will now aid and guide us," went on Balboa, "to conquer the sea and land we have discovered, which no

Christian has yet entered to preach the holy doctrine of the Evangelists."

The priest, one among the survivors, spared by God for his holy office, chanted the impressive *Te Deum,* and the lean, scarred sunburned men joined in the responses with heart and voice.

"By the favor of Christ," went on Balboa, as they crowded about him following their devotion, "you will be the richest Spaniards that have ever come to the Indies."

"Viva el rey Fernando! Viva España! Viva Balboa!" The men cheered.

The leader then called all present to witness that he took possession of the distant sea, its islands and surrounding shores in the name of his sovereigns of Castile. The notary of the expedition made a record of this to which all, to the number of sixty-seven, signed their names. Balboa then caused a tree to be cut down and fashioned in the form of a cross. This he set up on the spot from which he had first beheld the ocean. A cairn of stones was likewise piled up, and the names of Ferdinand and Juana were carved on neighboring trees.

Balboa camped his party for rest while scouts under Alonzo Martín de Benito, his lieutenant, descended toward the south to discover the best route to the golden beach. After two days these men reached the sea and came upon some abandoned canoes hauled far up on the wide sands. The tide began to flood with astonishing rapidity, whereupon Lieutenant Martín stepped into one of the canoes—the first European to be afloat in the new ocean.

Martín returned with his party, and Balboa, with all his men, marched to the coast. Again they noted the wide tidal flats. The place where they rested was inundated by the waters, as if the Great South Sea were rushing landward to bid them welcome.

Balboa, ever the dramatic figure, in full armor against attack by natives who had retreated into the brush and forest, grasped a silken banner showing an image of the Virgin and Child and bearing the arms of Castile and Leon. Armed with sword and shield, he waded knee-deep into the rising water, held his standard aloft, and declared physical possession. Against the warm sea wind blowing from the south out of the old Bay of Panama, the discoverer of the mightiest of oceans shouted the most grandiloquent of all historic claims.

"Long live the high and mighty monarchs Don Ferdinand and Donna Juana, sovereigns of Castile, Leon, and Aragon!"

Vivas from the beach came to him. He flushed and went on with his exalted message. "In their name I take possession of these seas and lands and coasts and ports and the islands of the south and all thereunto annexed; and of the kingdoms and provinces which do and may appertain to them in whatever manner or by whatever right or title, ancient or modern, in times past, present, or to come, without any contradiction; and, if other prince or captain, Christian or infidel, or if any law, condition, or sect whatsoever shall pretend any right to these lands and seas, I am ready to maintain and defend them in the name of the Castilian sovereigns, whose is the empire and dominion over these Indies, islands, terra firma, northern and southern, with all the seas, both to the Arctic and Antarctic poles, on either side of the equinoctial line, whether within or without the Tropic of Cancer and Tropic of Capricorn, both now and in all time, as long as the world endure, and until the final day of judgment of all mankind!"

Vivas and more *vivas* greeted Balboa as he returned to the shore, his face aglow with the triumph of his tremendous accomplishment.

Again the notary set it all down on parchment in legal words and phrases, and again all signed. They tasted the water, which was ocean salt. They carved a cross on a great tree, the roots of which were below high water. Lopping off a branch with a single stroke of his sword, Balboa bore it away as a trophy. Then he ordered his men to march back from the reaching tide.

More canoes were found, and in spite of warnings from some friendly Indians, who declared the season stormy, the very depth of the equinox, the Spaniards embarked in nine canoes. A tempest swept over the sea, driving them to a low island for refuge. At night the tide submerged their landings, rising to their waists. The canoes were broken to pieces or swept away. Then at low tide in the daylight, with great difficulty, they managed to regain the mainland.

After numerous raids against the caciques ruling that region, with little gold to show for them, Balboa retraced his march back over the mountains, arriving at the River of Darien on Jan. 19, 1514. He had accomplished an historic discovery, had revealed a great hitherto unknown ocean, and had claimed a hemisphere for Spain.

History has carved deep a date, Sept. 26, 1513, when the first European saw the great ocean, the South Sea, stretching south and west, extending to the uttermost ends of a new and undiscovered hemisphere. Balboa must have had some inner vision of the tremendous significance of his discovery. Since ancient times, the Dark Ages, the Middle Ages, and the Renaissance, Europeans had struggled through a half world. Balboa could see only to an horizon that looked much the same as do the rims of lesser seas, but something vast seemed to lift out of that inspiring ocean breathing before him to the endless West.

Man has no record as to when the Atlantic was first seen or when, in the dim mists of time, the first Egyptians, the early Chinese, or other voyagers of antiquity—perhaps the Phoenicians—beheld the Indian Ocean. There is no record of the discovery of the Arctic Sea beyond the legends of Pytheas, or the vague sagas of the Norsemen. The grim Antarctic—well, Francis Drake came as near discovering it as anyone; or perhaps the honor belongs to one of the unnamed ships of old

Comargo. But the Pacific, as we know it, greatest of earth's oceans, is definitely the discovery of that very human, roistering, ambitious, avaricious soldier of fortune, Vasco Núñez de Balboa.

Ferdinand, never too friendly, had created Balboa *adelantado* of the South Sea and governor of Panama and Coyba. There was no question of rewarding this soldier of fortune, for Balboa collected at the source. Vasco Núñez de Balboa was no shrinking violet. His men were devoted to him; his officers were brawling leaders; all had grown rich in raids against the gold-bearing Indians.

Over long periods of time, news filtered to the Indies of the boy King Charles I. What was happening in Spain? Old King Ferdinand, mightiest monarch of the Columbian era, conqueror of Granada, victor over the Moors; Ferdinand V of Castile, II of Aragon and Sicily, III of Naples, greatest empire builder of the age of discovery, clever, grasping, strong, died in 1516, the third year after Balboa's discovery and magnificent claims. And in Valladolid, the old capital of Castile, where sat the court, the young King Charles and his old advisers, word came of Balboa, growing richer and more powerful in the distant Indies.

God, having given immortality to Balboa, seemed to withdraw his favor.

So the cautious crown made Balboa subject to the authority of Pedrarias Davila, governor of Darien. With the ascension of Charles I, orders went to Pedrarias. "Get Balboa," would be a literal modern translation, "and get him quick."

The discoverer and his principal lieutenants—all swordsmen, profligate spenders, feared by men, and great hands with the women—were clapped in irons without warning and charged with treason against the crown. An alcalde, under orders from the governor, pronounced them guilty. Pedrarias, following instructions, condemned Balboa and his principal officers to death as usurpers of the territories of the crown.

The execution by beheading took place immediately in the public square of a small town near Darien in the initial year of the reign of Charles I. The governor of Darien watched the execution from between the reeds of a small house only twelve paces from the block. The influence of Balboa was so strong that he feared a revolt. Four of the discoverer's lieutenants were beheaded in quick succession after their leader in the twilight of a tropical evening in 1517.

Pedrarias Davila confiscated Balboa's wealth in the name of the crown and ordered his head to be impaled and exposed in the public square.

The fates, watching the consummation of a grand discovery, placed a memorable period at the close of its triumph.

Magellan: The Great Navigator

NO PHASE of the earth's unfolding story is more brilliant with the fire of heroic purpose than the first crossing of the greatest of oceans. After Balboa saw the Pacific, it was inevitable that some man should determine to conquer it, and Magellan's purpose to sail boldly over an unknown sea across a dread succession of doubtful longitudes was the high point in his circumnavigation of the world. Even the voyage of Columbus is trifling beside it.

Magellan was born about 1480 of Portuguese parents. He went to sea early and took part in some notable voyages before King Emanuel of Portugal, in 1515, rejected his proposal to make a voyage around the world. He did not know that there was a passage, but the news of Balboa's discovery must have reached his ears, and, good navigator that he was, he knew that there was a way around Africa—so why not around the land on which Balboa had stood, to the sea that Balboa had seen? Magellan, in disgrace in his own country, went to Spain and became a subject of Charles I. Charles was more sympathetic to Magellan's plans than Emanuel had been and gave him a fleet of five ships, the *Trinidada*, the *San Antonio*, the *Concepcion*, the *Vittoria*, and the *Santiago*. They were all small, the largest being 110 tons, and all were unsafe until Magellan made them seaworthy. On Tuesday, Sept. 20, 1519, they sailed from San Lúcar. And there started the greatest voyage ever made by man.

Magellan met resistance and even mutiny early in his voyage. Six months out from Spain he was far south on the coast of South America, his ships foul, short of provisions, in need of overhauling. There was no sign of a strait to the westward, and his crews were weary of cold and hunger. Three ships, the *San Antonio*, the *Concepcion*, and the *Vittoria*, were in revolt. Magellan had the ringleader stabbed and fought down the mutineers. He repaired his ships. Bands of natives, called Patagones, or Big Feet, by Magellan, began to appear, and some of them were captured. He wintered near the end of the continent and then put south again, and, on Oct. 21, 1520, St. Ursula's Day, they came to a wide open bight extending to the horizon in the west. A headland was named the Cape of the Eleven Thousand Virgins, and the strait was called the Channel of the Saints. But men know it today as the Strait of Magellan, and they call the clustered clouds of stars that hover overhead, in those latitudes, the Magellanic clouds.

Ferdinand Magellan was forty years old when he first saw the great Pacific. He was Knight of Santiago and Knight of St. James of the Sword, a proud, an arrogant commander, a square built man with a slight limp from an old wound, of middle stature, dark eyed, his black beard streaked with gray. He looked and walked like a sailor. On Nov. 28, 1520, his other ships having gone home or been wrecked, he led his little fleet, the *Trinidada*, the *Concepcion*, and the *Vittoria*, around the western promontory of Tierra del Fuego, commander of the first European ships ever to plow the Pacific.

Much history has been written of this bold departure into an unknown ocean. Scholar after scholar, through the centuries, has painted over the dim portrait until only bare outlines remain. Of the original surviving records, an abstract of the Journal of Antonio Pigafetta, patrician of Vicenza and Knight of Rhodes, sheds the high light of hardship, of superhuman endurance, on this ocean passage. Francisco Albo, Magellan's chief pilot, kept a terse seamanlike reckoning, entering the courses and each day's run, with the latitude by meridian altitude of the sun, measured by astrolabe. From this navigation log, accurate beyond belief, the way and progress of Magellan's ships have been preserved.

Although latitudes were accurate by observation, longitudes were problematical; charts carried by Magellan gave no indication of the actual distances of the vast ocean he was crossing. As sea birds might fly, 10,000 miles of ocean lay before him. As Magellan and Albo reckoned their departures, westward the ships made a distance over the mighty sea of at least 12,000 miles by log, ranging in latitude from Cape Deseado, in 50 degrees south of the equator, to 16 degrees north, for in their progress they crossed the Line and by the strangest of fates missed scores of unknown islands.

The disappearance of Magellan's personal journals, the disasters that overtook his ships and men and the innermost thoughts and plans of the great discoverer. Magellan had been in the Moluccas and was familiar with the Portuguese Indies, and he knew their longitude. He had voyaged twice to the Spice Islands, doubling the dread Cape of Good Hope four times, going and coming. Also, from his reckoning, he knew the approximate longitude of Cape Deseado. Magellan, who was one of the ablest geographers of his day, knew the approximate circumference of the earth. When he gave orders to stand across the South Sea, he had no delusion as to its mighty breadth. Whatever others may have thought, he at least knew the magnitude of the task lying ahead of him. It was Magellan's deliberate decision to take the supreme chance.

With the *Trinidada* leading, on that day of departure from Tierra del Fuego, the sun set behind a gray bank of western cloud, gusty southwest squalls held the pitching, rolling ships on their larboard tacks, with only lower sails and sprits trimmed to a heavy wind. White-bearded seas washed along their sides and slapped over their forecastles, cold water cascading into their waists. Anchors were still lashed on the bows, for at any moment in the coming night rocks or land might leap out of the black unknown ahead. The Captain General, his commanders, pilots, and the masters stood their watches with the keenest caution. That these men were superb sailors is proved by their beat westward through the unknown rock-strewn Channels of the Saints. They kept all ships, except one lost by desertion, grounding none and losing no anchors. Magellan Strait navigators, in the centuries that have passed, have realized more and more the superb seacraft of these ancient mariners.

Historians have told the meager details that have been left on this most hazardous and daring ocean passage, the repeated stories of their sufferings, but little enough of the obvious and certain actions of the commanders and their men.

Although the original expendable stores of the three surviving ships had been depleted by fourteen months of voyaging since the departure from San Lúcar, the navigational equipment, as allotted to the various ships, was largely intact. The parchment charts prepared by Nuño García, the portolanos (or *portolantos*, as old accounts have it) drawn on parchment, subject to large changes in size because of dampness or excessive drying, gave the navigators no hint whatever as to the course that lay ahead of them and only the most unreliable outline of the eastern islands of the Indies, the Moluccas, and perhaps the shores of ancient Zipangu. Of this last coast line the old cartographers had little more knowledge than that given by Marco Polo and his followers, few of whom were seamen or navigators.

Magellan and his pilots knew of the variation of the magnetic needle, and each clear day at meridian they observed the shadow of the sun thrown by a style across the cards of the huge dry compasses, of which one at least was mounted in a binnacle, set forward of the helm. A spare or two were also carried. Magnetic needles, which often varied in directive force, were strengthened by rubbing with a lodestone, and Magellan seems to have taken with him some thirty extra magnetized iron needles or bars. The Armada was well stocked with hourglasses, and each ship carried at least one timepiece supplied by Bernaldino del Castillo, from Cadiz. Whether the name was that of a maker or of an ancient ship chandler is not known, and probably the timekeepers were worthless, huge watches the size of buckets and not much more reliable. The sun, however, was their clock, as accurate then as now.

Magellan carried a globe, possibly a copy of the famous globe of Martin Behaim. Before leaving Seville, he spent 340 maravedis for a leather box to hold this precious proof that the world was round.

Of logs, for the measuring of distance made, there is no record. But the mariners, using an amazingly accurate sense of estimation, measured distance in leagues, possibly three or four miles in length, as usually reckoned.

Unlaying the ancient tangled coil, one comes to the most simple sort of navigation. The astrolabes, of which Magellan had the best instruments of bronze and a huge wooden sea astrolabe said to have been made by Martin Behaim, were huge circles graduated to degrees and parts of a degree, even down to minutes. These were suspended by a ring, and the beams of the sun were caught by pinules in a pivoted alidade, the circle, where the fiducial edges lay, measuring the altitude and zenith angle.

The declination of the sun, either north or south of the equator, or equinoctial circle, as it was then called, was given for each date in the tables of declination, those most probably used being the tables originated by Regiomontanus, the name adopted by a German astronomer, Johann Müller, of Nuremberg. These values of the sun's angular distance north or south of the equator were reasonably accurate, the inclination of the earth with respect to the sun's orbit being understood. Copernicus was contemporary with Magellan, though thirty years his junior, but *De Revolutionibus Orbium*, of Copernicus, was dedicated to Pope Paulus III, in the forties of the sixteenth century, long after the classic voyage of Magellan.

The navigation of the Captain General and his pilots rested on the use of that very ancient Arabian instrument, the astrolabe, developed in the first century. Geoffrey Chaucer clearly explained its use fourteen centuries after Christ: "Put the ring of thine astrolabe upon thy right thumb and turn thy left side against the light of the sun and move thy rewel up and down till the streams of the sun shine through both holes of thy rewel. Look then how many degrees thy rewel is raised from the little cross upon the est line and take there the altitude of thy sun."

And so, estimating their speed and distance, noting the true compass reading, watching the unfamiliar stars of the Southern Cross sink lower each night as they made their transits, observing their *alturias*, noting the courses and distances, the navigators, with Francisco Albo keeping the only log that survived, piloted the Armada northward. For Magellan, anxious to get out of harsh weather, made little westing during the first part of his ocean traverse.

On the morning of Nov. 29, the Armada was out of sight of the bleak lands they had quitted when leaving the strait. Mighty rollers tumbled in under them, and at daybreak signals were made to carry all possible sail. Reefed topsails were sheeted and hoisted, the helms were double manned, and in *La Diana*, the watch of the morning star, the flagship roomed ahead. For the wind held fair, and, sailing at the point of a triangle, the too lesser consorts clung to her quarters. They kept close, and during the night the consorts watched the faggots burning on the *Trinidada's* poop.

Whatever feeling the crews and their officers had as to dangers ahead, was kept in check by the strict routine of the ships, the washing down of decks, the preparation of breakfast, on the shortest of rations. But they were well stocked with wood; the galleys smoked, and the fish or penguin broth and a short allowance of moldy biscuit were served. Little remained aboard the ships of the delicacies carried from Spain, however. Figs, cheeses, the wine from Xeres, in 508 bottles, were nearly gone. The 420 casks of common wine were depleted; each ship had only a small quantity left in ullage casks, only partly full because of the evaporation. The Spanish anchovies were gone, but newly salted fish had been taken in abundance at the River of Sardines. The Captain General, aware of the state of provisions and water, estimated his chances of falling in with islands, of getting across the tremendous ocean.

Expecting a wide westerly trend of the shore, he was assured by and also astonished at the absence of land on his starboard. So the course was held to the north, the wind being drawn astern. The ships rolled out their wales, plunged and lifted like huge porpoises, and they noted a slight rise in the warmth. But for this they had no measure since more than a century was to pass before Réaumur invented the thermometer. But warmth there was, and the Captain General and his pilots noted a lightening of the wind. He changed course to the east of north. What had become of the great continent of South America? They had rounded it, but where was it?

On Dec. 16, they again made the land, for the morning sun rose behind the lofty Cordilleras, mighty blue peaks standing above the eastern horizon like the teeth of a shark. The American coast, which no European had yet seen in that latitude, trended almost north and south. There, also, as the sun lifted, were reflected ice and snow. Magellan, fearing for his dwindling stores and the unknown westward distance ahead, signaled to change course to the northwest. Few historians have given him credit for first sighting the mighty southern coastal Andes. What he set down in his own log of this north trending coast and its significance we can only guess.

Had Magellan stood a few points more to the westward or had he met with different winds, he would in all probability have sighted the high islands of Juan Fernandez rising 4,000 feet out of the sea! Well wooded and watered, rich in vegetation, abundant in animal life, endowed with safe and easy anchorages, these islands would have greatly aided him. Fernandez, who discovered the group of two chief islands, made his landfall in 1563, forty-three years after Magellan passed northeast and almost in sight of them, a scant 100 miles away—a close shave in a total distance of 12,000 miles.

North of the 34th parallel, a delightful change came over the wide blue stretches of Mar del Sur. The winds held steadily from the southeast, days of gentle breezes were succeeded by velvet nights of peaceful, starlit skies. The strange Southern Cross began to dip lower and lower, meteors burst out of the black skies like fiery lances splitting on a celestial shield, and the bellying courses, the great square lower sails, often caught sea swallows, as they called them—stray flying fishes.

The ships trailed their hame, or fishhooks, but with small result. Harpoons were ready in the heads, but few fish, it seemed, dared venture so far from the land. Great monsters spouted far off, but this was before the age of ocean whaling. When dolphins sported near, they dashed away again. One sun-drenched day followed another, always with the placid nights between, with their march of silent stars but never a glimpse of land. Sea birds kept giving hope of land to the mariners, for they skirted luscious coral isles, passing close northward of the Tuamotu or Low Archipelago, just out of sight of the myriad palm-fringed atolls seen later by their more fortunate followers. But the Armada's lookouts saw nothing but an empty sea.

Magellan, sailing for seemingly endless days, always into placid ocean, no longer beset by storms, except those of doubt, called this vast Mar del Sur the Pacific Ocean. The genius of this man is nowhere more apparent than in his christenings of an ocean, of lands and capes and islands. These Magellanic names have endured and will continue to endure as long as there are charts and men to read them.

A terrifying shadow of fear began to haunt the ships. Too many empty days were passing while they sailed onward across an ocean that appeared to be nothing but a waste of blue water rippling under the caress of gentle winds, and without end. The warmth increased, and the waxing and waning of the moon shed fitful shadows on the sea.

Now two burning months had passed over the dumpy little ships. Their crowded decks were like loathsome ovens, for vile fumes arose from the bilges, and the leaking seams only added to the damp corruption. The daily clank of the ancient back-breaking pumps sounded like a knell. The flap of idle sails when a lull came in the wind, filled them with added fear; the distant passing of thunderclouds maddened them. They saw waterspouts, and a few times they caught some rain in spare sails; otherwise they would have perished from thirst.

We have the testimony of Pigafetta, writing of Magellan: "Among the many other virtues that adorned him, one was especially remarkable, that he always remained exceptionally steadfast even amid the greatest misfortunes. He bore the pangs of hunger more patiently than did any of us."

On that harrowing passage there was no discrimination. All were "on the whack," as sailors say, from the Captain

General down to the youngest boy, Juan de Zubileta. And these sailors were young men mostly, in their early twenties, endowed by nature with ravenous appetites.

Their sunken eyes were burning with the dull madness of thirst and hunger, tortured eyes that had already lived a dozen lifetimes. Their bodies began to swell, their legs and ankles puffed to great size, their bleeding gums dropped over their loosened teeth, and ulcers formed in their mouths and on bodies already tortured by lice. Toes and fingers became like punk; the nails sloughed off. Their breaths were like sewers. Only the most vigorous could douse themselves with salt water.

The three watches were depleted by sickness; the binnacle lists (those unable to bear a hand) increased. We have no muster roll of the entire Armada—only the names of the final survivors and of those mentioned in the Pigafetta narrative. The total numerical strength, or, rather, weakness, remaining in the three ocean-crossing ships stood at about 150. At the start the vessels carried about one man for each two tons of burthen. Casualties cut down this manning by one half.

The one antiseptic of those days—vinegar—had long been exhausted in spite of 2,000 pounds taken from San Lúcar; but the wind, the sun, and salt water enabled them to lengthen their existence. These seamen, unlike others the Pacific knew, refrained from cannibalism. They clung to faith and prayer and discipline under three captains—Magellan, Serrano, and Barbosa.

Those who have made long sea passages under sail know how far science has advanced, but for centuries after Magellan, scurvy plagued the sailor. Wooden casks for water, warping barrels for dry stores, bottles with rotting corks for wine—these were their containers.

The crews, fighting vermin, also hunted rodents, and the starving men half roasted and swallowed this repulsive game. Sawdust was mixed with the decaying biscuits, and the mess was baked, the worms or maggots dying in the heat and adding somewhat to the nourishment.

As they rolled in the doldrums, between the trade wind belts, they began to strip all chafing leather, the hardened hides on the yards and stays. These had become so indurated with salt and so burned dry with the sun that they had to be towed overboard for softening before being cut up and rationed to the famished crews. During all this time the ships held company; the bells were struck, masses were said, prayers were offered, and the bearded Captain General and his pilots held their course while hopeless lookouts peered ahead for land.

Running between unknown and unseen atolls, a miracle of missing, they crossed the equator in longitude 158 west. For the first time in over a year they again saw La Tramontana, the Pole Star, lifting to the north, over the edge of the black horizon. On Jan. 24, 1521, came the cry, "Land ho!" shouted from the masthead of the flagship. They fired a bombard, the signal for land. The ships altered course. It was an island. The ships hove to, the weak people hoisted out boats in a sea alive with sharks snapping at the oars as they beached on a deserted islet lifting only a few hardy wind-bent palms. They found the spot of sand devoid of water, a desert waste. They called it St. Paul. Eleven days later they sighted yet another desert in the sea, also surrounded by sharks. They called it Tiburano. So feverish and so exhausted were the mariners that wild visions of springs, of fruits, and of rest filled them with mad hallucinations.

And Pigafetta set down the disappointments. "Since we found there neither people, nor consolation nor sustenance of any kind, the name of Desaventuradas was given them." That is, the Unfortunate Isles, for Magellan coupled the two, though they were many leagues apart.

Then, bearing straight to the west, with the Pole Star 16

degrees above the horizon, they moved before a brisk north-west trade, all on the verge of death, the command and the helm being kept by the utter will of desperation. Sooner or later, perhaps too late, Ferdinand Magellan knew they would be across or helplessly adrift on that terrible ocean of death, the dread Pacific.

Guam and the Isles of Spice

WHEN the second desert Island of Sharks dropped astern, on the night of Feb. 4, the Armada held course just northward of west, keeping the Pole Star abeam, checking the compasses by this reliable mark as well as by the sun. The latitude was 13 degrees, though old reckonings have given it as 3 degrees farther to the north. Perhaps the navigators, with their swollen lids and burning eyes, were no longer so accurate as before. Some rain must have helped keep them alive, and an unsinkable faith alone upheld them. The Captain General knew that mainland, or inhabited islands at least, lay somewhere not far ahead. A torturing month and two days, a time when even Pigafetta no longer remembered much besides the date, wore over them. The ships were foul; they leaked more than ever, especially the flagship and the *Concepcion*, and the crews no longer were able to do more than steer. The frayed sails could not be repaired;

canvas hanging from the yards was left to stand as best it might. All the disgusting powdery biscuit had been expended.

With long, matted beards, with torturing swollen joints, with death walking among them, the constant murmur of passing water sliding by and astern alone gave them hope. A calm—and this is no unusual thing at the lower edge of the northeast trade winds—would have soon left nothing but three charnel ships drifting aimlessly on the sea.

Pigafetta set down the words: "If our Lord and his Mother had not aided us in giving us good weather . . . we should all have died of hunger in this very vast sea, and I think that never man will undertake to perform such a voyage."

Rain, undoubtedly, had been their salvation, for the Knight of Rhodes omitted the word, the terrible word "thirst."

But never before and seldom since have ships been reduced to the utter extreme of endurance that was the fate of the Magellan Armada as it crossed the 145th degree of east longitude. The crews were so exhausted that no one knew whose watch it was. Men lay about the decks, half dead and dying. Only the strongest few were still mounting to the tops for lookout. The three captains were on their poops; the ships steered weakly, yawing points each way. A morning breeze blew in from the northeast. The yards were trimmed by the larboard braces, the flowing fuzzy sheets of hemp strained with creaking eagerness, moving in the dry bulwark sheaves.

As the Pole Star faded, cobalt colors of the sea began to lighten to that implacable empty blue. A line of pale green in the east crept under the night. The light of day fanned over their high sterns. But lookouts, as for many futile days before, were directed to the west. The *Trinidada*, wallowing far in advance of her consorts, her topsails glowing brownish gold, was shocked to life. "*Vigia, vigia* . . . " A feeble cry fell from the maintop. "Land! Land!" This incredible shout ran through the ship as its starving men rose to hang on bulwarks, and a few boys climbed the weather rigging. Off on the starboard bow was a dark shape.

"*Gunner! The bombard!*" Magellan gave the order. Old Master Andrew of Bristol, in the last stages of complete exhaustion, was still able to apply the match. A puff of smoke rolled from the flagship's side, and then a dull report echoed across the sea. The consorts were awakened to attention; then they, too, saw the land—it was no mirage. Answering guns boomed from the *Vittoria* and the *Concepcion*. The flagship hoisted her Royal Standard, the following ships bent on and flew their ensigns. Other islands opened off to port. Every leaping minute, as the sun beamed its level rays behind them, brought new sights. Swift moving, sharp headed lateen sails were seen. These queer craft approached with lightning speed, sailing miraculously close to the wind, their narrow hulls sustained by outriggers. The heavy bluff bowed ships, sogging before the wind, seemed as if anchored as the jabbering, brown skinned, naked crews cut by them, tacked and turned, while the land lifted as if a long promised curtain were going up, revealing an earthly paradise.

For ninety-eight days the seamen had beheld only blank horizons of despair. It was Mar. 6, 1521, undoubtedly the most dramatic landfall in the annals of the sea. Magellan had crossed the Pacific—at least he had arrived at the most outlying eastward islands of the Indies.

Moving into an anchorage that looked safe, off a village, along a swarming sweet smelling shore, amid clustering proas and canoes, the exhausted ships followed no ceremony of mooring. Halliards were let go by the run, the sails hanging in slovenly folds as the anchors splashed.

Nothing was done shipshape, but, at the order, a boat was hoisted out from the waist of the *Trinidada*, rising slowly as the entire crew tailed on the falls, their efforts so feeble that they got it over the side and then let it go by the run, dropping and sending waves among the crowding canoes.

Over the bulwarks came the savages, jabbering like curious monkeys. Aboard ship they took anything they could lift—belaying pins, buckets, knives, odds and ends of clothing—nothing could stop them. The starving men drove at the savages, sending them back into the water and their canoes. In a moment these thieves had hacked through the boat's painter and, swarming into it, paddled for the shore. When Magellan saw his precious boat headed for the beach, with the utmost energy other boats were hoisted out from the consorts. The *Vittoria* and the *Concepcion* manned their sides to repel these boarders. Boats were coming to the flagship. Magellan, hardly able to stand, but dressed in armored corselet, embarked forty men, while the *Trinidada*, springing broadside to the beach, fired her heavy guns after the retreating savages, the stone cannon balls ricocheting in the water, splitting and bouncing up the shore among the grass huts. As the thunders of this old artillery echoed across the island, forty starving Spaniards struggled toward the shore.

Birds screeched above the dark forests, natives cried in alarm, and the desperate men stumbled out of their boats and up unfamiliar golden sands. They approached the deserted huts, lifting the mats, peering into dim interiors. They found long golden yellow figs, sweet and delicious, and these they wolfed with ravenous impatience. There were also bananas, which they had never before seen, and huge nuts, the size of men's heads, which they cracked with great difficulty but with astonishing results, for a nectar (coconut milk) and sweet white meat rewarded them.

Seven of the bolder savages who crept back to their huts were killed without mercy. The stolen boat was recovered on the beach. A pig was found, and rapidly the boats were filled with bananas and coconuts, with bundles of sugar cane, and with quantities of dried fish. Breakers were filled with sweet cool water from a spring.

Back to the ships they went, laden with this providential

spoil. Nothing could stop the people from grabbing at the fruits, from gulping the water. Fortunately, divided among 150 men, the rations were small. There were screams from the pig being slaughtered over a basin. Smoke rolled from the flagship's galley. Then the Captain General, hoisting the signal for mass, stopped the orgy. In that twilight of the East, all knelt to pray.

As they were entering port, Magellan had made a note in his log: "Islas de las Velas Latinas"—Isles of the Lateen Sails. But this entry he crossed out when mass had been said and substituted the word that damned those distant islands for centuries—"Ladrones"—the Isles of Thieves. We now call the island at which he landed Guam.

Strength returning to the survivors they washed out their stinking water butts, coopered, and filled them. How many more leagues of ocean lay ahead they did not know. They raided the shore and took on board as much provision as possible. Many who had suffered too long died. They were given Christian burial.

Meanwhile the Ladrones were mustering in the wooded hills. The islands were aroused; war drums beat; swift proas were coming from the north. These natives who had never seen an arrow were preparing to descend upon the ships in overwhelming force. So backward were the savages that they would stand in astonishment when an arrow pierced them and draw it out by either end, staring at it until they died.

It was time to go. On Mar. 9 the ships made sail and again stood to the west, shaping course a point or two to the southward.

A week at sea with fresh fruits, abundant water, and increasingly frequent signs of land brought most of the shaky people a long way back to health. On Saturday, Mar. 16, land of large proportions loomed ahead. A small island called Humunu, by Pigafetta, the Isle of Good Signs, by Magellan,

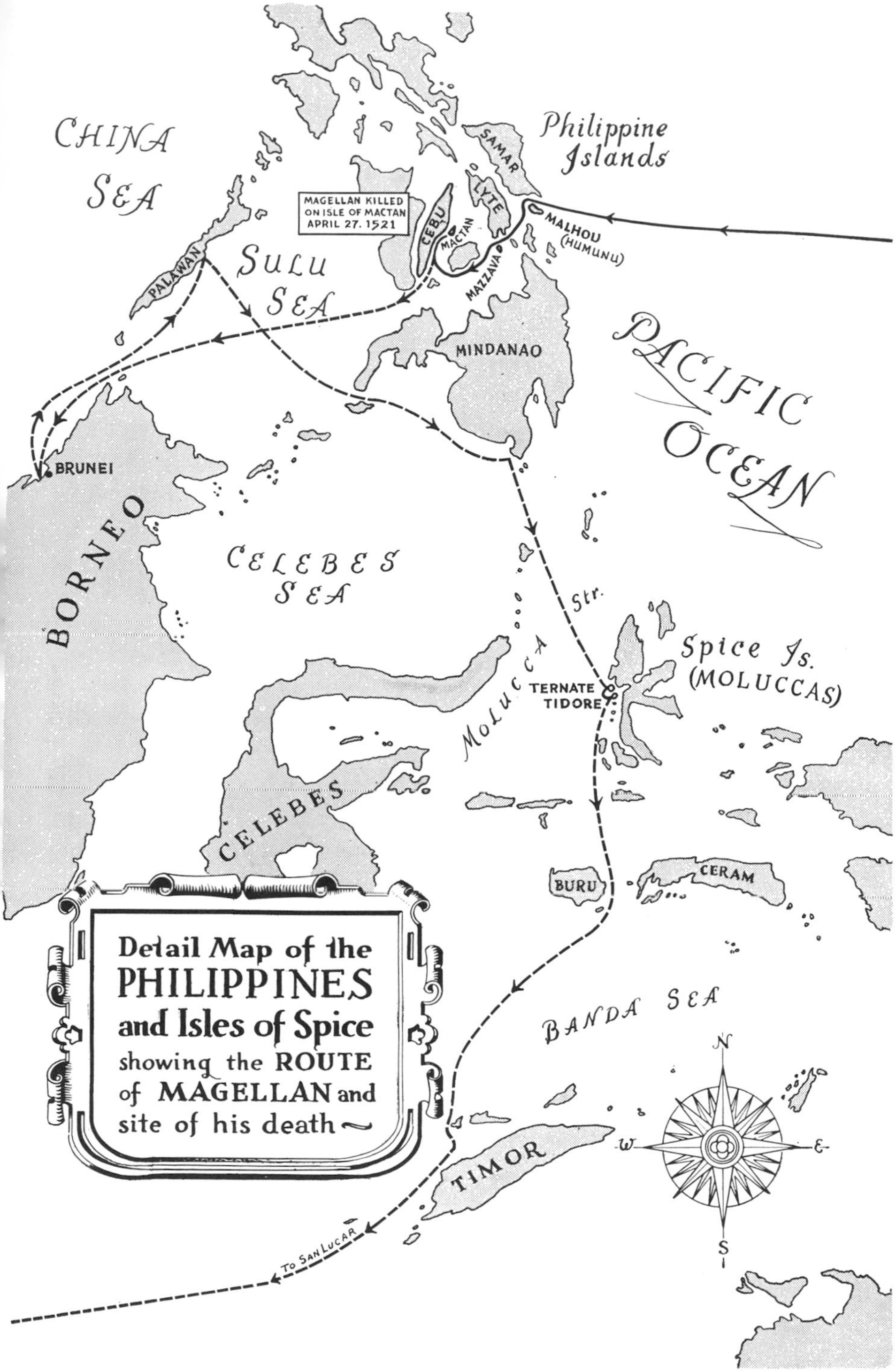

CHINA
SEA

Philippine
Islands

SAMAR

LYTE

MAGELLAN KILLED
ON ISLE OF MACTAN
APRIL 27, 1521

CEBU

MACTAN

MALHOU
(HUMUNU)

PALAWAN

SULU
SEA

MAZZAVA

PACIFIC
OCEAN

BRUNEI

MINDANAO

BORNEO

CELEBES
SEA

Str.

Spice Is.
(MOLUCCAS)

MOLUCCA

TERNATE
TIDORE

CELEBES

BURU

CERAM

Detail Map of the
PHILIPPINES
and Isles of Spice
showing the ROUTE
of MAGELLAN and
site of his death

BANDA SEA

N

W   E

TIMOR

S

To San Lucar

and now known as Malhou, rose to starboard. It was obviously uninhabited. Magellan made signal to anchor, and the three ships found shelter in a quiet cove.

Here was the first restful haven entered by the Armada, and also the last. The heady perfume of spices wafted from the shore; they were lulled by the drum of surf on a perfect crescent of sand. Gay plumed birds sang in the dark, cool forest. The leaves even rustled a welcome as the ships' boats were beached. Here, at long last, was peace.

Magellan's care of his people is nowhere more definitely attested than by his actions in the anchorage of Humunu. Two tents were made of sails, and the sick were brought to the shore on litters. A spring was found. Fruits in abundance yielded to search, and a life giving sea breeze came in across the ocean that had used them so cruelly.

Sunday passed in devotions and rest. On Monday a sail was sighted in the offing, heading for the anchored ships. The Spaniards on the shore stood behind their leader. Strict orders had been given not to speak without his permission or to discharge the arquebuses. The ships trained bombards on the frail craft, but no shots were fired. The boat, a proa, grounded on the white sand, and from it nine men landed and came directly to where Magellan stood. Five of them were richly dressed and made signs of welcome; the four others at once departed in the proa to return later with other natives who had been fishing in the offing. This meeting was one of friendship. All went to the ships, and gifts of bells, mirrors, and red caps were given the visitors, who, making signs of apology that they had only fish to offer, humbly presented a jar of palm wine and departed, promising to return.

On Thursday of that week so close to paradise, the proa came back carrying a venerable man, marvelously tattooed, wearing earrings and armlets of gold. This chief gravely bade them welcome. By signs he indicated that the land to the west was vast and important; he brought unworthy gifts, he knew.

But two canoeloads of coconuts, oranges, and palm wine, with which came a cock, were doubly welcome. These were the things his country afforded. There were also spices in plenty, he intimated, and, touching his bracelets—gold. He was taken aboard the flagship and shown the wonders of that huge craft, and, as an honor, a broadside was fired, that made the chief and his retainers grip the ship's bulwarks in fear.

By now great progress had been made in the recuperation of the sick. Swellings had subsided, eyes were brightening, and the skin of the sufferers regained its healthy hue. Songs were heard, high spirits prevailed, and the Captain General and his officers felt the uplift of success that comes with achievement and with the sense of power over those distant, backward, but friendly people. Already Magellan had discovered enough islands to warrant the marking of one for his own. On Monday, Mar. 25, the tents were struck, the camp was abandoned, and all repaired on board; the ships got under way; the people were eager to know what strange excitements lay ahead.

Having crossed the great Pacific, Ferdinand Magellan neared the completion of his appointed labor. He had shaped an heroic course over "a sea so vast that the human mind can scarcely grasp it" and, to quote further from the famous letter of Maximilian Transylvanus, had arrived at a seemingly perfect world. "Here everything is simple, and without high value, including peace, comfort, and spices. The best of these things, perhaps the best of earthly goods, to wit, peace, would seem, through the wickedness of man, to have been expelled from our world and to have taken refuge here."

The ships sailed between the islands. On Wednesday night a fire was seen on the shore bearing to the westward. They shortened sail and cautiously stood to the beach. Signs of a settlement were visible, and, as they anchored, a canoe carrying eight men lay idly by, watching the men furl their sails.

Summoning Enrique, his Malay slave, Magellan bade him address the natives.

Enrique called to them in Malay. They answered in kind!
The King's Armada had reached the Moluccas; of that there
was no doubt. And Enrique, at least, was back among his
people. So another important date was carved on the scroll of fame,
Mar. 28, 1521, when a brown man—Malacca Henry, the
sailors called him—established the fact that he was the first
human being to have sailed completely around the world.

The island they had fetched was Mazzava, an islet of the
Philippines. Enrique went ashore as ambassador, and gifts of
ginger and a large bar of gold were sent back to the flagship.
But Magellan declined the gold. The Spaniards came in
friendship, and without greed. All they asked was permission to
purchase food. The chief of Mazzava came on board the
Trinidada and embraced the Captain General, resplendent in
the tabard of St. James. The brilliant Royal Standard moved
in lazy undulation from the main truck, the ships were gay
with the flashing ensigns of Castile, Leon, and Aragon, and
long pennons flew from all mastheads. The bearded seamen
were in their whitest and best. And Enrique joyfully told of the
grandeur of Seville and the greatness of King Charles, their
master.

Departing to the shore, the native ruler and his court
witnessed a solemn High Mass. Magellan sprinkled them with
sweet-scented water and offered them the cross to kiss. On the
elevation of the host, he bade them adore the Eucharist, and
they did so with clasped hands. A large cross was brought from
the ships and set up on a high hill, the crucifix studded with
nails and topped by a crown of thorns. It would serve as a
signal to all future Christian navigators that they would be well
received at Mazzava.

In crossing the great Pacific and passing beyond its western
edge, Magellan was embarked on an even greater venture than
discovery. He was bringing the blessings of Christianity to

the idol worshipers of his new found empire of the East. Pigafetta, himself inspired by the vision of Magellan, records the succession of astonishing events. Gold, which so many of the world's conquerors deemed most valuable, was as dross to the crusading Captain General.

Never since has an explorer crowded so much sail toward the unknown shores as did Ferdinand Magellan during the twenty-one days from Apr. 7 to Apr. 27 of the year 1521.

From the idyllic haven of Mazzava the ships sailed to the greater islands, coming to Cebu on Apr. 7, where the Rajah Humabon, unable to understand his good fortune in becoming a vassal of King Charles of Spain, demanded common port dues of the Captain General. However, a friendly Siamese trader, a Mohammedan merchant then in port, whispered some wisdom to the ruler. These ships were dangerous, he said, and this Magellan was of the breed that had landed at Goa with fire and sword. The East still remembered Albuquerque. Accordingly, tribute was forgotten, and the Rajah deigned to visit aboard the *Trinidada*. Here he felt the terrifying shock of a full gun salute and listened respectfully when the great commander spoke of the might of Spain and of the even greater power of God.

Rajah Humabon, of Cebu, a practical prince, became fired by the evangelist Magellan. And a vast, suddenly profitable commerce began, for the huge trade cargoes of the Armada were still intact. Iron, that marvel metal, was fashioned before Rajah Humabon's eyes into instruments of war and peace. The strength of armor was demonstrated when a Spaniard, encased in mail and attacked by men with swords and lances, remained unharmed. Great banquets were provided. Pomp and power made their bow, but in peace.

Sunday, Apr. 14, in that lotus land of simple people, was fixed for a momentous ceremony. Father Pedro de

Valderranza, of the Armada, made ready for the Mass. Magellan, in the habit of a Knight of Santiago, prepared himself through prayer and confession to attain his worthy act of faith. An emotional throng crowded about a scaffold platform erected on the beach in an amphitheater of palms opening to the sea. Rich tapestries covered the platform, and branches of palm were festooned over the altar. Magellan assured Rajah Humabon that one of the great advantages of embracing the Christian faith would be an increased strength whereby he would more easily overcome his enemies, and the Rajah replied humbly that even without this new power he was disposed toward Christ.

The three ships, brilliantly dressed in flags, their yards squared, their sides clean, glistening with the rubbing of fresh paint, fired a general salute, the smoke lifting through their rigging and wafting over the shore like a gigantic cloud of incense. The Rajah and his Queen were baptized, and the Queen received the honored name of Juana, that of the mother of the King of Spain. She begged of Pigafetta that he give her an image of the infant Jesus to replace her idols. Magellan, acting as the Rajah's godfather, gave him the Christian name of Charles, in honor of King Charles of Spain.

The baptism of the natives of Cebu went on apace. Two thousand—some accounts say three thousand—embraced the faith, the first of whom, after the rulers, were the members of the royal household. Neighboring chieftains came to be sprinkled with the waters of the magical baptism.

But all the idols had not been destroyed. Some were kept to protect the Rajah's brother, who lay sick with a strange malady that robbed him of speech. Magellan averred that if all the idols were destroyed and the prince were baptized, he would recover. "And I pledge my head," he vowed, "that this will come about."

Enrique, the faithful, translated this promise. Many idols were smashed, and amid the greatest ceremony the Captain

General baptized the prince, his two wives, and his ten daughters.

Pigafetta reports, "He then asked him how he felt himself, and the prince answered, of a sudden recovering his speech, that, thanks to the Lord, he found himself very well."

And Magellan, with greater fervor than the rest, returned praise to God.

Idols were then committed to the flames in vast numbers and pagan temples built upon the margin of the Sulu Sea were demolished by the converted, and the newly made Christians danced about the island, crying at the top of their voices, "Viva la Castilla! Viva la Castilla!"

One village of idolators refused to be converted to the faith. The Captain General marched among them with his armored men, burned their houses to the ground, and erected a cross amid the smoking ruins.

On a Friday, that fateful day dreaded by sailors, Apr. 26, the *Trinidada*, tugging gently at her hempen cable off the Christian shores of Rajah Charles's island of Cebu, received a minor chief who held office subject to a rebellious chieftain named Chilapulapu. This petty ruler held the near-by small island of Mactan and defied the authority of Cebu's Rajah.

Having performed one miracle, the Captain General was now confronted by the need for further confirmation of the great strength of his beliefs. This, of course, was a simple matter involving nothing more than fighting savages.

Rajah Charles proposed to send his fighting men. The small island, visited shortly before by Magellan's sailors, bent on lechery and fights amid the grass houses of the pagans, had not been in the interest of their souls. Perhaps Magellan, a strict commander, did not know this. He was soon to sail, and he wished to leave Rajah Charles in complete authority over his immediate realm and its surrounding islands.

As midnight passed the Captain General, his captains,

Duarte Barbosa and Juan Serrano, his astrologer, San Martín, the faithful Pigafetta, and the slave Enrique, embarked in three boats with sixty armed men in helmets, wearing corselets of mail. The Rajah of Cebu, accompanied by the Prince, went with them, heading 1,000 men. And with them also was the Mohammedan merchant of Siam. This strong force in boats and canoes moved over the sheltered inland sea, arriving off Mactan three hours before sunrise.

The merchant of Siam was sent ashore to the rebellious Chilapulapu. "Submit to the Rajah and to Spain" was his message from the Captain General.

"We also have spears," came the reply.

This was ridiculous defiance. Magellan ordered the Rajah and his men to remain in his canoes. It was a job for warriors. Also, his new found Christians could see for themselves how Spaniards fought. The Mohammedan merchant shook his head—Allah preserve the luckless rebels of Mactan.

Dawn streaked through the treetops of the little island. The ship's boats pulled to the reef. Eleven armed men remained with the boats, and forty-nine, the Captain General at their head, in full and gleaming armor, waded through the shallow water. The crossbow men strung their barbs. A flying wedge of arrows sped at long range toward the Mactan warriors, 1,500 strong, moving them back. Rajah Charles, feeling great confidence in his defender, and the Mohammedan merchant, fearing for the natives (who, after all, had a right to their beliefs, and not a little cause for revenge), looked on.

The savages moved toward the invader, slowly surrounding the oncoming sailors. Arrows struck and stuck in the tough wooden shields. Gaining courage, the savages came forward.

"Cease firing!" the Captain General ordered and repeated his command, but without avail. The Spanish bowmen, cowed by the vast odds against them, shot feverishly and with careless aim. They could not hold their fire effectively. Panic seized them. The line of spears closed on three sides. Curdling war cries screamed over them. At their backs were the sea and no great guns to lay down a barrage of stone cannon balls, to hearten them by the thunder of the king's artillery.

But here let Pigafetta tell of the fight, for the Knight of Rhodes, wounded in the action by an arrow, is our closest witness.

"We jumped into the water, which was waist-deep, and then we had two long bow-shots to wade before we reached the land, while our boats could not follow us because of the reef. On the shore we found fifteen hundred of the islanders divided into three bodies, of which one opposed our advance, while others assailed us on the flanks. The captain, accordingly, marshalled his men in two companies, as affording a better means of defense. Our musketeers and crossbow men fired for half an hour from the boats, without effect, for from so great a distance our bullets and bolts and lances could not penetrate the wooden shields of the enemy, and at best could merely wound them in the arm. The captain ordered the marksmen to cease fire but his order was disregarded in the confusion. When the islanders realized that our fire was doing them little or no harm, they ceased to retire. Shouting more and more loudly and jumping from side to side to disconcert our aim, they advanced simultaneously, under cover of their shields, assailing us with arrows, javelins, lances with points hardened in fire, stones, and even filth, so that we were scarcely able to defend ourselves. Some of them began to throw lances with brazen points against our captain.

"To instill terror into the hearts of the enemy, the captain sent some of the men to set the islander's huts on fire. That only increased their ferocity. Some of them ran off to cope with the flames, which were raging in twenty or thirty of the houses, and there they slew two of our fellows. The rest attacked us with redoubled fury. When they became aware that, though our bodies were protected by armor, our legs were exposed, they aimed chiefly at these. The captain's right foot was wounded by a poisoned arrow, whereupon he issued orders for a slow and steady retreat. But nearly all our men fled headlong, so that no more than six or eight of us stayed with him, who, having been lame for years, could not withdraw quickly. Now we were exposed to lances and stones hurled from all sides, and we were no longer in a position to resist. The bombard we had in the boat could not help us, for the range was too great. Retreating, therefore, step by step, and fighting all the time, we withdrew from the shore, till we were a full bow-shot away, and the water already rose to our knees. But the islanders followed us sturdily, continually picking up the spears they had already cast, so that one and the same spear could wound five or six men in succession. Recognizing the captain, they aimed chiefly at him, and twice the helmet was struck from his head, He, supported by the few of us who stayed with him, fought like a valiant knight at his post, without attempting further retreat.

"Thus we fought for an hour or more, until at length an Indian succeeded in wounding the captain in the face with a bamboo spear. He, being desperate, plunged his lance into the Indian's breast, leaving it there. But, wishing to use his sword, he could draw it only half-way from the sheath, on account of a spear wound he had received in his right arm. Seeing this, the enemy made a combined rush on him, and one of them, with a long terzado, like a large scimitar, gave him a heavy blow upon the left leg which caused him to fall forward on his face. Then the Indians threw themselves upon him, with spears and scimitars and every weapon they had, and ran him through—our mirror, our light, our comforter, our true guide—until they killed him."

Disintegration of the first Pacific Armada was rapid after the death of Magellan. When the three ships sailed from tragic Cebu, dropping the little hornet island of Mactan in their wake, far on their larboard quarters, Captain Caraballo, senior commander, mustered the crews. One hundred and fifteen answered to their names. When the *Concepcion*, never the most seaworthy of ships, began to leak faster than the pumps could keep her free, she was beached at Bohol, stripped, and the two remaining ships shared her crew, equipment, and cargo.

The *Trinidada* under Espinosa and the *Vittoria* under Caraballo began a more or less aimless and piratical cruise that brought them to the coast of Borneo. The high purpose of Magellan lapsed into an inglorious enterprise. The ships, anchored off the great city of Brunei, sent five men ashore, whom the Sultan held prisoner, and when 200 war proas attacked, the ships slipped their cables and ran for it. Four unarmed junks appeared in the offing, two of which they captured. Aboard one of the prizes were the Rajah of Luzon, his suite, a treasure, and three beautiful women. The pirates —for they were no longer an Armada—divided the loot, released the Rajah, and Caraballo kept the women.

In Palawan, where they had touched before, they careened their ship, plugged the holes made by ship borers, caulked and covered the seams with lead, and set up their kettles, pitching the bottoms. Six weeks they stayed, working when the spirit moved and stopping in the villages at night. There was no powerful Rajah to restrain them in the Coral Bay.

An element of probity remained in the small squadron, however, for Caraballo was deposed and clapped in irons. The forthright Gomez de Espinosa remained captain of the *Trinidada*, and Sebastián del Cano took command of the *Vittoria*. On Nov. 6, the ships arrived at the Fortunate Islands, Ternate and Tidore, where they were laden with spices. There, however, the *Trinidada's* seams opened, and she began to founder, but by beaching and discharging they made her halfway seaworthy.

The stouter ship, perhaps because she was the smaller, the *Vittoria*, was deemed capable of returning to Spain, and this she did under Sebastián del Cano—the first craft to circle the world. Her cargo of spices more than compensated for the entire cost of the Armada, and del Cano was hailed as a national hero. His passage from Tidore to San Lúcar was hardly less terrible than had been the crossing of the Pacific and in the main was ably managed.

Two months out of Ternate, they were forced to put in at Timor, having met with heavy weather in the Banda Sea. Two months at Timor, patching and refitting, and the heavily laden ship again dared the open, sailing down the Indian Ocean. But this is really a story of that vast water between Africa and Austrialia (to give it the original spelling); the frightful rounding westward, against the heavy winds, belongs to the epic of the Atlantic Ocean.

On Feb. 13, the little brig (she is shown as a two-master in the one authentic print we have) put out from Timor. She carried, besides del Cano, Francisco Albo and the great recorder Pigafetta. Sixty people were in her, including thirteen natives of the East. When she arrived, all the Mohammedans had perished or been left at various places. Eighteen Europeans returned. Later thirteen men, abandoned at Cape Verde, reached Spain.

To quote once more the pious Pigafetta, "On throwing the dead into the sea, the Christians floated with their faces toward heaven, while the Mohammedans turned their faces the other way."

The passage of seven months across the two oceans ended in San Lúcar on Saturday, Sept. 6, 1522. The mariners had been away for three years and twenty-seven days and had sailed upward of 14,600 leagues.

The *Trinidada*, larger and deemed less seaworthy than the little brig *Vittoria*, refitted at friendly Tidore. She, it was decided, would sail back eastward across the Pacific to the shores of Panama, to the point from which Balboa had first seen Mar del Sur. Captain Espinosa chose this course, utterly in darkness as to the prevailing winds, the frightful harshness of the counter trades, the roaring forties of the crucifying eastward passage of this unknown sea.

The *Trinidada* stood out into the Pacific, away from the Moluccas. At Tidore word came to Espinosa that the Portuguese had given orders to capture them as pirates.

What this voyage was, how far to the east they got against the winds in a ship fitted only to lask along with fair breezes no one knows. The importance to history was her capture by the Portuguese and the finding on board of the only authentic word surviving from the great Magellan, his *Order of the Day*, given to the officers of the Armada, the recovered copy being the one possessed by the ill starred astrologer San Martín.

.V.

The Spanish Ocean

FOR a century after Magellan's voyage the Pacific was a
Spanish ocean. Drake, Cavendish, and Spilbergen merely
sailed across it, fighting and taking some treasure, being
of no more significance than are a few highway robbers in
some unsettled region. The ocean and its opportunities belonged to Spain. And for three centuries, more and more a
matter of dispute toward the last, Spain dominated the
islands and its shores. The first Spanish discovery, the Philippines, remained as the last Spanish crown colony until they
were taken by Dewey in 1898, 377 years after their discovery
by Magellan.

So vast a stretch of waters yielded its secrets grudgingly,
not to a few but to many succeeding navigators. A voyage in
the years of the late sixteenth and early seventeenth centuries
was no enterprise worth mentioning if it did not result in
geographical discoveries. And toward the last of this period

the remaining navigable waters not yet seen by white men were almost exclusively in the Pacific.

Politicians moved no faster in the days of Spain's glory than they do in our own expanded times. Three years elapsed after the little *Vittoria* returned to San Lúcar with her cargo of spices and her imperishable report before anything was done to develop trade with the Spice Islands and the way thither by sea across the Mar del Sur.

In 1525, the unheroic Commendator García Jofre de Loaysa sailed out of Spain to follow the course of Magellan. Young Sebastián del Cano, of great renown as the first circumnavigator to return to Spain, went as chief pilot, captain of a ship, and second in command. Loaysa was to remain in the East as governor of the Moluccas, after which del Cano was to become Captain General of the Armada.

A voyage into the Pacific, after the terrifying crossing of Magellan, was not to be undertaken lightly. A heavy Armada set sail from San Lúcar. The *Anunciada*, of 170 tons burthen, was lost in the Atlantic. The *San Gabriel*, of 130 tons, battered by storms, her people cowed by terrific omens of disaster, deserted the flagship, scuttling back toward Spain; she was never heard from again. The *Santi Spiritus*, a ship of 200 tons, commanded by del Cano, foundered in the Straight of Magellan, and del Cano transferred to the flagship, the huge *Santa Maria de la Vittoria*, of 300 tons. The two commanders, the aged Loaysa and the intrepid del Cano, entered the Pacific, accompanied by two caravels and a pinnace.

What their passage—second across the Pacific—was, only a reading of Magellan's voyage can suggest. They carried no recorder, no indomitable Pigafetta. But they did much to establish further Spanish claims against the Portuguese in the distant islands of the East. The heavy flagship was sunk at the little island of Tidore, east of the Molucca Passage, and here Commendator Loaysa died. Sebastián del Cano also perished in the Indies shortly after the death of the commander.

The earliest major mid-Pacific landfall came on a voyage in 1555. As with many other primary discoveries, the record is vague, and the details are missing. That the event was noted and that one Juan Gaetano sailed westward, coming to a group of large volcanic islands lying south of the Tropic of Cancer, 1,000 leagues westward of Navidad, is all we know.

What were his ships or his ship? Some day an old logbook may be found in the enormous archives of the Indies, in Seville, or possibly in Mexico. A vast amount of cataloguing, arranging, and research will eventually be done, and Gaetano's discovery may be verified. In any event, it belongs to the history of the Pacific in the first half century after Balboa. So mighty is this ocean that Hawaii remained hidden in its vast expanse for over two centuries after the voyage of Gaetano.

The first effective effort to open a trade route across the Pacific and set up a colony in the Spice Islands came in 1559, when an armada of five ships departed from Navidad, under Miguel López de Legaspe, a Basque, an official of the city of Mexico. It sailed with 400 men and reached the Islands of St. Lazarus, as they were called by Magellan, in honor of Mary's brother, for, like Lazarus, Magellan and his men had there been literally raised from the dead. By 1542, the archipelago had been renamed the Philippines, after Prince Philip, later Philip II.

Legaspe, accompanied by the aged friar Andrés de Urdaneta, who had piloted Loaysa to the Moluccas twenty-two years before and who had later taken holy orders as an Augustinian, stood westward with his ships. Philip II ordered that they try to establish a spice traffic and that no delay be allowed in trading, a contradictory instruction but possibly

an admonition for haste, since he wished the ships to report
expeditiously and to ascertain the best return route to New
Spain. "As much treasure as possible must be sent back with
the ship or ships that return with the news of the expedition,"
was his instruction. He also ordered Legaspe to take possession of all lands or islands in the group of the Philippines, to
labor for the conversion of the natives to Christianity, to
discover the return route, and to conserve all trade or its
profits to the crown.

In 1571, the aging Legaspe founded the city of Manila,
destined to endure, and, while the greedy merchants filled
their holds with spices to carry back to Philip, man's insatiable
curiosity again led him to take up the work of exploration.

Leading the van of explorers, between the conquests in
Peru and the colony in the west, were two of Spain's most
admirable navigators. Pedro Sarmiento y Gamboa, early
historian of the Incas, learned of their legends of lands to the
west, whence Inca Tupac Yupanqui had brought back gold
and silver and a copper throne and black slaves. He was also
said to have returned with the skin of an animal resembling
a horse. This voyage discovered two marvelously rich islands.
Where were these lands, or islands? Sarmiento was convinced
that the islands of legend were the outposts of a continent
stretching from Tierra del Fuego to within 15 degrees of the
equinoctial, somewhere in the Pacific. This obsession concerning a huge Pacific continent persisted for two centuries.
It was definitely part of the Pacific legend, the beginning of
which lay in the uttermost antiquity. For centuries after
Magellan, navigators hoped to sight this fabulous land.

Sarmiento was not only a seaman but a mathematician
endowed with inventive genius, and his calculations attracted
the notice of the Inquisition, as those of a subversive intellect.
The friendly Viceroy of Peru prevented his banishment and
arranged an expedition on which Sarmiento sailed. First in

command was the Viceroy's nephew, Alvaro de Mendaña, a youth of twenty-five. Two ships were fitted out, the *Los Reyes*, of 250 tons, and the *Todos Santos*, of 170 tons, carrying 150 men, half of whom were soldiers. Four Franciscan friars and a number of slaves were with them when they sailed westward in 1567, breasting into the unknown sea. They intended to steer for the fabled continent, convert all infidels, and form a settlement.

Mendaña, although no navigator, was a young man of character and humanity, a gentleman, if that term may be used, who had a feeling even for the rights of savages. The ships sailed from Callao on Nov. 19, 1567, and for twenty-six days stood westward without incident, except that, two days after leaving, the *capitana*, or flagship, struck a sleeping whale. Mendaña failed to consult with Sarmiento about the navigation; the pilots argued as to the direction of possible land from the flight of sea birds; their water grew scarce and unpalatable, then undrinkable. A few strange islands were sighted. Hernán Gallego, Mendaña's chief pilot, a man of experience, quick in resource, promised land. And in latitude south, sixty-two days at sea, they sighted land, the Isle of Jesus. Mendaña ordered a closer approach. Gallego held off, thinking it uninhabitable, but finally they saw canoes. A strong current swept them along. Another nineteen days, and they narrowly escaped disaster when a line of reefs, the seas breaking white, were strung across their course. And to add to their troubles, a typhoon swept them south. They were driven down to the Solomons, anchoring in Bahia de la Estrella, the Bay of the Star. And this land they called St. Isabel. They built a small brigantine for work among these islands.

Mendaña, with Gallego and Sarmiento, worked far to the north, into the counter trades, and eastward to southern California, into the port of Acapulco. They had not seen the continent of the Inca legend. Their sufferings were of the Magellanic order. They fetched anchor in Callao, port of the City of the Kings, in September, 1569, twenty-two months after sailing to the west. It was an enormous, empty voyage, beset by storms and marked by starvation.

The young Mendaña of 1569, discoverer of strange islands across the reaches of Mar del Sur, lived for fifteen years in the reflected glory of his achievement, engaged in supplications for further exploration, in favor and out of favor, and for a time held in prison. The Englishman Drake had raided up the coasts of Chile and Peru and onward to New Spain. For a time it seemed that enterprise to the westward, south of the equinoctial, might be forever ended, and yet nothing was known of that vast ocean. But in 1595 Alvaro de Mendaña sailed again in four ships carrying 400 men, and with him as chief pilot went Pedro Fernandez de Quiros, dark, tall, lean, a dreamer.

Mendaña carried his young wife, Isabel de Barretos, who, judging by her actions must have been a hussy. His three brothers-in-law went along and also a large staff of unnecessary officials. Fifty married men and their wives and families were of the people, and the holds of the fleet were stowed with goods and implements intended for settlement. Being short of provisions, even at the start, Mendaña attacked and captured a ship, renamed it the *Santa Isabel*, after his wife, and abandoned an old and rotten ship of the fleet.

According to the original plan, Mendaña was to establish three fortified cities in the new regions, was to carry cattle, horses, sheep, goats, and pigs for breeding, and was to be granted the absolute government of his new colony for two generations. He might have a large number of slaves and was to enjoy a customs exemption for ten years, with the right to coin gold and silver and to assume the title of Marquis. As in the case of so many of the early discoverers, the counting of the chickens before finding the eggs covered many sheets of parchment. This custom was very common in the Pacific

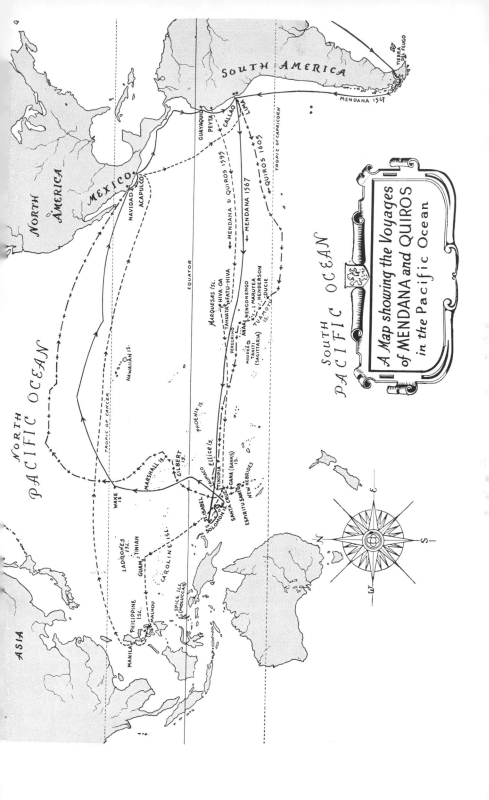

A Map showing the Voyages of MENDANA and QUIROS in the Pacific Ocean

expeditions, but the old ocean, although it seldom paid off the ones who placed the bets, invariably overpaid its promises to others.

On June 16, 1595, this considerable fleet sailed from Payta, in Peru, before the easterly trades. On July 21, they discovered an island that Mendaña named La Madalena, overjoyed because of the apparently quick passage to the Solomons. At first peaceful and cordial relations were established with the natives. But soon one of the seamen raped a young girl, and an outbreak started, followed by a retributive slaughter by the Spaniards.

These, so it seemed, were not the Solomons. A week after anchoring and after the sullen natives had been punished, Mendaña took formal possession of the islands, at Port Madre de Dios. There were prayers, a solemn High Mass, and the firing of a royal salute. The islands were then the property of the King of Spain. Mendaña named them Las Marquesas de Mendoca in honor of the Marquis of Mendoca. Tahuata he named Santa Christiana; Hiva-oa became La Domínica; and Fatu-hiva, Santa Madalena. But the name that has persisted is the Marquesas.

Of the women ashore Mendaña said, "Very fine women were seen here. Many thought them as beautiful as those of Lima, but whiter and not so rosy; yet they are very beautiful in Lima."

In the unrolling of the vast chart of the Pacific, there was no definite plotting of its islands. From 1570 to the end of the seventeenth century little was known of the boundaries or of the waters of Mar del Sur. We have seen what Sarmiento believed, or hoped, and at the time of this voyage of Mendaña the legend had increased. A famous map of 1570 shows the Strait of Magellan leading from Oceanus Aethipicus, the potato shaped South America, and Tierra del Fuego, which extended around the world as Terra Australis Nondum Cognita, and trending northwest into the Pacific of Mar del

Sur, limiting this mighty ocean. To land on a continent greater than all of Europe and to explore its magical surprises was enough to challenge the bold.

Never in the history of the Pacific had so wild and lecherous a rabble roamed among its palm covered islands. Old Mendaña failed, physically and mentally, sinking beneath his troubles and the lashing tongue of the dominant Doña Isabel, that full blooded female with the beauty of hardness. Arriving at an island, they called it Santa Cruz, since called Egmont Island by Carteret—a large land 100 miles in circuit, lifting a volcano, "a very fine shaped hill, from the top of which issues fire, and which often makes a great thundering noise."

Small boats rigged with sails, fifty of them, came out to the ships. The men were black, with woolly hair dyed white, red, and blue. They were a fearsome lot with red dyed teeth and painted bodies. The island offered no gold, but these savages had their arms ringed with bracelets of black rattan, and their necks were wound with beads and fish's teeth. Without provocation they discharged showers of arrows, and the ships replied by arquebus balls, killing one and wounding many.

But friendly relations were soon restored. An old chief named Malope, lean, gray, with a skin "the color of wheat," made friends with Mendaña. Perhaps this was the scene for the first of the Spanish fortresses. At any rate the village ashore was well built, had its wells, its communal meetinghouse, and its temple, or oracle. A Christian church was built, Mass was said regularly and in the usual manner. While interrupting the settlers at their lechery, natives were stabbed or shot.

The people intended as settlers wanted to leave this outlandish place and go to Manila, a city of Christians. But Quiros thought they should stay and carry on their work. The camp master ashore was in revolt. Doña Isabel urged that he be killed. And this was done. Quiros thought the time ashore one of license. Two soldiers were executed, and their heads were severed and hoisted on stakes. Doña Isabel hurried ashore and rallied around the shaky Mendaña. The old chief Malope was murdered. An ensign who went with the murder party was killed and beheaded. Three skulls festered on the stakes.

A sickness fell upon the Spaniards, a curse from heaven. Mendaña fell seriously ill and Don Lorenzo was made acting Captain General. Men died like poisoned rats. The vicar began to perambulate through the camp, calling on all to confess. Many had not unburdened themselves for years; one man had done so only once in his lifetime. The natives, mourning Malope, carrying the head of the ensign, attacked in force. And then Mendaña died.

Doña Isabel at once married her paramour, Don Francisco de Castro, the handsome weakling. Don Lorenzo was wounded in the leg and died. The vicar of the expedition perished five days later. Only fifteen men remained. Nothing in the chronicles relates to the women and children. The hardiest wenches remained on board the surviving ships. On Nov. 18 they left Santa Cruz, "in the claws of the devil," and the sick and dying on board the escaping ships called it "the corner of hell."

The vice-flagship had been lost among the islands. Old chroniclers merely hint at the trials of the voyage from Santa Cruz to Manila—carrying the corpse of Mendaña, the legal honeymoon of Doña Isabel, the reshuffling of the lechers, the desperate rations, and the lack of water.

Isabel held the keys to the ship's stores. In the uttermost extreme, Quiros, who seems to have had little enough determination, did induce her to issue two jars of oil for the people. He tried to conserve the fresh water, yet she used it to wash her clothes. "Cannot I do what I like with my own property?" she snapped at the pilot. The sailors grumbled that she washed her underwear with their own blood.

The expedition arrived at Manila. Doña Isabel and de

Castro returned to Peru as the heirs of old Mendaña. Quiros took passage eastward on a galleon and arrived in Acapulco in December, 1597. From there he also went down to Peru, to the city of Lima.

We know little enough about Quiros. A Portuguese, born in 1565, he served under the banner of Spain and Portugal, united in 1580 with Philip II as king. Quiros spent his boyhood in the slums of Lisbon and then became supercargo in a merchantman. He developed into an able sailor and pilot, but to understand his character a reading of Don Quixote might be advisable. The navigator and the knight, Quiros and Cervantes, were of the same time, both living in this world but dreaming of the next; impractical, indecisive, but unsinkable. Quiros sought a great thing that did not exist, the Pacific continent.

Those brooding waters of the West seemed to beckon Quiros to come and release the millions of heretical inhabitants of a vast land he believed to exist somewhere in the great Pacific, as told by the Incas, as believed by Sarmiento, and as shown by maps of the great Ortelius. It was a continent freighted with riches but, above all, the abode of people living in idolatry and consigned to hell unless saved through the blood of Jesus Christ. This was no theory, no mere proselyting obsession, but rose before Quiros as a duty transcending all of life. There was discovery to be made on a grand ocean for the propagation of the faith.

Quiros had no delusion as to the suffering entailed by the voyage he was promoting. Scurvy, thirst, and torture were to be their crown of thorns. To those who would authorize and pay the cost was offered the lure of such wealth as men could hardly dream of.

But Europe was in turmoil. The Netherlands had declared their independence in 1581, and with Philip II, then ruler of both Portugal and Spain, at the height of his power, no accretion of earthly wealth could seem impossible. The Dutch, after all, were negligible, and soon his might would crush Elizabeth and her piratical wasps. Philip II died in 1598. His invincible Armada had failed. Perhaps Philip III would be more amenable.

The Viceroy of Peru could entertain no such expense for the crown on his own account but recommended Quiros to the attention of Philip III if he cared to go to Spain and lay his vast ambition before the sovereign. Taking passage eastward, Quiros arrived in Spain during the great year 1600, when the Christian faith was celebrating its victories. He determined to begin his plea for the vast Pacific enterprise by first making a pilgrimage to Rome. He exchanged his few ducats for the garb of a pilgrim, fashioned a staff, and took ship to the coast of Italy, where he went on foot to the Holy City. There Quiros presented his credentials to the Duke of Sesa, the Spanish ambassador, who was so much impressed by the vital message of the navigator and by his deep sincerity that he called a council of geographers, mathematicians, and pilots to examine Quiros and consider his plans.

In the garb of humility, surrounded by these learned men of Rome, Quiros's eloquence transported them to the antipodes, sailing over burnished seas to the teeming Solomons, to an unknown hemisphere and its balancing continent, still undiscovered, still living in pagan darkness.

There were always two sides to every question, Quiros said, and nature shared equally its water and its land. So impressed were the learned men by this logic that the duke arranged a special audience for Quiros with Pope Clement, at which the sailor missioner again successfully presented his ideas, Clement blessing him. After two years in Rome amid interminable investigation and long devotions, Quiros journeyed back to Spain, carrying a piece of the True Cross, an epistle from the Pope, and letters from the Duke of Sesa to the King, backed by a huge report of the learned council.

The question then arose, was this poverty stricken, fanatical

Quiros a great enough personage, if he might so be called, to be placed in charge of an important mission? Was he practical? If so, why was he poor? The Council of State approved him, and the famous Council of the Indies disapproved. Finally a royal letter was given him to the Viceroy of Peru. Out of the royal revenues would come the cost of two ships, well fitted and supplied, and sufficient numbers of Franciscan friars were to be carried. Quiros was to have full authority. Departing for America with the letter but no money, he was shipwrecked in the West Indies. Finally Quiros reached Guayra in Venezuela, where he was forced to remain for eight months.

The king's letter impressed but did not move the colonial officials. His creditors sued him for debt; even his muleteer clamored for payment. In the midst of this distress he found two orphan nephews, whom he took under his protection.

Quiros attended a religious festival at the hospital in Panama. The upper story of the building crashed with the crowd, injured the navigator, and he spent ten weeks in bed. Partly recovered, he took passage to Peru in a zabra, or small launch, provided with scant water and provisions. Owing for this, he landed with his small nephews in Callao, walked to Lima, where, being penniless, they were given lodging by a charitable potter.

At last Quiros was able to present his formidable letters to the viceregal court. Don Luis de Velasco, the Viceroy, was impressed by the eloquence, the intense fervor of the supplicant. The letter of King Philip was a royal command. Philip III had ordered that Quiros should go in person upon an expedition, as the king put it, "among these hidden provinces and severed regions, an expedition destined to win souls to heaven and kingdoms to the crown of Spain."

Urged on by the indomitable Doña Isabel, her husband, Don Fernando de Castro, opposed Quiros, objecting to this expedition on behalf of a Mendaña claim to the Solomon Islands. But nothing could stop the progress of this inflaming

Quiros. The religious rallied to his support. Six Franciscan friars were to accompany him and four nursing brothers of the Order of John of God. Three hundred sailors were assembled—Spaniards, Portuguese, and Flemings—and three ships: the *San Pedro y Paula*, of 60 tons, the *San Pedrico*, of 40 tons, and a small zabra. By viceregal order provisions were taken aboard to serve them for a year. Barrels of biscuits and —with the contamination of water carried in casks in mind— many hundreds of earthen jars of fresh water were taken in the ships. Animals, goats, pigs, fowl, and some cattle cluttered the narrow decks. These were to be taken to stock new lands. Iron farm implements, goods for barter, fruit trees, seeds, and candles for the Mass were among the many items of lading. Never had the wide harbor of Callao beheld so tremendous an undertaking. The small ships were laden to the limit of flotation. The decks were crowded, the harbor was agog with the importance of the enterprise.

Quiros dedicated his small fleet to Our Lady of Loretto and dressed himself and his officers in the habits of Franciscan friars. On Dec. 21, at the period of the southern summer solstice, in 1605, after eight years of struggle, the seeker after a Pacific continent gave the order to sail out past San Lorenzo Island, that high yellow rock to the south of the bay. The quays, the ships in harbor, the housetops and galleries were crowded. The ships flung out their ensigns and banners, the sails bulged with an offshore wind coming down from the hills behind Lima. Bugles blared, guns thundered in salute, cheers arose. "We sailed with good will to serve God and spread our Holy Faith, and to bring credit to the King our Lord; all seemed easy to us," wrote González de Leza, one of the pilots.

Captain General Quiros, exalted beyond measure, merged more and more into the apostolic dreamer. He had the sole order of direction, and he mingled navigation with salvation as he set course to the west. His senior officer, Don Diego de

Prado y Tovar, captain of the flagship, became a bitter and an unscrupulous enemy. Luis Vaez de Torres, was captain of the vice-flagship. Bernal Cermeno sailed as master of the launch, or zabra, perhaps the most seaworthy boat of the fleet; and the chief pilot, Juan Ochoa de Bilboa, sent by the Viceroy against the wishes of Quiros, added to a confusion seldom found aboard ship before or since.

Between seizures of ill health, Quiros issued decrees of morality. In those close-packed ships, mingled with the bleating of fowl, the grunts of hogs, and the bellowing of cattle, were the stench of manure, the heat of tropic summer, of stinging flies, and the slat and creak of sails and blocks. The pilots kept the courses laid down by the Captain General. But so large were the ship's companies that idleness led to wicked diversions. Quiros ordered all gaming boards thrown into the sea, and all cards and dice. He issued voluminous orders, copied out by his faithful secretary, Belmonte Bermudez, a long suffering poet and friend. The orders of the day, on Jan. 8, 1606, were a mixture of piety, morality, advice on diet, and admonitions as to the treatment of natives, together with suggestions as to navigation and the recognition of signs of land.

They sailed across a coral sea in the latitude of Capricorn, the water often greenish blue as they sighted chains of desert islands while their supply of drinking water failed. An apparatus for distilling fresh water from sea water gave them fifty jars of it, and then their fuel was exhausted. This is one of the earliest mentions of the use of distillation at sea.

On the morning of Feb. 10, 1606, masthead lookouts reported land lying ahead. It was high land, as the early daylight disclosed. Nearing it, they saw wreaths of smoke ascending as a welcome or a warning. The ships hove to, and Quiros sent in a boat, a boat that lay off a fringe of breakers. Ashore, 100 natives had assembled on a beach behind the reef.

It was the island now known as Anaa, or Chain Island. Amid a confusion of Pacific atolls, of isles and reefs, sighted, landed upon, discovered by Quiros and rediscovered, come the names of La Encarnación (Ducie Island), San Juan Bautista (Henderson Island), St. Elmo, (Marutea), Las Cuatro Coronadas (Actaeon Group), San Miguel (Nengonengo).

And on Mar. 1 they came in sight of the Island of Beautiful People, Peregrino, or Gente Hermosa. The sex starved sailors approached the native huts. One tried to enter and was knocked down by a club, at which another of the violators ran the native through with a sword. Arquebuses were fired, and natives fled, leaving their dead. Quiros mourned them, " . . . for they had the faith of Christ at the doors of their souls."

Torres found enormous canoes, sixty feet in length and six feet wide. The peaceful people fled, abandoning beautiful mats, woven work, and tools of shell, with fishhooks of the same material. The Spaniards found dried oysters and a few pearls. A boat had been overturned in the surf, many water jars were lost, and Torres brought back no hostages. They sailed on again, in want of water, with discontent growing among the people. They were suffering and dying amid the plenty of that smiling ocean, while Quiros searched far for "the mother of so many islands."

Quiros tried to put down the recurrent gaming, even though the winnings were devoted to the souls in purgatory. He urged the people to better pursuits, to drills and exercises, and to reading and the serious study of the spheres and navigation.

Who can untangle the voyage of Quiros? The accounts vary with the winds. The course was no more certain than is the course of empire in a world of experts. Was he discovering a continent or only seeing its remaining peaks? He saw island after island that no one else had ever seen. The native chieftains waved their arms about the sea, indicating many other isles. Great green clad mountains, volcanic peaks, and circling reefs of coral confused the mariners. They sighted the islands of Tikopia and Nuestra Señora de la Luz.

On Apr. 26, Quiros was certain that at least he had sighted his mythical continent, naming it Tierra Austrialia del Espíritu Santo. A century and a half later de Bougainville sighted the land, which is entirely composed of islands, naming the group Grandes Cyclades, and Captain James Cook called them New Hebrides. Quiros named them Austrialia, in honor of Philip III, who was also Archduke of Austria.

At Austrialia del Espíritu Santo Quiros parted from Torres to sail that mighty course of incredible loneliness and hardship over the equator to 40 degrees northward and back down the coasts of New Spain to Acapulco, but with almost empty holds.

And yet, so he told the King, in the new land were people intelligent, docile, and capable of civilization. Bread grew on trees. The green coconut was further celebrated. The palms yielded spirits, vinegar, honey, whey, and toddy. The marvelous coconut also served instead of the artichoke and, when ripe, meat and cream. In its age it yielded oil, wax, and balsams, the shells furnished cups and bottles, the fibers made the best of cordage, and its oakum gave perfect slow matches for cannon. The leaves made their sails and thatched their houses. There was no end to the wealth of this paradise of the southern continent. The gardens yielded pumpkins and parsley with "intimation of beans." But it was not a vegetarian paradise alone. Hogs, sweet porkers thriving on nuts, fowl, capons, partridges, geese, turkeys, ringdoves, and goats all abounded. The land showed "intimation of cows and buffaloes." The treasures were gold and silver and pearls. Of spices there were nutmegs, mace, pepper, and ginger, "with intimation of cinnamon and cloves." The air at daybreak trembled with the harmony of thousands of birds—nightingales, blackbirds, larks, goldfinches, and swallows—besides the cheerful chirping of grasshoppers and crickets. Speaking of the morning, he could only grow more poetic, for the dews sent out the exhalations of orange flowers and sweet basil.

Quiros forgot to mention that tropic fish, the pargos, which poisoned him and many of his men in beautiful Austrialia del Espíritu Santo. Nor did he tell of hostile Indians blowing war notes on shell trumpets and shooting lethal arrows. Nor did he say he had left or deserted Captain Luis Vaez de Torres to go on as best he could in the lesser ship, the *San Pedrico*. And all account was neglected of the many deaths by scurvy, mayhem, and drowning. Of that land of Espíritu Santo, all he remembered were the rivers Jordan and Salvador, their banks a pure paradise.

In his great appeal for another voyage, having told of the ebony and infinite woods for shipbuilding, Quiros wrote, "I can show to a company of mathematicians, that this land will presently accommodate and sustain two hundred thousand Spaniards. None of our men fell sick from over-work, or sweating, or getting wet. Fish and flesh kept sound for two or more days. I saw neither sandy ground, nor thistles, nor prickly trees, nor mangrovy swamps, nor snow on the mountains, nor crocodiles in the rivers, nor ants in the dust, nor mosquitoes in the night."

Old Quiros, with that fiery look in his eye, that catoptric vision denied to home fed kings, to soft courtiers, was himself shaken by rheumatism. His teeth were rotted, and his scraggly beard was none too trim as he appeared in the cheapest of pilgrim garb. He brought back no glittering gold, and stories arrived at the court from Torres, who had reached the great commercial port of Manila, having sailed through a huge strait, Torres Strait, across the northern nose of a continent. Captain Torres sent word of an erratic Quiros and of his impractical, undisciplined command. His men raped the natives, gambled, and drank of palm wine, setting a pattern for the lotus land that long since has lured and eventually has overcome the white man.

Quiros was put off by Philip III and placed on a ship leaving for Peru in the retinue of a new Viceroy, who was instructed to keep the old man at home. He died in Panama, in 1614, 101 years after the discovery of Mar del Sur by Balboa. He is often mentioned by ancient commentators as the last of Spain's heroic navigators.

The Manila Galleons

A CHRONOLOGICAL history of the development of the Spanish Pacific, its discoveries, the propagation of the faith, the promotion of a great overseas trade, and the relation of these activities to conquests ashore, the establishment of colonies and countries, is as impossible as it would be to present all sides of a cube at the same time. While Mendaña, Sarmiento, Quiros, and others were voyaging, the settlement of the Philippines under Legaspe continued.

North of the line, above the islands of Hawaii (still to be rediscovered), rolls the widest stretch of empty ocean on the globe. This huge band of water, subject to mighty storms, is also swept by the northeast trades and ruffled by the boisterous counter trades to the north. It forms a magnificent two-way sailing route. It was to serve old Spain and her enduring eastern colony for two and a half centuries. The historic sea of the galleons plying between the Philippines and Mexico linked the ports of Manila, Navidad, and Acapulco.

The latter port has survived and prospered, but to the north of it Navidad no longer remains on the charts.

First of the galleons was the old *San Pablo*, sent east and to the northward under direction of wise Friar Urdaneta, sky pilot and sea pilot whose fame comes through the ages undimmed by venial weaknesses. This pathfinding ship left Cebu in 1565, commanded by Legaspe's grandson, Felipe de Salcedo. It suffered the waste and incompetence to be expected of an enterprise backed by a royal treasury. Finding the counter trades, the prevailing westerlies, was Urdaneta's distinction. The *San Pablo*, with a moderate cargo of cinnamon for crown account, laden in Mindanao, fetched Acapulco after a quick passage of three and a half months.

Andrés de Urdaneta, the aged Augustinian friar, discovered the best route eastward from the Spice Islands of Magellan. His reports to King Philip, the India House, and to the Viceroy of New Spain, with charts and full directions of sailing, laid down the course taken by 1,000 ships over a span of 250 years. It was westward in the trades, between 10 and 20 degrees of latitude, and homeward, arching north as far as 40 degrees, almost on the great circle of the earth between the Philippines and the coast of California. Then, making land between 40 and 35 degrees, they coasted down to Acapulco.

The galleons did not attain prime importance until after the founding of Manila by old Legaspe in 1571, when he established the seat of Spanish rule on the shores of Manila Bay. He died the year later, leaving Spain in safe possession of the archipelago, except for the islands of the warlike Moros, Sulu, and Mindanao, always in revolt up to the end of Spanish rule and for years later, even when under United States sovereignty.

Trade with China increased after the shift of government from Cebu to Manila. Junks sailed down across the Hwang-hai, the Yellow Sea, and the Tung-hai, or East China Sea, and came from the ports of lower China, from Canton east-ward over the Nan-hai, the South China Sea. Spaniards won the gratitude of Chinese merchants when they rescued the passengers and crew of a large junk foundering off Mindanao. The rescued merchants freighted a heavy junk with valuable cargo and entered Manila Bay the next year, early in 1572, finding a ready market at the new port and bringing other junks in their wake. Mexico began shipping silver, and cochineal in exchange for Chinese goods. For centuries the silver dollar, *mex*, has been a medium of exchange, especially in China. Mexican silver, freighted westward in the Manila galleons, largely originated in Peru. Cochineal, cacao, and copper, mostly Mexican products, were laden in Acapulco. The Spaniards of New Spain eagerly bought the silks of China and the rich merchandise of Coromandel, coming to Manila for ocean transport in the great galleons. Fans of ivory, boxes of sandalwood, ivory castanets, articles of jasper and jade, carved escritoires and boxes, chinaware, vases, bronzes, and women's decorative combs. And, although forbidden for a time, the jewels and jewelry of the East came ashore at Acapulco: enormous pearls, precious rubies and diamonds, pendants and earrings, finger rings, necklaces. The galleons brought back religious furniture made by heathen craftsmen, crucifixes, rosaries, and reliquaries. Uncut gems came to Acapulco. But mostly the cargoes consisted of silks.

The Chinese workmanship in silks, embroideries of gold and silver thread, Canton crepes, fine damasks, these filled chest on chest, duly numbered and manifested as they were struck below into the capacious hold of the lading galleon. The Spanish burtons creaked, the mules lifted the loads, the bales and chests were lowered from the bollards, and there were much shouting and whistling and watching by the talleymen and supercargoes. Boleros of silk and velvet, skirts, bedspreads, table damask, and vestments, cloaks and robes and finery were of these cargoes.

Spices and aromatic herbs were stowed in the capacious holds. Java, Ceylon, and the Moluccas sent their products. Drugs were shipped, camphor, musk, borax. Great cargoes of chocolate from Guayaquil went westward, and teak came back, and later the famous Segars made in Manila. Slaves were often carried, but not as in the slavers of the African trade. These people were brought from the Philippines, mostly as servants, and later sold into bondage in New Spain until this was prohibited in 1700.

This sea trade was a natural flow. The need for these commodities by the people on opposite sides of the Pacific was mutually complementary. New desires grew with the expansion of trade. The oldest of civilizations came in commercial contact with one of the newest of lands. Manila became a magazine for the richest merchandise of the East. It drew traders westward from Mexico; its Spanish overlords grew in power and wealth, the walled city was built, and within this citadel stood the monasteries of the Augustinians, the Franciscans, and the Dominicans. Manila built the good Convent of San Andrés and also Santa Potenciana; the mothers, nuns, and sisters became famous for their help to the women and girls of the seaport. The *residencia* of the Jesuits was erected, and the work of salvation begun by Magellan has been carried on through the centuries.

The prosperity of trade across the Pacific slowed most other Philippine activities. Profits from the galleons made for luxury among the wealthy, and few royal officers saw much use for other means of livelihood. Shipbuilding, the construction of the ever growing ships, became the most considerable of Philippine industries outside the galleon trade.

Master Francis Pretty, a gentleman accompanying Thomas Cavendish, (or Candish, as it was sometimes spelled) noted events concerning the Manila trade as encountered on that voyage, the third circumnavigation of the world. "On the foure and twentieth day of August 1587," Master Pretty wrote, "our Generall with 30 of us went with the pinnesse unto an haven called Puerto de Natividad. . . . We took a Mulatto in this place, in his bedde, which was sent with letters to of advise concerning us along the coast of Neuva Galicia, whose horse wee killed, took his letters, left him behinde, set fire on the houses, and burnt two newe shippes of 200 tunnes the piece, which were building there on the stocks, and came aboard our shippes againe."

Cavendish's *Desire* measured 120 tons burthen, the *Content*, 60 tons, and the *Hugh Gallant*, only 40 tons; so the craft being built at Navidad were heavy vessels by comparison and most probably galleons intended for the Manila trade. But whatever building was done on the Mexican side of the ocean was small by comparison with greater craft launched in the Philippines.

When they had passed through the region of typhoons off the inhospitable coasts of Japan, the dangers of the stormy eastward passage that arched up along the great circle close to the Aleutian Islands took toll of ships and lives and rich ladings. The answer, it seemed, was to build stouter, stronger, and more seaworthy ships, and the better and more enduring woods of Asia made Manila and its environs a shipbuilding center.

The main building ways were at Cavite, on Manila Bay. The hardwoods of the Philippines were the best material possible for the construction of ships. Teak, that enduring timber, often formed the framework of keel, stem, and stern pieces. Master shipwrights came from Spain from the naval dockyards to work these great balks of teak and the natural knees that bound the fabric together as a whole. The keels were enormous squared logs, carefully scraped. The aprons behind the stem pieces, the stemsons and breasthooks and keelsons lying over the huge ribs, all were fashioned by the adz and bolted through with heavy wrought iron fastenings.

Hundreds of native workmen and Chinese smiths were employed.

Forward, the gripe, the part of the stem that met obstructions, might be of ironwood. And just as strong were the after ends, the deadwood and aprons and huge stern hooks. The rudder posts were built of solid teak, the iron gudgeons were the heaviest of forgings, and the rudder, hung on its pintles, would be a piece of selected teak, strapped with wrought iron, a metal that defies the action of sea water. The beams supporting decks were of teak.

The planking was usually of lanang wood, an unsplinterable timber that resisted small shot or took heavy cannon balls and imbedded them. All planks were bent in steam and fastened carvel fashion, caulked and double caulked and pitched. These craft, so heavy as to defy destruction, deep and broad of beam, rode like strong castles on the sea. Safety, not speed, was the desired end. It often took half a gale of wind to move them, especially when foul with weeds and barnacles toward the end of a year at sea, drouthing across the mightiest of oceans.

Manila hemp, that strong silken abaca, known to this day as the best cordage in the world, was spun and layed in the rope walks at Cavite. Sail canvas was woven from eastern hemp, extra strong and pliable. The construction of a large galleon, plank on plank, was built up at the bends to the thickness of three or four feet in the heaviest ships, rising with a tumble-home to the huge bulwarks. This was the work of many months stretching into years. The high topgallant stern castles, the galleries for the general, the forecastle, and the deep waist gave these monsters an appearance of solidity seldom seen on the oceans.

Many cabins were fitted for the commander and his officers; there were quarters for officials, for important passengers, and cubicles for the merchants and petty officers. Others slung in hammocks or curled up on mats. The range in size of these historic ships is given by William Lytle Schurz in his excellent history, *The Manila Galleon:*

Tonnage	Length of deck, ft.	Length of keel, ft.	Beam, ft.	Depth of hold, ft.	Number of guns
1534¼	174	145	49	25	80
1095	156	130	43	22	70
990¾	140	126	42	21	60
488½	120	100	34	17	50
410½	112	73	31	15	40
303½	102	85	29	15	30
199½	88	73	25	13	20
144½	78	65	22	11	10

Roughly it will be noted that a galleon was about one third as wide as she was long on the water line, and her depth of hold was one half as great as her breadth. That is, she was thoroughly stable and not built for fast sailing or capable of easy maneuvering. As stay sails did not come into use at sea until a century after the establishment of this trade, most of the earlier ships were intended to lask along with fair winds at not more than five knots with the most favorable winds. Tacking was well nigh impossible, and a capable command, meeting head winds, could only hope to sail some seven points from the wind, adding a point or so of leeway; that is, the ship made no headway.

In the months of May and June, 1755, the huge galleon *Santísima Trinidad* had been prepared at the royal arsenal in Cavite. She was hove down, caulked, and pitched after six months of lay-up and neglect. Her refitting had paid a handsome sum to the thieving alcalde and his officials. Half a million pesos it cost to get her ready for the voyage. Her masts were scraped, her yards were crossed, the standing rigging of heavy hemp was set up and tarred, and through her clumsy blocks was riven the golden cordage of abaca. The yellow brown sails were bent. The ship was newly painted a dark bottle green, her poop carvings and forward scrolls gilded, precious gold leaf glittering with the red and yellow trimmings. She had been at her mooring for many weeks, surrounded by junks and sampans. Boxes and barrels were taken in and struck below. Her water butts were filled, her bread room stowed, her cabins furnished. The casks of salted meat were over the lower tier of the less perishable cargo, dunnaged off with mats.

The great ship *Santísima Trinidad*, of 2,000 tons burthen, was down to her deepest lading. Hold hatches had been battened and sealed against pilferage. Soldiers, under their captain and lieutenants, were standing watches over these, over the bread room, the spirit room, the water butts, and, most important of all, the magazine. The guard was stationed aft to keep inviolate the quarter-deck and the poop. The pilot mayor, a grizzled veteran of the Pacific passage, was giving his last instruction to the minor pilots and admonishing the old quartermasters. The heavy helm had been swung to starboard and port as the pilot mayor watched the adjustment of the tiller tackles, great purchases riven with rawhide rope. The great rudder moved slowly but smoothly under the eyes of the pilots who watched from a banco boat under the stern castle. In the dark half deck over the rudder head, where the tiller was housed, hung the relieving tackles in beckets, ready for instant use. This engine for the direction of the galleon was of utmost importance.

The pilot mayor himself saw to the taking on board of the bronze astrolabes and the new cross-staff from England. He had the last issue of the tables of declination and of eclipses sent from Seville and the newest portolanos of the Pacific, together with maps of the eastern harbors. The great chart with its marked courses leading out from Manila Bay, through Boca Grande, into the South China Sea was spread on the pilot table in the coach house at the break of the enormous poop. The *Santísima Trinidad* commanded its helm with a huge double wheel. Two steering binnacles were but forward of this on either side, and overhead on the poop stood the large navigating compass.

The pilot mayor, Don Maria y Santestevan, was making his last voyage homeward to Acapulco. He had accumulated a fortune as a pilot during ten voyages in the galleon trade. With good and bad luck, he had been at sea for forty years. It was time he retired, for the great responsibilities of the sea had driven him gray and stiffened him with rheumatic pains. But he was still under sixty, a resolute man. Of course the Commandant General, who would make a vast fortune out of one voyage, the Marquis de Balsantoledo, was no seaman; he and his staff had no reason to be. He was going by favor of the King and his colonial governor. The great ship and its remunerative voyages supported an imperial city—old Manila.

The boatswain and his mates were clearing the tanglement of running ropes, long triced up above the sheer poles. Tagal stevedores were being sent ashore. On the foreyard, tackles were hoisting in the cattle; the sheep and pigs and great coops of fowl were taken in and stowed near the galley and kept under guard. The cackling of hens announced the dropping of eggs. The General's servants secured these for the cabin mess. On the mizzen the burtons to larboard were whipping up the last stores, the special wine, and fruits for the General and his suite. The women of the general, those veiled creatures destined for no one knew quite where, had come aboard in the night and stood in the quarter galley under a duenna, looking out across the harbor. Slaves of the governor attended them. There were much laughter and the strumming of instruments and the clinking of glasses. Ladies, ignoring the female voices below them, stood on the poop deck, but most of these were to return to the shore to the walled city decked with flags.

The galleon's great pinnace had been hoisted in and rested

on the booms over the waist, and her quarter boats were stowed. Shore boats, the state barge of the governor, and many bancas swung at the booms or were hovering close by the ship. There was constant calling back and forth from women bidding good-by to their friends.

Four hundred officers and men manned the ship. The hundred seamen, topmen, and waisters were at their posts. The gunners were ready at the saluting cannon. Half the armament, forty great pieces, had been sent ashore so that more cargo could be taken on board. There was no danger to so great a ship; she still had forty guns mounted ready for action. The carronades on the quarter-deck were ready, the captains standing by with their slow matches.

Amidship, the master's mate stood by the main capstan. The great cable had been taken around the barrel and led down to the grating tier through a round gate in the deck. Hauling tackles were hooked, and the many long bars, like the legs of a circular spider, were swiftered in, and men stood ready to heave up. Part of the shore gang not yet over the side were held to help weight the best bower, already at a short stay. On the bowsprit cap stood the master. The Commandant General, being spoken to by an orderly, nodded, "Yes, yes. Of course." So the pilot mayor gave the order to heave in, and the topsails were sheeted and the yards hoisted as the heavy iron anchor broke out of the Manila mud.

Then at another nod, the *Santísima Trinidad* shook as the guns thundered a salute, the governor having left the ship amid a fanfare of trumpets and the roll of drums. Smoke drifted above the harbor and over the city as the forts answered gun for gun. The galleon, with flags and pendants flying, was under way.

The southwest monsoon was blowing, and the ship had trouble working out of the Boca. But by watching the puffs and standing ready with kedges, she rounded the Corregidor. Hauling her bowlines, she sheeted on the larboard tack standing to the north, the first galleon to try the new route, upward and into the Pacific through the Ballintang Channel, thereby saving many useless miles, formerly lost when sailing to the south, through the Embocadero out between the islands off to the ocean.

A seemingly impossible confusion prevailed on board. The screaming of pigs and the crowing of cocks were as much part of it as the calling of harsh sea commands, the shrill of the boatswains' pipes, the cries of the children, and the moans of the seasick, for the mighty galleon rose and fell to the sea's breathing as if itself alive. Filth was being washed into the sea from the cumbered decks; splashing water sluiced into the scuppers down over the wales. Many hearts were sore; many ashore had their all, their loved ones and their hopes, aboard the stately ship. But she was safe, safer than any of the many Acapulco ships. Since the passing of Anson, ten years before, the sea had been free from all enemies except pirates, and she could defend herself from these. No ordinary cannon shot could penetrate her sides.

On the third day out, with the strong monsoon driving her, boiling through a singing sea, her high poop glinting in the evening sun, the pilot mayor, Don Maria, heard the hail from aloft. They had sighted Cape Bojcador on the northern coast of Luzon. The night came over them like a hood. They shortened the mizzen canvas and furled the fore-topsail, taking in the sprit. Already many of the passengers were coming on deck, having recovered from *mal de mer*. The Marquis's suite were up, and some of the ladies and women had been seen in the gallery as men and boys looked down from the poop. But this coming night held a terrifying promise. The great swells rolling in from the Pacific against the wind gave the ship an unusual motion. Old seamen shook their heads. They were to clear the island of Ballintang in the dawn to come, running northward of it and south of Batan. Many dangerous reefs and vigias were shown on the portolano.

As the galleon rolled, her wales going under, the great stars came out and then were suddenly covered, thunders rumbled, but without lightning. The priests on board crossed themselves, as did the devout, and holy water was sprinkled on the square ports of the great cabin.

"What think you of this, Don Maria?" one of the pilots asked of his chief.

"I saw this once before in the *Sacra Familia*, when we lay off the Marianas, and it took us nine months to cross."

By midnight, as the watches were changed, the wind fell, and a rumbling came up out of the deep. The sea grew thick and phosphorescent. Buckets were cast over the side, and a grayish stew of floating pumice was hauled on board. The air became sulphurous. The galleon trembled; the sails slatted through the middle watch. The huge poop compass began to sway. Dark clouds hung over the mastheads. No one slept, not even the tired watch. Candles were lit in the cabins. What was to happen?

But with the coming of daylight, a bloody threat out of the eastern sea, sharp winds swirled in from the south and east, and the *Santísima Trinidad* bent under the blasts with close reefed courses, double watches at the wheel, while her high sides took the pound of the breaking seas, the veils of spray rising and lifting over her like clouds. The pumice sea had gone, and the galleon surged on, close by dangerous Raza Isle. But she was a stout ship, that heavy craft, so nobly built and so ably manned. Through the weeks, as she hammered away, always east and north, the astrolabes and the cross-staffs each day gave her more latitude. It grew colder, cruelly chill, but the thick sides retained the heat of Manila for weeks. The life on board settled to routine; the Commandant General became more used to the sea. The novelty of the ocean never palled, but the settled work of the ship made one day seem so like another that only the gradual lessening of fresh meat, the killing of the last fowl, the slaughtering of the last pig marked the time, and the water began to taste of the casks, to be less in quantity as the pilot mayor strictly supervised the allowance, the master and his mates having the ordering, with the guard of soldiers always at the provision hatch.

The first death—a child—came on a Sunday. Burial was before the mast, and the body was committed to the deep. Then others began to fail, as was the usual thing on the long crossing to Acapulco. Burials were in the early morning, just after sunrise. Heavy weather·from the north sent them scuttling 5 degrees to the south to a warmer latitude. And when the wind again became more westerly, Don Maria held the ship northward lest the wind begin to fail, for, like the western ocean, this still vaster sea has its horse latitudes, those uncertain stretches between the trades and the counter trades.

The Black Current, that dark stream off the coasts of Japan, had helped them on in spite of baffling winds.

Three months out from Manila, the great galleon's pilots noted those ominous signs of the coming of another equinoctial storm. The topmasts were struck and the topsail yards sent down to be lashed across the bulwarks. Heavy preventer braces were sent up to the yardarms. The courses were close reefed, and that new sail the English called a spencer was laced to the mainmast. The heavy tiller tackles were eased by the relieving tackles. Hatches were battened, except the access hatch to the main deck, where the people lived. Heavy hatch hoods were rigged. The boats were double gripped. And then, sogging in the sea, taking it on the bluff bow, the *Santísima Trinidad* wallowed, hove to, being driven more to the north. As thundering seas and the level drive of spume and wind hardened the last remaining canvas, it split free in the squalls, and she rode under bare poles, the high poop holding her into the wind. Truly the height of naval architecture had been achieved. Fires were out in the galley, the stench of roiled up bilges permeated the ship, but her people were becoming seasoned by the passage and did not mind. Only the Commandant General never got over his sickness of the sea. Now they were halfway across, the pilots said, thank God!

Like all things, a great storm at last comes to an end. The pilot mayor took advantage of a favoring slant to run south again before making more easting. He would avoid the fogs and strive for a better wind. Those who had been below were pasty and pale, and the seamen who had been on deck began to suffer from salt water boils. Veterans of the eastward passage knew that the hardest part of the voyage lay ahead.

But things had improved greatly in the galleon trade. The older men told of the legends handed down. No less than sixteen storms had swept over one of the earlier galleons. The great pilot Tozal and the heroic Father Esteban Carillo, of the *San Andres*, had carried her through a dozen devastating North Pacific tornadoes, one after another, handling the great ship with skill and encouraging her people in their many weeks of suffering. After each storm it was the custom to make votive offerings to the patron saint of the galleon. But these were old voyages, a century before. Ten years previously the huge *Santa Domingo* reached harbor on the coast of New Spain, making land in February, having also passed through sixteen punishing storms. Her planks were opened; she leaked so all hands labored at the pumps, and her poop and upper works were shattered by the pounding, her masts were sprung, and she made port just in time to avoid foundering at sea.

Many of the earlier galleons, when the southern passage was made out past the Philippines, fetched the Ladrones, crippled and sinking, and stories of them had come down. But the *Santísima Trinidad* was strong. The weather grew fine, and the people, in spite of their suffering for lack of food, made merry of a night on the broad decks, singing under the moon. Most of the restrictions of ship life had lifted. Even the women of the general's suite mingled in the fun. Although water was scarce, wine was still plentiful for those who had it.

Our great ship *Santísima Trinidad* made the coast of California and stood down past the Farallones. The great Bay of San Francisco was still unknown. She sailed past Navidad and entered Acapulco safely, as many lesser craft had done before her.

Never before or since has so mighty a procession of commerce continued over the same ocean route, under the same management, as that of the Manila and Acapulco ships, flying the flag of Spain and owned by the crown. Antonio de Morgo, the historian, wrote: "These vessels make the voyage from the Philippines to New Spain with great difficulty and danger, for the course is a long one and there are many storms and various temperatures." And Morgo himself had ample knowledge of the passage.

But in spite of the " . . . eternally doubtful and dangerous navigation of these seas," as Philip Thompson, an Englishman, wrote from his own experience as a pilot of galleons, comparatively few of them foundered—say, thirty or so—during the two and a half centuries of their existence as argosies of trade.

Capture by enemies was also infrequent. Cavendish took the *Santa Anna* in 1587; Woodes Rogers, the pirate, took the *Encarnación* in 1709, both of these captures off the coast of California. In 1743, Commodore Anson, flying the British naval pennant on the *Centurión*, captured the great galleon *Covadonga* off the Philippines. Last, the English took the great *Santísima Trinidad*, in 1762, when running back to Manila after damage in a storm. The percentages of missing and of captures would not have caused much concern to modern underwriters of shipping.

So these great strong ships plied, regardless of all other Pacific voyagers and oblivious of the teeming clouds of undiscovered islands lying far to the south.

Drake Enters the Pacific

AN OVERTAKING fate was to come into the great South Sea of the conquistadors, especially along the mountain fringed seashore stretching from 50 south to the line and northwestward to the coast of New Spain. Cortés and Pizarro had done their work less than a half century before. Spanish rule was well established, and the drive for Inca gold had brought forth vast quantities of easily negotiable wealth. Shipping, largely unprotected, freighted unheard of treasures safely on the sea. Not an enemy had yet dared sail in that distant ocean. Mendaña had returned to New Spain in 1569 from his dimly known voyage to the Solomons, when Pedro de Sarmiento served with him as second in command.

And then came that stretch of a quarter century during which there were no notable Spanish voyages to the westward. It was before the years of Mendaña's second fatal expedition, before the coming of Quiros. Off to the setting sun an ocean of mystery bounded the world with its voids. But the west coast cities of South America, the treasure ports on the Spanish longshore seaway, lay open for trade and transport undisturbed. The region was so distant that none but a Magellan could reach it except across the Spanish-held Isthmus of Panama. Spain accepted its inaccessibility as a guarantee of her perpetual sovereignty.

On Sept. 6, 1578, three English ships emerged from the Strait of Magellan, entering the Pacific, the first keels to fly there the colors of great Elizabeth. They stood bravely to the northwestward, Captain General Francis Drake leading in his flagship *Pelican*, a carrack of 120 tons. After him came the *Elizabeth* and then the small bark *Marigold*. Not a soul along that tremendous stretch of sea, the longest coast line north and south on earth, had the slightest apprehension that the first privateering cruisers had entered the eastern Pacific. Where Mendaña was impractical, a dreamer and no great shakes as a seaman, this Drake was one of the world's most experienced navigators, a ruthless sea fighter, a man of such extraordinary ability, force, character, and, withal, piety that the combination of qualities has seldom if ever been equaled in the annals of the sea. What he did in this historic raid has been smothered in the lists of loot. What the implications were and what were the results thereof extended through a century of world events, leading eventually to the downfall of Spain and the establishment of a new sea power that has survived to the present day.

Drake makes all the pirates of fact and fiction look like pickpockets by comparison. He carried the commission of the excommunicated Queen Elizabeth, his partner in the loot, and the Pacific Ocean was his oyster, its shores rich with silver and gold and rare merchandise. This is not imagination, it is sober history.

Before we follow Francis Drake in the taking of various prizes, the sighting of small ports on an ancient coast lying at the feet of the towering Andes, listen to the cries of despoiled Spaniards, the howls of dogs and Indians, and watch the hoisting in and tallying of pieces of eight, let us look at our Captain General, then at the vigorous, experienced age of thirty-eight.

He was born about 1540 in the sleepy little village of Tavistock, the eldest of twelve offspring begotten by the Reverend Edmund Drake. The fog-weathered Devon countryside nourished young Francis where the river Tay leads down to the seaport of Plymouth. Early he took to the sea, serving under his kinsman, Sir John Hawkins, not then knighted. Captain Hawkins traded in slaves, carrying them from the Bight of Biafra to the West Indies. From this Hawkins drifted naturally into enterprises against the Dons, and Francis Drake joined him and had a long experience in the hard realities of piratical warfare. He cruised with Hawkins in the Bay of Mexico, but mostly without success.

The times of Elizabeth were tense with an ever-growing hatred between Catholics and Protestants, a fever it has taken centuries to cure. Spain and Portugal, by papal bull, shared the world between them and wallowed in the riches thereof. England, and later Holland, the have-not nations, were to dispute this doctrine, not by argument but by force. Great Elizabeth, having been judged illegitimate by the Church of Rome, an insult her captains never forgave, adhered more strongly to her Protestant beliefs. The band of seamen who served her, among them Francis Drake, struck many a deadly blow in behalf of their Virgin Queen. It was like a comic opera on a gigantic scale; only the cannon balls and cutlasses were real. Broadsides crashed through many an oaken wall, death went to sea, and blood washed in the scuppers.

Drake, after fruitless attempts at plundering the Spaniards, at last made a great haul of treasure outside the little port of Nombre de Dios. Capturing a mule train, he took only the gold, being unable to carry the great weight of silver over the mountains. Shortly after this, in 1572, Drake ascended a mountain in Panama and, climbing a high tree, looked over the Pacific. He vowed to sail the first English keel upon that vast expanse of ocean.

Having returned to England laden with treasure, an arrow wound on his face and a Spanish arquebus ball lodged in his leg, the redoubtable Drake, the Queen's valiant and expert capitaine, fitted out three frigates at his own expense and cruised against the rebellious Irish. During this enterprise Francis Drake kept in mind his ambition to sail the Pacific in the service of Elizabeth. A plan was formed under the patronage of Sir Christopher Hatton, Vice-Chamberlain to the Queen, and later Chancellor of England. With the powerful backing of this noble, aided by his own high reputation for valor, Captain Drake was able to fit out a stout fleet of five ships and barks. These were got ready at Plymouth, and many gentlemen eager for glory attached themselves to the enterprise. Drake embarked most of his fortune, and a very substantial share in the venture was taken by the Queen.

His flagship, the *Pelican*, a ship of the French pattern with tumble-home sides, built with two closely fitted sheathings of planking, was sumptuously appointed. She had a high charged stern castle and stepped three masts. Her foremast near the prow rose out of a forecastle, and below this extended a billet head. Her bowsprit was long and had a decided stave—that is, was tilted upward; under it she swung her spritsail yard. The mizzen mast had no square canvas but hoisted a long crossjack yard, from which was set a sail after the lateen pattern. Like ships of her time, she was unprotected below the water line except by pitch, and her seams were covered with strips of lead, nailed on to hold in the caulking.

This was the flagship that sailed around the world and that was for many years kept in the Thames at Deptford as a shrine until at last she rotted and a chair was fashioned from her timbers that today stands at Oxford University.

The plan of Drake's voyage was kept secret. It was reported that he intended cruising in the Mediterranean to Alexandria. The seamen had no knowledge of the tremendous length of the contemplated venture. On Dec. 30, 1577, the *Pelican* led four consorts out through Plymouth Bay. Since we are concerned primarily with the flagship, the other ships and their various fates are cited in the order of their ending. The *Christopher*, a pinnace of 15 tons, and the *Swan*, a fly boat—that is, a supply ship—of 50 tons, were unladen and their stores distributed among the rest. The *Maria*, a canter captured in the Cape Verde Islands, was also discharged of her lading. Then these three, off the Patagonian coast, were set on fire. This left the *Marigold*, a bark of 30 tons, and the *Elizabeth*, viceflagship, of 80 tons, to follow the *Pelican* into the Pacific.

Drake's entry into the Pacific and his stormy sweep to the south by stress of weather, parted from his consorts, into the sub-Antarctic, resulted in the discovery of an island in 57 degrees south and 74 degrees west, an island where his single remaining ship, the *Pelican*, anchored for four nights, his people spending three days visiting the shore, on Oct. 25, 26, and 27, 1578. The Island was long shown on old charts, somewhat west of its position in longitude. But then, no island being found there, with very deep water over the spot, the ancient "Port Sir Francis Drake," as the old charts named it, was quietly forgotten. In the storm transverse the *Elizabeth* was driven back into the Strait of Magellan. Supposing the Captain General to have foundered, she returned eastward through Magellan Strait to England with the bad news. The *Marigold* did founder, parting company with her two consorts during a great storm near 57 degrees south, never to be seen again. Drake, however, was unsinkable and unbeatable. Striving for better weather, he stood to the northward along the grim coast of Chile, which he found to lie north and south, not northwest and southeast. Magellan's discovery of this fact had not yet been transferred to charts.

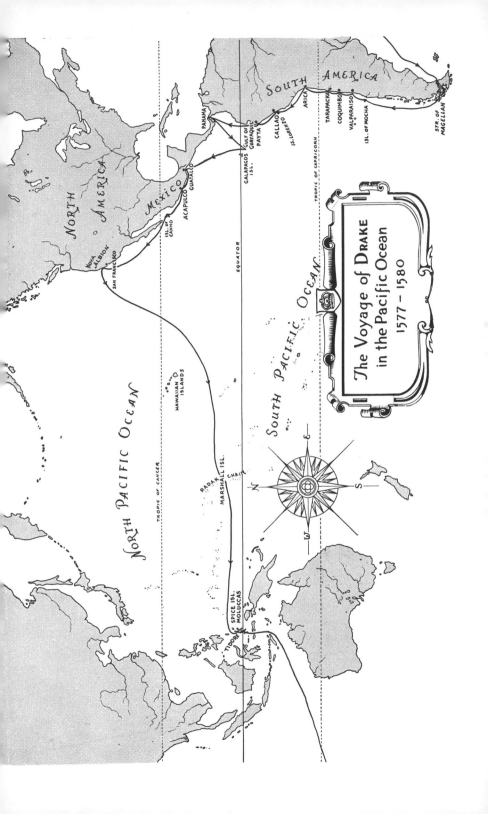

Drake was provided with the best navigating instruments of his time. Silver and bronze astrolabes of fine workmanship were part of his equipment, and the remarkable accuracy of his recorded latitudes attests their excellence and also his skill as a navigator. He carried books on navigation, one in English and another in French. Also, he had a third book, a volume of directions, of Magellan's discoveries, presumed to have been a copy of the narrative of Antonio Pigafetta. The declination tables of those times, giving the angular distances of the sun, north and south of the equator, the lunar eclipses, etc., were carried by Drake as he worked northward along the coast.

On Nov. 29, 1578, the *Pelican* came to the island of Mocha off the coast of Chile, lying in 38½ degrees south, being about ten leagues off the main shore of the land. "Here our Generall hoysing out our boate, went with ten of our company to shore, where wee found people, whom the cruell and extreme dealings of the Spaniards have forced for their owne safetie and libertie to flee from the maine, and to fortifie themselves in this Island."

When Drake approached La Mocha in that distant November, without charts, his lookouts descried land, lifting like a blue cloud to the north. For fifty miles this thing kept growing to the height of 1,300 feet, looming greater because of its limited extent, being only seven miles long. Its south part rose abruptly from the sea, tailing down to the north. It lay like a lion, off the coast of Chile. Far eastward were silhouetted mountaintops, seen when the weather cleared and the sun came from behind. A reef broke to seaward as the *Pelican*, under shortened canvas, moved carefully in toward the island. They anchored in seven fathoms over sand and found themselves sheltered from anything blowing out of the north. Of the five stout ships that had left Plymouth over a year before, only one remained, the ship of Drake.

Drake himself was in need of rest. His force was weak, as his actions show, for on many occasions he was compelled to run rather than engage forces that to him at least must have seemed contemptible. A spell of fair weather gave them the chance to recuperate and refit as far as possible at sea, setting up rigging and reeving new running gear. The powder kegs were dry, but the provisions were low, and fresh water was almost gone.

Running in through the surf to a bad landing at La Mocha, Drake himself, at the head of his boat's crew, parleyed with the islanders, " . . . who came downe to us to the water side with shew of great courtesie, bringing to us potatoes, rootes, and two very fat sheepe, which our General received and gave them other things for them."

Fresh water was their dire need. The next day, landing with casks, two men carrying barrels, going in search of a spring, were attacked. Indians who mistook them for Spaniards, " . . . to whom they use to shew no favour if they take them, layde violent hands on them, and as we thinke, slew them.

"Our Generall seeing this, stayed here no longer, but wayed anchor and set sayle towards the coast of Chili."

This drab, inhospitable island was Drake's initiation to the great South Sea of Spanish rule. Unlike many other explorers before and since, he did not seek revenge against the Indians, who had made a natural mistake. They, too, were Spaniard killers and in a way his friends. But the prospect, as he saw it then, was drear enough.

Closing with the land, Drake came upon an Indian in a canoe. Thinking the *Pelican* Spanish, the native gave word of a place called St. Iago, where, he said, a great Spanish ship laden from the kingdom of Peru lay at anchor. Drake, always kind to the Indians, gave him some trinkets and took the native on board to act as pilot. It was southern summer, when the blue and yellow coast of Peru is fanned by warm breezes from the southwest, a fair wind to the *Pelican*. The toughened mariners basked in the sun, glorying in the gentle weather.

Fresh green patches showed ashore as they came up with Angeles Point; smelling the good land, they opened a wide and peaceful bay, sheltered from all but winter northers. The haven lay asleep on that supreme December day.

A large deeply laden ship was riding safely at her anchor, with only eight Spaniards, a Greek, and three Negroes on board her, a mere anchor watch. These men curiously lining the bulwark were eager to meet with another ship. They saw an able looking craft wafting in, her topsails down, the sheeted crossjack holding her close to wind as she struck her spritsail, squared the forecourse and rounded to close by—as pretty a piece of sailoring as could be seen. She hung her mainsail, and a boat was hoisted out; her anchor plunged into the bay.

Here was news, perhaps from far Cadiz or San Lúcar! She was a strange deep sea ship, not a coaster, not a clumsy Manila galleon. In that dull summer bay, while the captain and the merchants and most of the men were ashore, the stand-by people would have the real excitement. They welcomed the boat coming toward them by beating a drum. They greeted her with shouts of joy and made ready a "bottija of Chili wine to drinke to us."

Swinging under the quarter of the Spaniard, Drake's boarders climbed into her main channels and over the high bulwark, led by Master Thomas Moon, who began to lay about him " . . . and stroke one of the Spaniards and sayed unto him, '*Abaxo, perro!*' that is, in English, '*Goe downe, dogge!*' "

One of the friendly men, dropping a glass of wine, crossed himself and dove into the bay, swimming fast toward the little hamlet of San Iago. He spread warning of the arrival of a rover. Moon and his people clapped the remaining Spaniards and the Negroes under hatches.

Drake, leading another boat ashore for the little town, found there only nine households, a chapel, and a warehouse. The inhabitants had fled. The English sacked the poor place. In the tiny chapel were a silver chalice, two cruets, and one altar cloth, "the spoil whereof our Generall gave to M. Fletcher his minister."

Here was a miserable act of pilfering, and the gift of the spoil to the cringing Fletcher was a token of disdain. They did find the warehouse stored with wine of Chile and many boards of cedar, which they took to the *Pelican* and split for firewood. But aboard the ship, which Thomas Moon had captured, was plenty of loot. The Spaniards were put ashore, but one man, a Greek called John Griego by Haklyut's account and later referred to as Sant John de Anton in a copy of Drake's letter, was kept with the ship. Manned by a prize crew, presumably under Thomas Moon, she weighed and stood to sea with the *Pelican*, for the ancient bay of Valparaiso, the Vale of Paradise, was by then astir, and many boats were being manned along the shore. Soldiers dashed about, the sun glinting on their arquebuses and crossbows. It was no place in which to stay and fight.

Off the coast and well away toward the north, Drake rifled the prize, the ships lying with topsails backed, bobbing in a brilliant sea, while chests and bags were tallied over the side of the *Pelican*. First came leather pouches of Baldiva gold, pure and glittering like warm fire, these to the amount of 25,000 pesos, valued at 37,000 ducats of Spanish money. They also found in her a good store of Chile wine. If they were short of water, at least they had plenty of that mild and stimulating beverage. But there was no drunkenness or unseemly conduct or irreligious blasphemy aboard a ship commanded by Captain General Francis Drake. In his cabin he pondered the treasure, the first golden fruits of his enterprise to the benefit of the Queen. That evening he dined with his principal shipmates, young John Drake at his side, and the music of viols came out of the great cabin and across the decks. The men were smoking the weed brought to England by Raleigh, for some of this had been found in the ship, and an extra ration of Chile wine helped. There was much merry talk of prize money, of the rich haul.

Hereabout, on that very December night, perhaps on the eve of the Nativity, Captain General Drake addressed the ship's company. Their brave storm beaten *Pelican* was thenceforth to be known as the *Golden Hind*. They drank to this renaming and cheered. Then Parson Fletcher, under the eagle glance of his employer Drake, said, "God bless the Queen."

So *Golden Hind* she was, and her name taken from the idea of her first freighting of golden treasure, thereby making the expedition a success, has come down through the centuries. But some say the name was suggested by a golden hind on the device of Sir Christopher Hatton, Drake's influential patron.

The two ships, the prize most probably under command of Thomas Moon, stood northward to Coquimbo. Here Drake went for fresh water, their great necessity. John de Anton had told them it was one of the finest bays on the west coast. Three centuries later it became a favorite anchorage for ships of the British Navy on the South Pacific station. Drake entered and sent fourteen men ashore with casks.

Word had gone northward along the shore by courier. Swift runners had carried dread news of a pirate ship. Five hundred Spaniards were assembled on the beach behind a rise, 300 of them horsemen. As the seamen landed, rolling ashore their cumbersome barrels, the soldiers charged, slaying one of the men with an arquebus ball. All retired to the boats, carrying their companion. The next day Drake, in armor, his ship within range, her guns bearing, landed in force to bury their shipmate. The Spaniards sent down a flag of truce. But Drake, embarking, still short of water, sailed away. He had fought Spaniards too long to parley.

So desperate was Drake for fresh water that ten leagues onward he again anchored and sent some of his people ashore to fill a few casks. Seeing a horseman, they immediately embarked. The pilot, John the Greek, then carried them to

Tarapaza, or Tarapacka. They had by that time outdistanced all possible along-the-shore couriers, for Drake cracked on sail with such a fair wind that the two consorts covered 10 degrees of latitude in little more than three days. No foot runner or horseman could do that. In addition, the Andes, rising in majestic steepness, their foothills reaching down to the sea, made difficult paths and roads. The grandeur of the scenery, the land seemingly reaching to the sky, disclosed the highest mountains these Englishmen had ever beheld. It looked as if a rampart of impregnable rock stood on guard before the mines of the Incas. But how to get at more gold?

Anchoring in the dull little bay, a place without promise, Francis Drake, walking along the quiet shore, came upon a Spaniard fast asleep in the shade of a bush. Lying at his side was a leather pouch containing thirteen bars of silver " . . . weighing 4,000 ducats, Spanish!" They took the silver and let the sleepy Spaniard go.

"Not farre from hence going on land for fresh water, we met with a Spaniard and an Indian boy driving 8 Llamas or sheepe of Peru which are as big as asses; every one of the sheepe had on his backe 2 bags of leather, each bagge conteining 50 lb. weight of fine silver; so that bringing both the sheepe and their burthen to the ships, we found in all the bags 800 weight of silver."

Sant John de Anton, the Greek (to give him the name bestowed by the jolly Drake), directed them a little way northward along the mighty rampart of coast into a still more salubrious sea, where they reached Arica, now within the Chilean boundary. Here was a small bay formed by a precipitous bluff lifting 700 feet from the sea. It dwarfed the ships; it hung over them like a brown shadow. Here the Andes throw up Titanic snow-capped peaks, gleaming like the silver that seemed so plentiful, red as molten gold in the sunset. Drake knelt each night and morning, asking God for blessing on his enterprise. At Arica they found three small barks and promptly rifled them, finding in one fifty-seven wedges of silver, each weighing twenty pounds. In these small craft they discovered only a single person, the crews having fled to the shore on approach of the English sails. Two hundred *botijas,* or Spanish pots of wine, were in these ships. Drake preparing to land, or, as the record states, to "leape ashore," with a force of thirty-seven armed with arquebuses and crossbows, saw a cloud of dust kicked up by a force of horsemen thundering down toward the raiders. Taking a Negro, found hidden in one of the barks, asleep in the hold, they returned on board and, with prize crews, stood out of Arica, accompanied by two of their captures. One bark they burned, and the other joined with them.

Now this astonishing coast, its llamas laden with silver, with sleepy Spaniards dozing harmless beside great stores of loot, was also awake. Some tremendous effort of intelligence had caught up with them. Holding the ships off shore, Drake embarked in his pinnace, a small swift sailer, running close inshore just outside the breakers, the ships a league to seaward. As da Silva wrote, "Having in that manner sailed about five and forty leagues, they found a ship that lay at anker in a haven, who about two hours before had bene advised of an English pirate or sea rover, and had discharged eight hundred barres of silver out of her, and had hidden it on the land, which silver belonged to the king of Spaine."

Here Drake was disappointed. He was on the verge of ballasting the *Golden Hind* with silver, tons of it. The ship held no more than three pipes of water, and these they took; then, slipping her cable and hoisting her sails, they stood off shore and "let her drive" (that is, without a crew) back onto that rumbling rocky coast. The Captain General abandoned the ship taken in Arica, and she, too, was turned adrift. The few prisoners were transferred to the ship captured in Valparaiso.

The *Golden Hind* moved gently before a southerly breeze beneath a canopy of blazing stars. Drake, under shortened canvas, his topsails hung in their gear, his mainsail and foresail hoisted by the buntlines, the sprit and crossjack giving him command of her, hauled the wind abeam and stood boldly toward shore, close by a steep island (San Lorenzo) and on toward a mighty wall of distant mountains defined by the jagged blanking out of rising star dust in the east. All was quiet on board, for they were approaching a position of some strength, the capital of Peru, the seat of Viceroy Francisco de Toledo. It was a rich bay, that of Callao de Lyma, lying at the mouth of the Rio Rimac. Pizarro had founded a city three leagues inland only forty-three years before, and since 1541, the date of his assassination, he had lain at rest in Lima, his City of the Kings. It was a strong place to be attempted by a force as weak as that of Captain General Drake. Men-of-war might be swinging at their moorings in the bay.

Nevertheless, the silent corsair, lights extinguished, closed with the shore and into the unknown anchorage. Drake and his officers were in armor. All hands were at quarters. Both broadsides were shotted and run out in battery. The crew, with boarding pikes and cutlasses, were ready, with matches lit, boarding nettings and close-fights triced up. Leadsmen on either side whispered their soundings. No tenser night had ever been known. As Pilot da Silva put it, " . . . being within three houres within the night, sailing between all the ships that lay there, being seventeene in number."

Few of the great naval commanders have ever equaled the intrepidity of Captain General Francis Drake entering that unknown bay on the night of Feb. 13, 1579.

He lost no time in putting over his boats to examine the ships in Callao. There were no men-of-war. Drake searched for a ship that had treasure but was told that this had already been laid ashore. At the same time a merchantman, with lights lit, coming up from Panama with Spanish wares, ghosted to an anchorage. A customs boat had put out from the shore to board this new arrival as she anchored close by the *Golden*

Hind. The shore boat, spying the corsair, hailed, and one of the Spanish prisoners (the inference is that it was none other than Drake's faithful da Silva) answered and said, "We are the ship of Michael Angelo, come up from Chili."

The customs men sent a boarding officer, who quickly became suspicious and, frightened by the hostile appearance of the *Golden Hind*, hastily stepped back into his boat. As soon as the merchantman was aware of the danger she put to sea. Drake immediately shipped some of his men in a pinnace, and they followed her, bidding her strike. She refused and with an arquebus shot killed one of the Englishmen.

Drake, in the meantime, having hastily searched the anchored craft and finding no loot, cut the cables of the ships and the masts of two of the greatest craft, vessels that might embark a force and follow him. Returning to the *Golden Hind*, he broke out anchor, setting all sail in chase of the Panama merchantman, picking up the pinnace and her slain man on the way.

In the pearl dawn outside Callao they overtook the running ship as she held close inshore. The Spaniards in panic hoisted out their boat, tumbled into her, and rowed swiftly, beaching through the rumbling fringe of huge Pacific breakers. A boarding party leapt aboard the merchantman, righted her helm, set canvas, and ratched off to join the flagship.

Again the coast was afire with alarm. A large boat under sail was seen making toward them, and they judged her a spy, for presently two great ships loomed to the south, pressing all sail, as if armed and coming to fight. Drake sent John the Greek and two Spaniards taken in Callao to the Panama ship and let her drive, but not without consideration for the pilot, who was given a letter of safe conduct in case he should fall in with the *Elizabeth*, of which Drake had no knowledge.

What became of the undermanned ship of Sant John de Anton is not known. Most likely she was picked up by the pursuing Spaniards, and it went hard with John the Greek.

The *Elizabeth*, when the letter of safe conduct was written, was well on her way back to England, without honor or glory and with doubtful tidings of the Queen's valiant Captain General, Francis Drake.

Aside from Drake's early concern about fresh water, which he soon overcame, his provisioning from prizes and the shore gave all hands an abundance of fresh meat, fruits, pots of butter and honey, and such vegetables as the country afforded. And there was always the liberal allowance of wholesome Chile wine. Some of the ships taken were laden with fish, as was a Panama ship encountered shortly after the adventure in Lima, when they touched at the haven called Payta. In her they also found forty bars of silver and eighty pound weight of gold. The passengers, including two friars, were sent ashore in a boat. One of the crew of the captured ship stole two plates of gold, which he would not confess taking, but after these were found about him Drake promptly hanged this rascal to the yardarm. Then, having secured all booty, they let the ship drive.

Word come to Drake of a treasure ship that had sailed toward Payta, but, not finding her there, he chased her northward across the Gulf of Guayaquil. She was heading for Panama to transship her wealth over the Isthmus and thence eastward to Spain, according to the custom of those days. In the pursuit northward the *Golden Hind* overhauled a bark laden with ropes and tackle for ships. Drake took her and also found in her eighty pound weight of gold and a gold crucifix "with goodly great emeralds set in it." With this prize he gained a large supply of cordage for his own ship as well. But the treasure galleon still eluded him, and they were coming close to the Line, sailing under brazen skies. In little more time, unless he made her out, the quarry would get into the Gulph of Panama. Da Silva tells of trimming the *Golden Hind* with pots filled with water hung from the stern. Her sailing suffered because she was too far down by the head with weight of silver and gold. Lookouts were alert, but made more so by Drake.

"Whosoever first descries her," he offered, "shall have my chaine of golde." And from then on there was great sport to see who should pick up the sail ahead, while the *Golden Hind* boiled through the warm Pacific beneath a press of canvas day and night. White whiskers of foam spread out from her prow, and in the dark she seemed to part a sea of fire. But at three o'clock in the afternoon, young John Drake, hanging at the mainmast truck, sent down the cry, "*Sail Ho! Sail Ho!*"

So swift was the pursuit that by six o'clock the *Golden Hind* came abeam of the chase, and Drake ordered her to strike, which she refused to do. "Then fire!" And a great piece aimed at her mizzen by Oliver, the master gunner, brought it down.

"Well done, my Oliver—well done!" cried Drake. Then the crossbow men sent on a shower of arrows, wounding the master of the treasure carrack. She yielded, and Thomas Moon led the boarders. They were close to Cape San Francisco, on the coast of Ecuador, abreast of the distant Galápagos Islands. And Drake, fearing pursuit, stood off to the west under press of sail that night and the next day and night, making all the way he could, held back as he was by the slower, injured galleon.

On the third day they hove to on a placid tropic sea and rifled the prize. Da Silva tallied fourteen chests with "ryals of eight and with gold." Hakluyt gives her "thirteen chests full of royals of plate, four score pound weight of gold, and six and twentie tunne of silver." Da Silva noted 1,300 bars of silver, 300 of which belonged to the King.

The capture was the ship *Cacafuego*, or *Spitfire*. The lift of a great tumbling sea danced in the sun as the ships dipped and rolled. Now Drake's men had grown rich; the flush of victory and satisfied revenge put them all in high good humor. Even the losers seemed to be enjoying themselves. A ship's boy of the treasure carrack said to Drake, " 'Our ship shall no longer be

called *Cacafuego* [*Spitfire*], but *Cacaplata* [Spitsilver].' Which
pretie speech of the Pilot's boy ministered a matter of laughter
to us, both then and long after." And Drake was kind to the
boy, as he was to all men and boys who did not cross him.

The pilot of the ship, Don Francisco, had among his belong-
ings "two very faire guilt bowles of silver." To him Drake said,
"Señor Pilot, you have here two silver cups, but I must needs
have one of them." The pilot wisely obeyed the request and
then, being a clever man, added the other cup as a voluntary
gift.

Drake cast off the emptied treasure ship, keeping a few
hostages, just in case, as he stood toward the coast of New
Spain. On the way he met another ship laden with China silks
and China dishes. She had on board a Spanish gentleman from
whom Drake took a "Fawlcon of golde, with a great Emeraud
in the breast thereof." Holding the gentleman and her pilot, he
also turned this craft adrift.

They were then in the North Pacific, closing with the coast
of Mexico. The pilot taken with the last ship brought them to
the harbor of Guatalco, on the shores of Tehuantepec, eastward of the galleon port of Acapulco. This pilot told Drake
that the place had but seventeen Spaniards.

"As soone as we were entered this haven, wee landed, and
went presently to the Townehouse, where we found a Judge
sitting in judgment, in associate with three other officers, passing upon three Negroes that were accused of conspiring to burn
the Towne."

Drake, who enjoyed his comedy, took charge of both judges
and prisoners, ordering court adjourned in the name of the
Queen. He carried these astonished people aboard ship, and
the chief judge was caused to write a letter instructing all to
leave the town at once so the English might safely water there.
This letter being written, the Negroes were turned loose with a
word of commendation, and their prosecutors were un-
ceremoniously set ashore. The sailors then landed, watered,

and, before departing, ransacked the town of Guatalco. In one house they found a "pot of the quantitie of a bushell, full of reals of plate, which we brought to the ship."

In this place our vigorous friend Thomas Moon chased a Spanish gentleman up a dusty street as he was fleeing out of the town and, searching him, "found, a chaine of gold about him, and other jewels, which he tooke, and so let him goe."

Before leaving Guatalco, Drake made a change in his personnel, a change of extraordinary historical interest. Nuño da Silva, the Portuguese pilot, and expert navigator, taken in the Cape Verde Islands with his canter the *Maria*, and who had served the Captain General loyally, was put ashore, together with the various hostages picked up on the way northward along the coast. Thence onward the *Golden Hind*, heavily laden with loot, was manned solely by Englishmen.

Drake sailed off to the west, leaving da Silva and the others to the Spanish authorities, who took them into custody.

Drake, with his English crew, sailed to the Isle of Canno (most probably the Las Tres Marias, off the coast of Mexico, in about 21 degrees and 30 minutes north). Here Drake brought the *Golden Hind* to the beach, set up a camp, discharged his cargo and stores, tallied his treasure, and careened. He restowed and filled his water butts. The ship was then stocked with a sufficiency of wood. No sooner had she been made ready than a sail was descried, and the approaching craft was overhauled and searched. Aboard were a Spanish governor and two pilots. She was an outbound Manila ship, but without treasure. Drake took some of her merchandise, but not much, since he was already laden deep, and he let her go. But he did get her sea cards, or charts, showing the route to the East.

In this most historic of all ocean raids, profitable beyond belief, Drake came to some philosophical conclusions. Hakluyt gives this pious homily.

"Our Generall at this place and time, thinking himself both

in respect of his private injuries received from the Spaniards, as also of their contempts and indignities offered to our country and Queen, sufficiently satisfied and revenged; and supposing that her Majestie at his return would rest contented with his service, purposed to continue no longer upon the Spanish coasts, but began to consider and to consult of the best way for his Countrey."

Drake's raid stirred up a mighty storm of protest and activity. Swift zabras by sail and sweeps carried the news up from Chile and Peru to the Isthmus of Panama. Fast caravels were hurrying to great Spain with alarming dispatches from the Viceroys. New Spain was afire with indignation. The eastern shores of the Pacific from Acapulco to Magellan Strait were in a state of terror. If one ship could do such damage, how about an entire fleet? Drake was called "the scourge of God," and Bernardino de Mendoza, ambassador to the English court, in his protests to Elizabeth, termed him "the Master Thief of the unknown world."

The Spanish crown would deal severely with its colonial governors for their negligence. Philip II was no one to trifle with. Don Francisco de Toledo, Viceroy of Peru, in October, 1579, the year of the great raid, sent his ablest commander in pursuit of Drake, none other than Don Pedro de Sarmiento y Gamboa, who had sailed with Mendaña. Sarmiento put to sea with two heavy ships. Drake had disappeared from the coast of Mexico, and the Spaniards were sure he was again heading back via the Strait of Magellan. Sarmiento's orders were: "If you meet or get news of the ship in which sails Francis Drake, the English pirate, *you will do your best to capture, kill or cripple him by fight, at any risk whatever.*"

As Sarmiento sailed south to catch Drake on his disastrous attempt to fortify the Strait of Magellan against other raiders, Drake made his bold decision to sail across the Pacific. "He thought it not good to returne by the Streights, for two speciall causes: the one lest the Spaniards should there waite, and attend for him in great number and strength, whose hands, hee being left but one ship, could not possibly escape. The other cause was the dangerous situation of the mouth of the Streights in the South Sea, where continuall stormes reigning and blustering, as he found by experience, besides the shoalds and sand upon the coast, he thought it not a good course to adventure that way; he resolved therefore to avoyde these hazards, to goe forward to the Islands of the Malucos, and there hence to saile the course of the Portugals by the Cape Buena Esperanza."

Drake's Pacific adventure also had another object, namely, the search for a northeast passage from the Pacific into the Atlantic and around North America homeward by that long sought way. He was to sail northward, locate the fabled Strait of Anian, and so home. For two centuries after Drake this vision of a northward passage around America prevailed.

Drake sailed " . . . toward the pole Arctike." On June 5, "We found the ayre so colde, that our men being greviously pinched with the same, complained of the extremities thereof, and the further we went, the more the colde increased upon us. Wherefore we thought it best for that time to seeke the land, and did so, finding it not mountainous, but low plaine land, till wee came within 38 degrees towards the line. In which height it pleased God to send us into a faire and good Baye, with a good winde to enter the same."

Old voyage narratives are among man's most honest records. Marco Polo, long regarded by the ignorant as a romancer, has become a veritable well of truth. Pigafetta, barring some misinterpretations, was most truthful in stating what he saw. Drake's voyage was written most probably from word of mouth accounts by Richard Hakluyt, and the story set down by old Chaplain Fletcher is truthful. Wherever latitudes are mentioned by Hakluyt, they check closely with present-time positions.

When Drake entered the "good Baye," just north of the Golden Gate at San Francisco, he named the country Nova Albion. It was a discovery: "It seemeth that the Spaniards hitherto had never bene in this part of the Countrey, neither did they ever discover the land by many degrees, to the Southwards of this place."

This was a country inhabited by friendly Indians, a land rich in herds of deer, the whole country "being a warren of a strange kinde of Connies, their bodies in bignesse as be the Barbary Connies, their heads as the heads of ours, the feet of a Want, and the taile of a Rat being of great length."

The people of Nova Albion ate these "connies" and made coats of their fur. The white banks and cliffs, still to be noted on the coast of California, that lie toward the sea reminded Drake of Albion " . . . because it might have some affinity with our Countrey in name, which sometimes was so called."

They were at this place in June. Around the middle of that month, in the year 1579, says the narrative, "There is no part of earth heere to be taken up, wherein there is not some probable shew of gold or silver." Quite a guess, 270 years before the gold rush of '49! Then at last, having formally taken claim and having accepted homage and exchanged presents with the native king, Drake caused a brass plate to be prepared.

"At our departure hence our Generall set up a monument to our being there, as also of her Majesties right and title to the same, namely a plate, nailed upon a faire great post, whereupon was ingraven her Majesties name, the day and yeere of our arrivall there, with the free giving up of the province and people into her Majesties hands, together with her highnesse picture and armes, in a piece of sixe pence of current English money under the plate, whereunder was also written the name of our Generall."

In 1938, this plate was found, exactly as described, a plate of brass with a hole wherein the sixpence might have been set. The plate is now in possession of the University of California. Never in the great history of recorded voyages has more direct corroboration come to us from beyond the centuries.

Drake, with aid of the charts taken from the ship "going for the Philippines," left his anchorage and set a course westward over the Pacific through the northeast trades, out past the Golden Gate, missing this discovery. The date was near the middle of June. On Oct. 13, 1579, the *Golden Hind* sighted her first land, being four months in the crossing. The passage was uneventful and, because of ample provisioning, free from scurvy. Making his landfall at some islands in 8 degrees north, Drake missed the islands of Hawaii, probably sailing to the southward. His landfall were islands, the Radak Chain, or the Marshall Islands, according to the latitude. They were thickly inhabited and afforded cocos and fruits, and the swift canoes of the natives caused admiration among the mariners.

Drake's fresh provisioning, his strict discipline, and his superb seamanship carried him through the coral-studded seas. A month later he was in the Moluccas, and then on to Tidore. As the chronicle goes, "Wee continued our course by the Islands of Tagulada, Zelon, and Zewarra, being friends of the Portugals, the first whereof hath growing in it great shew of Cinnamom." They provisioned and exchanged some of their silver for spices.

Drake returned to England on Nov. 3, 1580, having been away for three years, the first commander to circumnavigate the globe in his own flagship.

After many adventures, including the famous defeat of the Spanish Armada, he set sail in 1595 on what was to prove his final voyage. Second in command to old Sir John Hawkins, he went to the West Indies in an attempt to mend his fortune and his glory. Sir John Hawkins died in November off Porto Rico, and after that ended the career of the great Pacific navigator

Sir Francis Drake. He died of a flux at seven o'clock in the morning, Jan. 29, 1596, off Porto Bello, at the age of fifty-six.

The next day Sir Thomas Basherville, who succeeded in command, carried him a league off shore and buried him in the Spanish Main.

The Taking of the Santa Anna

TEN years after Drake, a scant stretch of time in the Pacific, the third circumnavigator fared that way. This was on what Hakluyt calls "the admirable and prosperous voyage of the Worshipfull Master Thomas Candish of Trimley in the Countie of Suffolke, Esquire, into the South Sea, and thence round about the circumference of the whole earth, begun in the yeere of our Lord, 1586 and finished 1588. Written by Master Francis Pretty lately of Ely in Suffolke, a Gentleman employed in the same action."

The title tells the story, and the prosperous part of it was the taking of the first Manila galleon by Candish, or Cavendish, as we now spell it. His three ships, the *Desire*, admiral, of 120 tons, the *Content*, vice-admiral, of 60 tons, and the *Hugh Gallant*, rear admiral, a bark of 40 tons, followed a course, nearly paralleling that of Drake, northward along the coasts of Chile and Peru. But Cavendish, aside from many adventures ashore, found little or no gold of Baldivia lying in the holds of defenceless ships, no Spaniards asleep alongside bags of silver, and llamas laden with the white metal were not to be seen. He entered the ports of Acapulco, of old Navidad and Mazatlan, gaining knowledge of the Manila ship, the annual galleon heading toward New Spain across the wide ocean lying to the west. For nearly eight months Cavendish had cruised the coast up from Magellan, and on Oct. 14, 1587, fell in with Cape San Lúcar (Cape St. Lucas) at the southern tip of Lower California. It reminded him of the Needles of the Isle of Wight. For want of men, because of casualties in scrimmages and from sickness, the *Hugh Gallant,* their rear admiral, had been purposely sunk some months before. The *Desire* and the *Content* took her surviving people. They cruised back and forth across the course of the Manila ship, when, on Nov. 4, between seven and eight of the clock in the morning watch, the trumpeter of the *Desire,* laying aloft to observe the sea, espied a sail bearing toward the Cape of San Lúcar. Never in the history of the Manila galleons had one of them been disturbed, and the huge weedgrown craft sagged on before a fair wind, close to the end of her mighty course.

The trumpeter cried out, "*A sayle! A sayle!*" at which the master, Thomas Fuller, of Ipswich, and others lay aloft, and these shouted down the happy news to their General, Thomas Cavendish.

The approaching galleon was a great ship, of at least 700 tons, heavy, with high sides although she was deeply laden. A foul bottom made her slow and sluggish. The *Desire* and the little *Content,* like killer whales after leviathan, gave chase, pressing sail, while the General ordered that all be put in readiness for attack. The great guns were freshly served with powder and shot, arquebuses were at the bulwarks, and in the tops lay the crossbow men; pikes and cutlasses were handy, and the grappling irons were made ready to cast. The nettings were triced, and all was in order aloft, with preventer slings and braces rigged. Nothing they could think of was neglected.

They sanded their decks, and tubs of sea water were at the hatches.

There was tremendous excitement aboard the privateers. Great Manila ships were thick of side, and solid great shot could not always harm them. They carried upwards of 400 or 500 men. And no attempt had ever been made to attack them.

"Master Fuller, how stands the chase?" Cavendish called from the great cabin where he was shaving and dressing in armor. Young, excited, and not too experienced, he nevertheless was determined.

"Right on head, General. We shall reach him soon."

"What! Is all ready?"

"Yea, yea, General. All is manned." he replied and, to the helm, "Mind your luff. Steady the course."

They closed, the two small ships to windward. Cavendish, in armor, came on the poop.

"Oh, ship of Spain!" hailed the General. "Whence come you?"

Flags were flying. The colors of Castile and Aragon rose to the mizzen of the wallowing galleon, her green weeded bilges lifting as she rolled. Her men lay behind the bulwarks, and the *Desire* and *Content* held their weak crews below the nettings and close fights. Cavendish listened for a reply.

"Give her a chase piece," he ordered the gunner. The shot fell short. "Run a good berth ahead of him, Master Fuller."

"Yea, yea, a berth ahead! Steady there the helum, steady, men! And ready with the matches. Mind your locks. Mind your bowes."

They gave her a volley of small shot. "Now, gunner. *Fire!*" And a broadside thundered into the great *Santa Anna* galleon, for it was she, inbound from Manila with treasure and rich merchandise for Acapulco. The balls hit her sides and dropped, but the small shot tore through her rigging and cut the sails.

"We do her no harm, Master Fuller."

"None, General Candish, none. We are too far."

"Lay her aboard! All ready!" The ships closed in the afternoon sea, the heavy Pacific swell lifting her like a great strong fort, and the General's ship, at the signal, came to her high sides. With cries, "St. George for England!" the *Desire* threw her grapnels while the tops of both ships discharged showers of arrows and fired their clumsy arquebuses.

Fifty men were told to board her, but the *Content* lay off, firing but not boarding so that she might be close in case of a bloody repulse.

Shouts and the rolling of drums, the blaring of trumpets sounded down on the English. Above them on the galleon a great company of soldiers stood at arms. Stones were hurled down on the corsairs. The Spaniards, behind their strong poop and forecastles and amidship, were sheltered by her close fights. None could be seen while the lances and their javelins worked against the men clambering up the slippery wales and the heavy chains. Then they came hand to hand on the wide deck, already blooded. Rapiers flashed, and the English were repulsed, casting off with two men slain and four or five wounded. A loud cheer of derision came from the *Santa Anna*.

"We new trimmed our sailes, and fitted every man his furniture, and gave them a fresh encounter with our great ordnance and also with our small shot, raking them through and through, to the killing and maiming of many of their men." So the two corsairs kept pounding them, and there were no great guns to keep them off.

Aboard the huge *Santa Anna*, all became confusion. She was a half year out from the Philippines. Many of her people were sick, her women screamed in terror, weeping over their dead, and her soldiers were disorganized. The few great guns she had were below, stowed in the cargo.

The *Desire* again attacked her huge quarry, strong only in her bulk, her height of hull. "Our General encouraging his men afresh and with the whole noise of trumpets gave them the third encounter with our great ordnance and all our small shot to the great discomforting of our enemies, raking them through in divers places, killing and spoiling many of their men."

The fight had gone for six hours, and some of the round shot had holed the galleon between wind and water. Being unable to reply and fearing foundering or a boarding in the night—for the corsairs grew more bold—the *Santa Anna* threw out a flag of truce, the white folds rising in her tattered rigging. Cavendish ranged close alongside, ceasing his fire. The Spanish captain parleyed for mercy, asking only that their lives be spared. The English might take their goods, and they would presently yield.

"Abajo! Abajo!" Down came the colors of Spain.

"Our General," wrote Master Pretty, "of his goodness promised them mercy, and willed them to strike their sayles and hoise out their boate and to come on board which news they were full glad to heare of, and presently strooke their sailes, hoysed their boat out, and one of their chief merchants came aboord unto our Generall: falling downe upon his knees, offered to have kissed our General's feete, and craved mercie."

What a scene that must have been on the small deck of the *Desire*—the powder blackened men, stripped to breeches, barefooted; the wounded with their rude bandages; the coxcomb Cavendish, flushed with victory and the sight of wealth beyond counting. It was getting on toward dark. Care had to be taken lest the *Santa Anna* elude them in the night.

Pretty adds a touch to the picture: "Our Generall most graciously pardoned both him (the merchant) and the rest upon promise to their true dealing with him and his company concerning such riches as were in the shippe: and sent for their Captaine and their Pilote, who at their coming used the like dutie and reverence as the former did. The Generall of his great mercie & humanitie, promised their lives and good usage."

A prize crew were thrown on board the galleon, people from the *Desire* and the *Content*, while the captain, pilot, and the chief Manila merchant were kept as hostages. That night the

English carpenters aboard the prize plugged the dangerous shot holes, and the seamen repaired the cut rigging, casting in shroud knots, reeving fresh running gear. A guard with arms put the people below hatches, having cast their dead into the sea. The wounded were taken care of as best they could, and small arms, pikes, javelins, and other weapons of use were sent into the boat or cast into the sea, along with the powder, shot, and stones. Lights were rigged on the *Santa Anna* to keep her in company while the two corsairs ranged on either side, all being hove to under shortened sail.

That night the chief merchant brought aboard the manifests, the specie list, and in the cabin of the *Desire* was set forth the extent of the loot riding so close to them, the first and only big prize of the long cruise. But what a list it was, with its long tally of cases and chests of rich Eastern goods! So many chests of silk, bales of satin, and of damask, so many parcels of musk in casks. And there were ivories and choice pieces for the altars. Pretty says she was laden with "great store of al maner of victuals with the choyse of many conserves of all sortes for to eate, and of sundry sorts of very good wines."

But the main item of loot was gold. "An hundred and 22 thousand pezos of golde." (That is, pieces of eight.)

But history looks upon this tally with some suspicion. The letter sent to the Right Honorable Lord Hunsdon, Cavendish's patron, and given to the public, detailing an account of the action and the booty taken, left the amount of treasure and value of merchandise to be guessed. Here is the paragraph.

"Right Honorable Lord:

"I navigated along the coast of Chili, Peru and Nueva Espanna, where I made great spoils; I burnt and sunk nineteen sail of ships small and great; All the villages and towns that ever I landed at I burned and spoiled; and, had I not been discovered upon the coast, I had taken great quantity of treasure. The matter of most profit unto me, was a great ship of the King's, which I took at California, which ship came from the Philippines, being one of the richest for merchandise that ever passed those seas, as the King's Register, accounts and merchants did shew; for it did amount in value to .... in Mexico to be sold. . . . (my ships were not able to contain the least part of them). . . .

"All which services with my selfe I humbly prostrate at her Majesties feet, desiring the Almighty long to continue her reigne among us: for at this day she is the most famous and victorious prince that liveth in the world.

"Thus humbly desiring pardon of your honour for my tediousnesse, I leave your lordship to the tuition of the Almighty.

Plimmouth this ninth of September 1588.
Your honors most humble to command,
Thomas Candish."

To manage things better, Cavendish, the day after his action, fetched the Mexican coast and put into a harbor that the Spaniards called Aguada Segura, or the bay of San Lucas, at the very tip of southern California, then a wild place, uninhabited. Master Fuller, of the *Desire*, noted, "We ankered in 12 fadoms water."

The surviving Spaniards, both men and women, were taken out of the galleon to the number of 190; half of her original complement must have been slain. They were treated with some consideration. "They were set ashore where they had a fayre river of fresh water, with great store of fresh fish, foule, and wood, and also many hares and connies upon the maine land. Our Generall also gave them great store of victuals, of garuansos, peason, and some wine. Also they had all the sailes of their shippe to make them tents on shore, with license to take such store of plankes as should be sufficient to make them a barke."

Having disposed of their prisoners, the eighty odd pirates—

for that is what they were—set about the business of "hoysing out our goods, sharing of the treasure, and alloting to every man his portion."

Cavendish, being somewhat of an amateur privateersman and not the sailor Drake was by a long count, did not hold a tight command. He left the division of prize money to a proper admiralty court. As in other of Cavendish's decisions, he was weak. "In devision of spoils the eight of this moneth, many of the company fell into a mutinie against our Generall, especially those who were in the *Content*, which neverthelesse were after a sort pacified for the time."

Cavendish hung in San Lucas anchorage for some time, getting his ships restowed, careening before making the full transfer of treasure. With the Spaniards in camp, the many women, the warm climate, in a land plentifully supplied with game, much merriment went on between the sea weary people of the galleon and the now rich privateers. On Nov. 17, in that year 1587, they celebrated "the happy Coronation of her Majestie, our Generall commanded all his ordnance to be shot off, with the small shot both in his owne shippe where himself went, and also in the *Content*, which was our Vice-admiral. This being done the same night we had many fireworks and more ordnance discharged, to the great admiration of all the Spaniards which were there: for the most part of them had never seen the like before."

Both ships being well stowed and ready for sea, the privateers gave a last celebration. Cavendish was a dandy, a courtier with the graces of London's elite. He entertained the merchants and the few ladies of quality aboard his little ship. That last night in San Lucas saw the treasure laden ships, with hatches battened over bursting cargoes, ready to sail. The people said farewell to their friends, not without some weeping on the part of the *señoritas* and *señoras*. But they would leave a great treasure behind them, in the partly discharged *Santa Anna*, so the Spanish captain knew.

And on the next day Cavendish gave the captain a royal reward, as the old records show. He gave him both swords and targets, or shields, for defense against the Indians, with some pieces and powder and shot, all to his great contentment. Then the Englishman took out of the great ship two young lads "born in Japon." Christoper, twenty, was the elder, and the other, Cosmus, was seventeen, and "both of very good capacitie."

Cavendish also took three boys born in the isles of Manila, one about fifteen, the other thirteen, and the youngest nine. These were Alphonso, Anthony de Dasi, and a child unnamed, who was taken to London and "remaineth with the right honorable Countesse of Essex," the "dear Lettice" of notorious Tudor times.

Also, with an eye to information, Cavendish held "one Nicholas Roderigo, a Portugall, who hath not only bene in Canton and other parts of China, but also in the islands of Japon being a countrey rich in silver mynes, and hath also bene in the Philippines.

"Hee tooke also from them a Spaniard whose name was Thomas de Ersola, which was a very good Pilote from Acapulco and the coast of Nueva Espanna unto the islands of Ladrones."

Then, to the utter dismay of the Spaniards, on Nov. 19, as the two ships were about to sail, Cavendish set fire to the *Santa Anna,* sending a good 500 tons of rich merchandise up in flames.

"We saw her burnt unto the water, then gave them a piece of ordnance and set sayle joyfully towards England with a fayre wind which by this time came out of the Eastnortheast: and night growing neere we left the *Content* asterne of us, which was not as yet come out of the road. And there thinking she would have overtaken us, we lost her companie and never saw her after."

Was the little sixty ton *Content* boarded by the Spaniards?

Did she go back for one more night on that fabulous beach, or did she stand across the great Pacific, laden with her share of loot, to founder or go ashore on one of the many unknown islands? Just another lost ship in a vast ocean of mysteries. So it was and has been from the beginning to the present and will be forever onward while the salt seas last.

The *Desire* fetched the Ladrones "with a faire winde for the space of 45 dayes, and we esteemed it to be between 17 and 18 hundred leagues. The 3 day of January by sixe of the clock in the morning wee had sight of one of the islands of Ladrones called the island of Guana (Guam) standing 13 degrees ⅔ toward the North." They had made a remarkably fast Pacific crossing. Only sixty-seven years had passed since Magellan's distressed old *Trinidada* fetched the Isles of Robbers. Cavendish sailed on past Guam and the obstreperous natives.

The *Desire* ran into a tremendous storm on Jan. 14, lying ahull all night when by break of day they fell in with a great headland in the Philippines, Cabo del Spirito Santo. They had crossed our Pacific.

The unknown East had its great surprises. On the night of Jan. 15, while they were anchored in the Moluccas, Nicholas Roderigo, the Portuguese, sought a secret audience with Captain Cavendish, coming aft in the dark under the cramped poop in that little ship so crowded with intrigue and treasure.

Roderigo, vowing truth and faithful service to his captors, was informed that the pilot Thomas de Ersola, taken out of the *Santa Anna*, had written a letter to the governor of Manila and secretly sealed it and locked it in his chest on the main deck, that Ersola meant at the first chance to convey to the Spaniards. The letter told of the two English ships and their piracies along the coasts of Chile, Peru, and Nueva España and what they had taken and spoiled. He warned the governor to make strong their bulwarks, their two galleys, and any provision they might possibly make. He gave the anchorage of the *Desire* at an island called Capul at the end of the island of Manila and reported her as a single ship with a small force in it.

And that night the English crew seized and carried the Spanish pilot aft to the great cabin. In the stuffy space under the silver lamp they charged and tried him. The letter was found, and the unfortunate Thomas de Ersola was double ironed and confined. Captain Cavendish willed that he be hung in the morning. So on Jan. 16, he swung to the port fore yardarm, to the roll of drums, at the island of Capul. His body was cut down and snapped up by the sharks.

Much had been going on in the European world during the cruise of the gentleman from Trimley in the Countie of Suffolke. The deeply laden *Desire*, sea worn but brave, fetched the port of Plymouth, coming into the historic bay under a suite of sails made of the heaviest silk, gleaming in the sun of England. They stood up Plymouth Sound on Sept. 9, in the year 1588, that of the great Invincible Armada of Spain. But the Armada had been beaten, and all England was rejoicing when Thomas Cavendish returned, laden with Spanish gold, with a mighty story to tell. He was the third circumnavigator and the second Englishman to round the world, returning with plunder. His silken sails were not a mark of vanity entirely but the result of his having lost his worn out canvas in a tempest on the way up from the great cape Buena Esperanza, or Good Hope, at the tip of Africa.

Cavendish had made equable distribution of the booty among his men. Young and dashing, with a personal fortune large enough to have bought an earldom, he cut a gallant figure in the court of Elizabeth. There was no question of his right to Spanish gold. The Tudor Queen knighted him forthwith; all Britain hailed him. And yet Sir Thomas Cavendish was a mere shadow of the man that was Sir Francis Drake.

Cavendish, to wind up his Pacific glory, soon scattered his pieces of eight. Three years later, in August, 1591, he again departed from Plymouth under Captain John Davis. He died of a broken heart on the towering South Atlantic Island of Ascension.

.V.

The Struggle for the Pacific

FROM 1400 to 1600 stretched a brilliant era of primary oceanic discovery. The two heroic centuries saw Bartholomew Diaz sail far down the west coast of Africa past the distant column built by Diego Cam at the mouth of the Congo. Then Columbus stood out into the challenging West to a new world. Vasco da Gama sailed around Africa. And, greatest navigator of them all, Magellan pierced the most southern end of the new world through the strait that bears his name and sailed across the world's mightiest ocean. Magellan's Pacific beckoned to the dream of Quiros; it lured the valiant privateer, Sir Francis Drake, and it saw the centuries of high discovery end in an era of plunder.

Discovery had always been associated with possession. The white races, through some self-deception, thought they owned the earth and the fullness thereof and extended their ownership by simply annexing the lands and possessions of those who had lived there for hundreds, perhaps thousands, of years. But, since the Mayas drove out a primitive people and the Aztecs drove out the Mayas in Central America, perhaps the white race is not so different from all other races. We pity the lowly savage when the white man takes his land, but the lowly savage had no qualms about taking land from his enemies. It is only now in this twentieth century that man is asking himself—white, black, and yellow man—whether this method is as praiseworthy as it might be in the eyes of God, or Allah, or some other deity.

The history of the Pacific is no different in this respect. Perhaps the Polynesians found a race there that they exterminated; certainly some Polynesians made war upon their neighbors that they might have possession. And when the white man entered the Pacific, he fought, also: the Dutch with the earlier Spanish, the English against the galleons of Spain, all of them against the Polynesians, and, finally, the Americans against the Spaniards and the Filipinos—and warfare, in various forms, still goes on. But probably the most dramatic moment was the long-ago and far-away period when the Dutch, the Spaniards, the English, and a few pirates sought for spoils on the gold-rimmed lands of this ocean. For every new country is a rich country, despite what men do to it afterward.

The distribution of discoveries among the Western nations in the Pacific was at first confined to the strong Catholic powers, Spain and Portugal, then the greatest seafaring nations. When they were united, the Pacific became a closed ocean, later to be challenged by the English and, still more strongly, by the Dutch. The great Pacific was to see a century and a half of fighting along its shores and across its wastes, accompanied by minor discoveries and rediscoveries, for in any such body of water islands are mislaid and then found again. Men still search for some of the lost ones.

The wealthy world empire of Spain expired slowly. It was first challenged by the Dutch toward the end of the sixteenth century. Then for a very short time they put up a fight that made a dent in many a Spanish bulwark and stronghold. The tough little nation that once swept the British Channel and signified its defiance of England by sailing up and down that busy body of water with a broom tied to a masthead was not to be frightened by the power of Spain. It had a foothold in the Far East, and the west coast of South America, with its stores of gold, looked good to the merchants of Rotterdam. Jacob Mahu's fleet did not do so well when it arrived off the coast of South America in 1598, but the stories of the wealth of the Incas persisted.

Oliver van Noort, a native of Utrecht, had retired from the sea to become an innkeeper " . . . in the flower of his age with a strong passion for glory," as an old chronicler puts it. He went to sea with the *Maurice* and the *Henry Frederick*, two tall ships, and the yachts *Concord* and *Hope*. He sailed from the Texel in the same year that Mahu sailed from Goeree, in 1598, putting to sea in September. He worked westward through the Strait of Magellan, massacred some Fuegians, and marooned his vice-admiral, Jacob Claesz.

He was a tough disciplinarian, this van Noort, possibly because he had been an innkeeper. There is a tradition in the army that the most hard-boiled commissioned officers are those who have come up through the ranks. Off the port of Valparaiso he fell in with the *Buen Jesús*, which he took, only to find that her holds were empty. Later he was to learn that there had been a vast treasure on the *Buen Jesús*, that it had been thrown overboard—three tons of gold. Van Noort searched the *Buen Jesús* again without finding anything and then, as an afterthought, searched the pilot. He found in his breeches a big bag of leather containing one pound of gold. Disgusted, red-faced Admiral van Noort retired to his great cabin aboard the *Maurice*, called for his schnapps, and drank it with the small bag of gold on the table before him. There was probably no greater maritime headache in history, and if van Noort had obtained all that gold the Dutch would have made a much greater attempt to conquer South America.

But despite his ill luck—and this was in the days when men like him were freebooters—he was a first-class fighting seaman. He sailed to the Ladrones and then to the Bay of Cavite, on which is the city of Manila. It was off Cavite that Admiral Dewey defeated the Spanish fleet and so won an international political headache for the United States.

In the morning, off Manila, on Dec. 14, 1600, two heavy galleons were sighted bearing down on the *Maurice* and the *Concord*, all that were left of his ships. Van Noort had 80 men on the two ships, whereas the Spaniards had 100 apiece. The Dutchman kept to windward, but because of the breeze he could not use his lee ports, which he had to keep closed, and so the Spaniards luffed into him and boarded him. The crew of the *Maurice* were driven from their deck to below. The *Concord*, thinking the admiral's ship had surrendered, tried to escape. Van Noort, with the Spaniards masters of the deck, was not beaten. He thundered at his crew.

"Up you go after them, or I'll fire the magazine, and we'll all go up together. Wy zyn al verdomd!"

They went up, pushed the Spaniards overboard, and sunk the galleon, after which the boats were lowered, and the swimming Spaniards were stabbed. Not very nice, but that is the way the Pacific was in those years. In retaliation, the Spaniards took the crew of the captured *Concord* on shore and hung them all. Van Noort quit those seas and went home to contemplate his empty leather purse in his tavern and to think of the tons of gold he had lost. It was a good story and probably cost many a round of drinks.

The Dutch finally got tired of pothouse admirals and men like Mahu who did not uphold their national prestige. So the great Dutch East India Company, gaining control of Java and Borneo, which Holland retains to this time, decided to enter the picture. It already controlled a vast empire in the East, had millions of subjects, and ruled with soldiers, forts, and trading fleets that were really men-of-war. Joris Spilbergen, who had successfully fought their fleets in the East Indies, was put in command, and Spilbergen was a man.

Six sail were ordered to be made ready, armed, and provisioned. The fleet consisted in part of the heaviest ships of that time, carrying great ordnance to the extent of fifty pieces of the largest. These craft were the *Great Sun*, admiral, the *Full Moon*, vice-admiral, the *Huntsman*, and the *Sea Mew*, all of Amsterdam, and the ships *Aeolus*, of Zealand, and the *Morning Star*, of Rotterdam. Admiral Spilbergen chose his own officers, men of courage and ability. Aboard the flagship he carried a large force of soldiers and marines commanded by Captain Rowland Phillips, with his lieutenant, Francis de Chesne. These are the only names that have come to us out of that distant time. The fleet went through the Strait of Magellan and out into the South Sea on Apr. 6, 1615. It was not long before Spilbergen heard of a fleet of heavy Spanish ships intended to repel the Dutch invasion of waters that Spain looked upon as her own.

This fleet was commanded by Admiral Roderigo de Mendoza and carried a formidable armament. Mendoza sailed in the great *Jesu Maria*, mounting 24 brass cannon and manned by 460 men. She had cost the King 158,000 ducats. The *Santa Anna* was vice-admiral, a ship only slightly less powerful, carrying 300 men. Besides these two great ships there were the *Carmelite*, with eight pieces of brass cannon and 200 men, the *St. James*, of equal force, the *St. Francis*, which carried no ordnance but had 70 musketeers, and the *St. Andrew*, with 80 musketeers. There was also an eighth ship of uncertain furniture.

With this fleet, Admiral Mendoza stood to sea from Callao, word having come from fleeing merchant craft that the Dutch, in force, with heavy ships, were approaching the bay. "Two of my ships," said Mendoza to the Viceroy, "can take all England, and much more easily these hens of Holland, after so long a voyage which has spent and wasted them."

"God grant you are right, good Roderigo," the Viceroy smiled. It was a brave fleet of the Royal Navy of the Ocean Sea that sailed out of Callao Bay.

Toward the night of July 17, 1615, the Spaniards descried the square topsails of the Dutch and closed with them under full press of canvas. The ships approached and held their fire as they showed their ensigns.

Admiral Spilbergen, being Dutch and regular and finding himself confronted by a piece of business after business hours, hailed the Spaniard.

"If you so desire, Señor," he cried through his great brass trumpet, "I will withhold my attack until dawn!"

"*Dawn! Attack? You hens of Holland! I will fight you now.*" Roderigo de Mendoza shouted this defiance and a broadside from the *Jesu Maria;* twelve brass cannon sent their balls ricocheting on the water close across the bow of the *Great Sun.*

Spilbergen had luffed just in time to avoid the shot. Smoke rose through the rigging of the Spaniard, and the vice-admiral ranged in line, the lighter ships holding off to engage when the moment came. The Spaniards sponged and charged their guns.

"*Hens of Holland!*" Joris Spilbergen, purple with rage, almost burst at the insult, stamping up and down his poop, adding a string of Dutch profanity, while the seamen grinned, standing by their guns with matches lighted. The *Great Sun* filled away, flying the red signal to engage as the *Full Moon* followed her, both ships, closing with the heavy Spaniards, discharging their first broadsides as they bore. A shock ran through the ships, and the second crash of great ordnance thundered over the Pacific.

About ten o'clock on that volcanic night, the guns grown hot, the heavy *Jesu Maria* lay aboard the *Great Sun,* and the two flagships, as they closed, exchanged point blank broadsides, the shot crashing through their wooden sides. Trumpets blared between the roar of artillery. The rash *St. Francis*, standing up next in line, attacked the Dutch admiral with small arms but was forced to sheer off. At that time in the great fight, the *Sea Mew* ranged close by the *St. Francis* and sent her to the bottom with a single broadside, amid the splintering of her timbers and the howls of her musketeers. When this happened Mendoza luffed, and the *Jésus María* sent a crashing broadside into the little *Sea Mew*. Spilbergen, seeing her distress, sent a boat's crew to her aid, for most of the *Sea Mew's* people had been knocked down. He signaled the *Full Moon* to do likewise.

The *Huntsman*, coming up in the dark, seeing the boat from the *Great Sun*, rowing amid the smoke as revealed in the flashes of fire, mistook her for an enemy. Laying a great piece, she hit the boat and sent her down. Only one man escaped. By then the action had progressed beyond midnight; the smoke became so thick that friend and foe were no longer distinguishable, and the ships drew off, their cockpits full of dying men, their sails and rigging cut and their sides wounded.

In the heaving Pacific swell the battered men-of-war lifted and rolled. At early daybreak the Spaniards signaled Mendoza that they would run for it, there being only five battered ships left. But here the Dutch admiral and vice-admiral set upon the Spanish admiral and vice-admiral, the four ships closing in deadly combat. The *Aeolus* then joined battle, pouring her broadsides into the Spanish flagship.

The battle went well into the ensuing day, and the admiral and vice-admiral of the Spaniards were lashed together for greater resistance, their sides grinding in that turbulent sea awash with wreckage. All topmasts and some lower masts were shot away; shrouds hung in tangled shreds; yards held by their chain slings swayed as the braces were gone. Carpenters worked to plug shot holes. The guns were stinging hot;

water was being hauled up to cool the pieces, to put out fires and wash away the blood. Corpses, dismembered and ghastly, were tossed into the sea. Such were the scenes in both the Dutch and Spanish ships. But always the ensigns were kept flying. Curses rang through the day, cries of agony and of defiance, and faint cheers came down the wind in that off-shore battle, with the blue peaks of the great Andes far to the east. Sharks lashed about, and smoke rose in brown and bluish clouds above the mastheads. The smell of burning canvas, of hemp and tar added a pungent odor amid the sulphurous fumes of gunpowder.

Joris Spilbergen was like a sea lion during that terrific battle. His marines fired constantly and with precision, their ranks thinning. Were the Dutch hens? He shouted the taunt back again and again after every effective broadside, and the cry was taken up by the crews. That insult cost Roderigo de Mendoza many men.

The Dutch are a phlegmatic people until aroused, when they grow bellicose. Here they fought like demons. It is a pity no great artist like van de Velde was there to depict those high pooped ships in the deadly grip of war. Their billet heads were smashed and carried away, ornate quarter galleries were wrecked by shot and collision: a magnificent picture of horrent hell lay spread over the wreck strewn sea.

The people of the *Santa Anna*, being pounded by the guns of the *Full Moon*, leaped aboard the *Jésus María*, and some hauled up a white flag. But these cravens were shot by their officers, who struck the signal, the Spanish preferring to die rather than yield. The Dutch, seeing this sign of weakening, pressed them the more. On the Spanish flagship hardly fifty were alive. Surging back to the Spanish vice-admiral, the crew, in desperation, attempted to board the *Full Moon*, lying close, the ship's yardarms locked. Back they were driven, and Mendoza ordered the cutting adrift of the *Jésus María*. By benefit of returning night he spread all possible sail before a freshening on shore breeze, running for Callao. But the great and battered ship was mortally wounded. The decimated crew hoisted whatever sail they had. As the Dutch followed her, the great *Jesús María*, leaking from many shot holes, her pumps carried away, shrouds and gear trailing astern, filled and plunged under the waves, her heavy guns carrying her down with her remaining people, her cockpit full of shattered, suffering men.

Soon another Spaniard foundered, and the *Great Sun* and the *Aeolus*, swinging back upon the *Santa Anna*, renewed the battle. On the second night the Spanish vice-admiral flung out the white flag of surrender. The Dutch vice-admiral, the *Full Moon*, sent two boats to fetch the commander of the *Santa Anna*, but he refused to leave his ship, saying that he would stay that night in his disgrace. One of the seamen from the *Aeolus* had taken the Spanish ensign, and the boats shoved off, but ten or twelve Dutchmen remained on board, contrary to command, thinking they might be first at the spoil. Night covered the stricken ship, and her people, together with the Dutchmen, did what they could to save her. Finding her about to founder, they lighted many flares and lanterns and cried out for help. But this was hopeless, and the *Santa Anna* sank in sight of the Hollanders, being quenched in the dark and the cries of the crew were drowned. At daybreak the Dutch admiral put over four boats, and these picked up thirty men, the sole survivors. The fleet of the Spanish Royal Navy had been severely punished. A few of the lighter ships had fled to Callao with news of the disaster.

A hundred and eight Dutchmen were killed and wounded, the proportion about half and half, many dying from their injuries. Admiral Spilbergen sailed with his battered ships for Callao, and there a piece of great ordnance on the shore, throwing a thirty-six pound shot, hit and almost sunk the *Huntsman*. Ashore, the Viceroy was prepared for them with an army of 800 horse and 4,000 foot.

The tough old admiral—and of course he was not so old, probably in his forties—sailed the coast northward, coming at last to that ancient port of Navidad. He took no prizes worth the mention; a ship laden with salt and eighty jars of syrup were tallied. But he gathered a deal of valuable knowledge about the lands, coasts, harbors, customs, governments, products, climate, and possibilities for trade and plunder. The Dutch East India Company was concerned with the larger view. Musty reports in its vast archives may be dull reading but are shot through with flashes of vital plans. The great action was shown in a concise statement of property losses, detailed damages to the ships, and the dead were listed so that their names might be promptly stricken from the pay roll.

Spilbergen in his action had taken many prisoners and others along the coast. In New Spain he exchanged them for sheep, fruits, and other provisions. In Acapulco, Melchior Hernando, a nephew of the Viceroy came aboard "to take a view of the fleet which had vanquished the King's." He was kindly entertained by the admiral. But the castle at Acapulco was well defended by seventy brass guns; the Spaniards knew eight months before that Spilbergen and his victorious fleet were on the way. Force respected force, nothing else.

On Nov. 20, 1615, the Dutch sailed from the little port of Navidad. They had been there ten days for final provisioning and water. Standing westward on Dec. 3 "to their no little wonder" they saw two islands at a great distance in the sea, and the next day passed a mighty rock in 19 degrees, lying fifty leagues from the continent. These were what we now call the Revilla Gigedo Islands, and the sighting constituted Spilbergen's geographical discoveries.

He crossed the wide ocean without recorded incident, arriving at the Ladrones. Thence he went to the Island of Capul, "where the Indians wear long coats like shirts, and are noted for the extraordinary respect they pay to clergymen, before whom they will prostrate themselves on the ground, and take it for a mighty honor to be allowed to kiss their hands."

Spilbergen spent a year in the East. His fame had preceded him westward by galleons from Manila. The Dutchmen were respected and feared, and he had done more for the prestige of Holland and the Dutch East India Company than all other voyagers combined. But great fleets were coming from Holland, sailing around Africa. In May, Spilbergen with his six ships, some prizes and replacements, met with Captain Castleton, commanding four English ships. From the Englishman he heard of the Dutch General, Dirkson Lam, who had sailed from the Island of Banda the year before with twelve men-of-war and a large body of soldiers. Lam had taken the Island of Pulo Wai, the richest in those parts, "of which he made himself master with great ease." And so went the taking of the Dutch East Indies, the fighting with Spaniards and Portuguese. And in time the ships, too badly damaged for a westward beat around Africa, remained in the Indies.

Admiral Spilbergen sailed home in the great Company ship *Amsterdam*, accompanied by the *Zeeland*. He was the fifth circumnavigator, and a famous man.

In the steerage of the *Amsterdam*, or in some obscure cabin of the half deck, were Captain Willem Schouten, the two young Le Maire brothers, and the captain's brother, John Schouten. They were being returned to Holland, stripped of their ships and goods, culprits in the eyes of the great India Company.

These men had made the greatest geographical discovery ever made by the Dutch, the passage around Cape Horn. The powerful Dutch East India Company had obtained a monopoly from the States-General of Holland forbidding all Dutch ships but their own from trading to the East, either by way of the Cape of Good Hope or through the Strait of Magellan and so across the Pacific. Since no other way to the East was known, all Dutch ships not owned by the company were barred from this rich trade.

But old Isaac Le Maire, of Amsterdam, who had resigned from the directorate of the company, had an idea that there might be another passage. The canny merchant must have had a better knowledge of geography, or perhaps a stronger instinct for exploration, than many of his contemporaries. So he formed a company in the little port of Hoorn and fitted out two ships to sail under command of Captain Willem Schouten. These were to reach down to the Strait of Magellan and test his theory. On board them went his sons, Jaques and Daniel, and Captain John Schouten, Willem's brother, who took charge of the smaller ship, the *Hoorn*. The other was the *Unity*. The little *Hoorn* was burned accidently while being careened in Port Desire, Patagonia, and her crew and salvaged stores were transferred to the *Unity*.

They sailed south, past the entrance to the Strait of Magellan, into unknown seas, and on Jan. 29, 1616, they discovered and rounded a bold headland, which they called Cape Hoorn (or Horn). So the genius of old Isaac Le Maire overcame the legal restriction of the monopoly, and stout Captain Schouten opened up a new passage to the Pacific around the stormiest cape in the world. After two weeks they came abreast of the western end of the Strait of Magellan, drank a cup of wine, and named their discovery the Strait of Le Maire. Then they stood northward into the Pacific. Schouten's crossing of the great ocean has been dwarfed by his earlier achievement and his later misfortunes, but because of the outstanding humanity of its conduct, a quality often lacking in the voyagings of other and far lesser navigators, it deserves high place in the log of the Pacific.

Schouten gives us our first glimpse of the famous Islands of Juan Fernandez, on one of which Alexander Selkirk, the prototype of Defoe's Robinson Crusoe, lived for several years. Schouten came up to them on Mar. 1. He tried to anchor on the wrong side, the western, but did send some of his weary sailors ashore. They brought out fish, lobsters, and crabs, and then, finding the island inaccessible, stood to the northwest. They found an islet that had nothing on it but a silent species of dog "that would neither bark nor snarl nor make any noise at all"; so Schouten called it Dog Island. This was one of the Tuamotu group. On another island they found some natives, who were so bold that they came alongside and tried to pull nails out of the cabin ports. They were treated kindly and given wine. Schouten remarks on their tattooing with snakes and dragons "and such-like reptiles." They found another island so filled with flies that the men could hardly open their mouths without a fly entering. After coming to a few other islands, they neared the Solomons, which Schouten gave a wide berth, fearing to fall in with the dreaded New Guinea coast, and after a time they came to the Dutch port of Bantam in the East Indies.

On the way they had traded diligently, filling their hold with spices and knowing that by rounding Cape Horn they had beaten the legal restriction of the Dutch East India Company. But tough old Admiral Spilbergen called them trespassers; their claim was disallowed, their ship and its cargo confiscated, and they were sent home to face the courts of Holland. So Spilbergen and Schouten, the fifth and sixth circumnavigators of the world, went back home on the *Amsterdam*, one full of honors, the other under a cloud.

Spilbergen had so strengthened the Dutch by his victory over Admiral Mendoza and so powerful had Holland become in the East Indies that thought naturally was given by Prince Maurice and the States-General to a further adventure along the American coasts of the Pacific. The Dutch were the first to take advantage of Cape Horn for the dispatching of a powerful fleet into the Pacific, a fleet that could never have hoped to work its way westward through the treacherous Strait of Magellan.

Although the Hollanders were stubborn in their extension of trade, they were far from being precipitate. It was six years after the return of Schouten and Spilbergen before they sent out their next and most powerful armament to soften up Chile and Peru. Admiral Jacques Le Hermite, an able and accomplished sea commander long in the service of the East India Company and one well accustomed to an extensive command, was given control of a costly fleet of eleven ships. No such armada had yet penetrated to the Pacific, and heavier ships had only sailed eastward to the Indies.

The ships were supplied by the admiralties of Amsterdam, Zeeland, Holland, North Holland; the Dutch East India Company contributed no ships but shared in the expense and assigned many of the officers, including the admiral. Most of the cannon were of brass, thought superior to cast-iron ordnance in those days.

It was intended to set up strong defenses in lands taken from the Spaniards. Besides the principal officers, there was a large staff. Mustered in the ships were 1,637 men, of whom 600 were regular troops in five companies of 120 men each, with an artillery equipment of 294 pieces of brass and iron cannon.

The Prince of Orange was strongly behind this movement, for the government, under the States-General, was at that time losing much of its character as a republic, being more of a monarchy. A very considerable sum of money was invested in this enterprise, its main object being to subjugate the lands of Peru and Chile and so to make the wide Pacific a Dutch ocean through control of its eastern as well as its western shores.

This armada, called the Nassau Fleet, sailed from Goeree Roads on Apr. 29, 1623. The ships rounded Cape Horn successfully, the first ever to anchor there. By the time they came bravely into the Pacific, they consisted of sixteen sail, having been augmented by the capture of some Turkish corsairs in the Atlantic.

Admiral Le Hermite expired in the Bay of Callao after a long illness. Schappenham took charge, and the constant fighting along the coast continued. The Dutchmen, meeting no great sea force which they could overcome, had to fight against land forts and armies. The Spanish plate fleet, which they might have intercepted, had sailed northward and was well on its way to Panama when the Nassau ships appeared off Chile.

An earthquake greeted them in Callao de Lima, this happening a week after the death of their admiral. They tried to treat with the Spanish Viceroy, having taken prisoners. His reply was that he had nothing but powder and ball at the service of the Dutch. He would enter into no negotiation with the invaders whatever for the ransom of prisoners, and if any of them presumed to land at the port of Callao with another flag of peace, he would order them hanged with the flag about their necks.

On June 14, 1624, the Dutch admiral decided to answer this insolence by hanging all of his Spanish hostages. On the next morning, therefore, in sight of a vast multitude who were standing on the shore, the poor Spaniards were hung, one after another, to the number of twenty-one, from the port mizzen yardarm of the flagship.

Three old men were spared, being sent ashore with a message to the Viceroy advising him that, since they were to receive no quarter, he need expect none to any who fell into their hands.

The ships sailed up to Acapulco and beat down again to Chile. Their councils grew unsteady after the death of Le Hermite, however, so they sailed across the Pacific, and the ships were dispersed to serve in the East. Admiral Schappenham, grown desperately ill, embarked in the *Concord*, sailing for home; he died on the way, "worn out with care and labor." The *Concord* alone of Le Hermite's ships completed the great circumnavigation in 1626.

Holland suffered from the failure of this Pacific enterprise. Historians glorifying the Dutch navigators often ignore the mighty but ineffective Nassau Fleet.

The last Dutch venture into the Pacific was carried out by Jacob Roggeveen, sixty-two years old, who had already made a great success in the East Indies. The only real importance of his voyage is that he discovered Easter Island, off the west coast of South America, that strange remnant of a past civilization. The Dutch sailors saw, in the morning light, natives prostrating themselves before their idols, facing the sun, and offering burnt sacrifices. The natives resented a landing, and the Dutch fired on them, killing many. "They brought us," says the chronicler of the expedition, "in return for the dead bodies we have given them, vast plenty of provisions of all kinds." Men, women, and children presented themselves with branches of palm in token of humility.

In this way Roggeveen found an island that has become one of the mysteries of archeologists. It lies 2,000 miles from the coast of Peru and 1,500 from the nearest inhabited island, excepting Pitcairn. If the secret of its idols were known, the whole mystery of the Pacific might be solved.

After the early discoverers and the battle for supremacy between the Spanish and the Dutch, it was natural that the Pacific should attract the sea rovers, those daring pirates who had made the Caribbean their hunting ground and ships carrying wealth back to Europe from New Spain their prey. There were many of these sea rovers, but the most famous was perhaps the poorest pirate of them all, William Dampier. Dampier loved adventure. He clung to the sea most of his life and was a mariner of mariners; but as a buccaneer he was a failure.

Much has been made of Dampier, for he was one of the most contradictory creatures who ever hoisted the Jolly Roger. He would have been a great naturalist had opportunity opened the door for him, a scientist of distinction. He was always more interested in the flowers, the trees, the natives and their habits and customs, in the winds and tides and currents, in bearings and landmarks and charting reefs than he was in loot. Not that he did not like to rid a captured vessel of its precious cargo, but even while he coveted the gold he despised the method and men with whom he was associated. His dissertation on winds is a much more valuable treatise than anything he has to say about piracy, and his methods of navigation and his observations have added more to his fame than his futile attempt to capture a Manila galleon. He was a brave sailor, a staunch fighter, and often held his men together by the desperation of his efforts; yet he was a bad leader, for his heart was not in what he did.

Dampier was, in fact, an anachronism. He adopted piracy as a profession, served it honorably according to his lights, and wrote several books that were distinguished by their vigorous English. When he was nearly sixty he walked ashore, an embittered and disappointed man, to sink into obscurity. What became of him after his last voyage nobody knows. But in his day he wrote his name large in the annals of the Pacific freebooters.

As a young man he went to sea on a few voyages, fought against the Dutch off the English coast, and then went to Jamaica and Yucatan, where he hoped to chop out for himself, literally with an ax, a profitable and highly respectable career. That he did not do so was because of a Captain Hodsell, who took a liking to the tall, powerful, straight eyed young man and persuaded him to enlist with the pirate fleet at Jamaica. And so he was in at the taking of Porto Bello and also in the trip across the Isthmus of Panama with Captain Sharpe and others of his tough company, ten years after Henry Morgan had sacked and burned Panama on the Pacific side. They did not attempt to capture the rebuilt city but made their way south in a captured ship. They attempted to take Arica in northern Chile, but, owing to dissension, failed to do so. Then they split into two groups, one led by Sharpe and the other by Dampier. Somehow the cutthroats made their way back along the coast in small boats, with few provisions, until they got to Panama and then traveled again across the Isthmus. They came back empty handed. They captured another ship, and, after divers adventures, Dampier made his way to England.

But after eight years he found patrons in such men as Charles Montagu, afterward Earl of Halifax, and Thomas Herbert, Earl of Pembroke. And in 1699 he was appointed captain of His Majesty's ship *Roebuck*, of twelve guns and fifty men, in which he made a voyage to New Holland, or Australia. This was Dampier's only real command, and he had difficulty because of his intolerable temper and impatience. A picture of him shows a man with long black hair, a glowering, dark, and oval face, piercing eyes, and a general demeanor that speaks of anything but patience. He was also gloomy and pessimistic, a dour person if there ever was one, not the best disposition for a commander of a ship in unknown waters, pressed by circumstances.

He sailed with several other ships, of which one was the *Cinque Ports*, Captain Pickering, who died on the way out and was replaced by Captain Stradling. On the ship was a man named Alexander Selkirk, one of the ablest sailors aboard but also a man of irreconcilable disposition. At Juan Fernandez, in the Pacific, there was trouble on the *Cinque Ports*, and Selkirk was left behind to become the prototype of Robinson Crusoe.

The ships went about their business of capturing merchantmen but were beaten off by a Spanish galleon. It was not a profitable voyage, and it is notable only because of Dampier's voluminous writings and descriptions of islands, for he was a good observer. Curiously enough, he was not a good explorer, or he would have pushed his inquiry into New Holland far beyond his cursory examination. He was one of those men who sell an idea splendidly to their patrons, start off full of zest, and then become lukewarm when their voyage is only half over. But nothing could stop his pen or his keen penetration of physical phenomena or human characteristics.

His next voyage was as pilot to Captain Woodes Rogers in the ship *Duke*, accompanied by the *Dutchess*, privateersmen both. Dampier was taken along because of his acknowledged ability as one of the greatest navigators of his day. It was the rescue of Alexander Selkirk, a small part of their adventures, that makes the voyage worth remembering. Dampier took the ships to a high southern latitude off Cape Horn. After they rounded that stormy point, they made up for Juan Fernandez, which they reached on Feb. 1, 1709. A boat was lowered and set out for the beach. It grew dark, and lights were seen, a great fire on a beach. The boat was lost in the dark, and the *Duke* fired a quarter-deck gun and hung out lights in the mizzen and foreshrouds. At two in the morning the boat returned, the light ashore having scared them off. What might be there the morning would disclose. They stood at their guns and with their sails to the mast lay off the island. Frenchmen or Spaniards may have been on the shore; an engagement was imminent.

But imagine their surprise. There were no ships at anchor. With shotted guns they approached. There were no enemy troops lined on the shore. They anchored and sent in a boat. On the shore stood a solitary man, of hairy face.

"Immediately our pinnace returned from the shore and brought abundance of crayfish with a man clothed in goatskins, who looked wilder than the first owners of them. He had been on the island four years and four months, having been left by Captain Stradling of the *Cinque Ports;* his name was Alexander Selkirk."

The tale, told throughout the ships lying at anchor there off Juan Fernandez, is remarkable enough. Selkirk, who had been born at Largo, the County of Fife, Scotland, and bred a sailor, "had been left ashore with his clothes and bedding, a firelock musket, some powder and bullets, tobacco, a hatchet, a knife, a kettle, a Bible and some practical pieces and his mathematical instruments and books. . . . He provided for himself as well as he could, but for the first eight months had much ado to bear up against melancholy, and the terror of being alone in such a desolate place.

"He built two huts with pimento trees, covered them with long grass and lined them with skins of goats, which he killed with his gun, so long as he wanted and his powder lasted, which was but a pound, and that being almost spent, he got fire by rubbing two sticks of pimento wood together upon his knee. In the lesser hut, at some distance from the other, he dressed his victuals; in the larger he slept, and employed himself in reading, singing psalms, and praying; so that he said he was a better Christian, while in the solitude, than ever he was before, or than he was afraid he should ever be again.

"At first he never eat anything till hunger constrained him, partly for grief, and partly for want of bread and salt. Nor did he go to bed until he could watch no longer; the pimento wood, which burnt very clearly, served him both for fire and candle, and refreshed him with its fragrant smell. He might have had fish enough, but would not eat them for want of salt, because they occasioned a looseness, except cray-fish, which are as large as our lobsters, and very good. These he sometimes boiled and at other times broiled, as he did his goat's flesh, of which he made very good bróth, for they are not so rank as ours. He kept an account of 500 that he killed while there, and caught as many more, which he marked on the ear and let go. When his powder failed he took them by speed of feet; for his way of living, continual exercise of walking and running, cleared him of all gross humors; so that he ran with wonderful swiftness through the woods, and up the rocks and hills, as we perceived when we employed him to catch goats for us. We had a bull dog, which we sent with several of our nimblest runners, to help him in catching goats; but he distanced and tired both the dog and the men, caught the goats and brought them to us on his back.

"He told us that his agility in pursuing a goat had once like to have cost him his life; he pursued it with so much eagerness, that he catched hold of it on the brink of a precipice, of which he was not aware, the bushes hiding it from him; so that he fell with the goat down the precipice, a great height, and was stunned and bruised by the fall, that he narrowly escaped with his life; and when he came to his senses, found the goat dead under him. He lay there about twenty-four hours, and was scarce able to crawl to his hut, which was about a mile distant, or to stir abroad in ten days.

"He came at last to relish his meat well enough without salt or bread; and in the season, had plenty of good turnips, which had been sown there by Captain Dampier's men, and have now overspread some acres of ground. He had enough good cabbage from the cabbage trees, and seasoned his meat with the fruit of the pimento trees, which is the same as Jamaica pepper, and smell deliciously. He found also a black pepper, called *malageta*, which was very good to expel wind, and against griping in the guts. He soon wore out all his shoes and clothes by running in the woods, and at last, being forced to shift without them, his feet became so hard, that he ran everywhere without difficulty; and it was some time before he could wear shoes after we found him, for, not being used to any so long, his feet swelled when he came first to wear them again.

"After he had conquered his melancholy, he diverted himself sometimes with cutting his name on the trees, and the time of his being left and continuance there. He was at first much pestered with cats and rats, that had bred in great numbers, from some of each species, which had got ashore from ships that put in there for wood and water. The rats gnawed his feet and clothes whilst asleep, which obliged him to cherish the cats with goat's flesh, by which many of them became so tame, that they would lie about him in hundreds, and soon delivered him from the rats. He likewise tamed some kids; and to divert himself, would, now-and-then, sing and dance with them, and his cats. So, that, by the favour of Providence, and vigour of his youth, being now but thirty years old, he came, at last, to conquer all the inconveniences of his solitude, and to be very easy."

And there is the true story of Alexander Selkirk, alias Robinson Crusoe. He had no "Man Friday"; that superb servant of fiction could never have been born into this world and rebounds to the genius of Defoe.

After the rescue of Selkirk, who was made lieutenant, or mate, of the *Duke*, at Dampier's request, they took one rich prize, the *Nuestra Señora de la Incarnación y Desengaña* (Our Lady of the Incarnation), but were driven off when they tackled a larger galleon, the *Begonia*, perhaps because the *Begonia* had on board a number of pirates sailing home with their own loot as peaceful men of business. And they fought very well in defense of it. The ship with the long name was renamed the *Bachelor* and returned with the others to the Thames.

Figures were given out as to the total plunder taken by this expedition, a loose estimate being between £300,000 and £400,000; after allowance was made for all deductions, the remaining profit amounted to £170,000. This was not so bad, although some said (and much was concealed in those days) that the real net profits were £800,000. We have the note that Selkirk's prize money was £800, and, since most of the plunder was taken after he joined, this may be a fair appraisal of the sum earned by the junior officer.

At this point Dampier vanishes. Whether he went back to his old home in Somersetshire or whether he went to sea again is not recorded. But of all the pirates who sailed the sea he was one of the most remarkable, not for his piracy but for the qualities that made him a poor pirate.

Heroic Anson

ADMIRAL ANSON has been celebrated by his successes, his immense wealth, obtained as prize money won in actions at sea, and his elevation to the peerage. High honors were heaped on him in his latter years. But the trial of his soul, the proof of his great heart and resolution, and the character of his officers and crews were brought out in the Pacific Ocean, far from the sinister beginning and the glamorous ending of his most famous voyage.

Let us forget the Admiral of the Fleet, Lord Anson, Baron of Soberton, who served, in 1751, under Pitt, as First Sea Lord of the Admiralty, instituting and prosecuting many reforms in the Royal Navy, especially in its fiscal administration, then rotten with the foulest graft. Let us concentrate on the sailor.

Here is the start of Anson's adventurous voyage to and across the Pacific. The year 1739 saw England again at war with Spain, and it was decided to surprise the enemy by sending a considerable force of ships into the Pacific. At first this was to consist of two fleets, one sailing east and the other west, rounding the great capes and meeting in the Indies. Captain George Anson, a naval officer of experience, just returned from a cruise to the coast of Guinea in the *Centurion*, was chosen to command the fleet sailing to the east. It was to be a sudden and unexpected blow. But delays, wranglings at the Board of Admiralty, wire pulling, and what not eliminated the fleet supposed to sail westward to meet him, and in the final lash-up the plan was cut in two. Anson was ordered to sail around Cape Horn without a force to meet him in the East Indies.

The surprise idea exploded, for the scheme became widely known, especially in Spain. The fleet was long in getting started, and the stories concerning the weakness of the ships and their poor manning made the Spaniards suspect a ruse. Not only did the Admiralty do the worst job of its kind but the victualing contractors, the grafting dockyards, and the pernicious paymaster traders lived upon and infested the enterprise.

Six ships assembled at the Nore, an anchorage off Sheerness dockyard at the mouth of the Thames. The year was one of great naval activity with many British fleets at sea commanded by admirals and officers all senior to Anson. He had the greatest difficulty in obtaining men. It was a time when seamen for the navy were impressed—that is, captured—anywhere and conveyed against their wills into the King's service. Officers, from admirals down, competed for crews. The news of a long, hard voyage around the world had no attraction for most enlistments. Anson grew desperate because of the delay in manning. During this time a proposal was made to fill his holds with trade goods, to be disposed of by the pursers and thus to reduce the expense of victualing. Salt horse and pork of the poorest quality were sent to the fleet; bread as hard as stones, destined to rot in the casks, was supplied, the sea tack being made of part flour and part other less valuable materials. But the main difficulty lay in getting crews. Anson sent press gangs ashore, taking men from merchantships when possible, or from grogshops. He accepted jail deliveries, enabling local jails to rid themselves of rascals. Even in this way he obtained less than 200 men for his fleet.

The months dragged, and the ships were slowly recruited. The Admiralty then had a grand idea of drawing on Chelsea Hospital, up the Thames, sending aboard, under protest, a large draft of disabled sailors and soldiers. So 500 out-invalids, most of them crippled and some demented, many veterans, pensioners ranging from sixty to seventy years old, were put into the ships. Those who had any sparks of energy left, deserted, risking their necks at the yardarms in preference to undergoing a world-round voyage.

Then, to fill up, the Admiralty sent Anson a large draft of marine recruits, raw boys who had never fired a musket or been a day at sea. Some old sailors, many fine officers, and warrant ranks who had sailed with Anson before joined up because of loyalty.

Finally these ships stood out from the Nore and tided down to Spithead against a contrary wind, a punishing job in itself. The fleet consisted of the *Centurion* (flagship), 60 guns, 513 men; the *Gloucester*, 50 guns, 350 men; the *Severn*, 50 guns, 350 men; the *Pearl*, 40 guns, 250 men; the *Wager*, 18 guns, 140 men; the *Tryal*, 16 guns, 80 men; and two supply ships, chartered merchantmen, the pinks *Anna* and *Industry*.

Anson anchored off St. Helen's, Isle of Wight, where his deplorable command hung on for many weeks while he discovered and attempted to repair the dishonest jobs done at Sheerness; rotten spars and defective rigging were but a part of it. The contractors had prevailed, and the pursers had cluttered him with worthless trade goods. His invalids, exhausted by the tiding, the constant weighing of anchors, filled the sick lists.

Time, however, hammered his raw boys into seamen. And fortunately, among his former shipmates were many superior officers and men. The venture had also attracted a few wild spirits, some of whom were destined to fame, among them the Honorable John Byron (to become grandfather of the poet and later to sail a great voyage), who was entered as a midshipman in the *Wager*. In spite of the motley crew, the fleet was commanded by one of the greatest sailors of that time, Commodore George Anson.

They sailed on Sept. 18, 1740. A heavy Spanish fleet under Admiral Don Joseph Pizarro was sent to dog them and sink them in the Pacific. But Cape Horn took care of the Spaniards, dispersing and foundering most of them. Anson, with dwindling man power (the *Centurion's* log alone noted from one to four corpses a day dumped overboard) rounded Cape Horn. Two of his ships, the *Severn* and the *Pearl*, parted company after being blown back into the Atlantic. Anson thought them lost until long after, when he reached the Indies. There news reached him of their going home. The little *Wager* was wrecked, running ashore in Chile.

Life in a heavy ship showing two tiers of guns, topped by thirty cannon on her quarter-deck, a ship of the line of the second class, sent on a long and difficult voyage, the heaviest warship to enter the Pacific up to her time and for many decades after, is worth considering. The terrible conditions incident to this great sea, and, indeed, to all oceans of the mighty era of long-voyage sailing ships, remained static for a vast span of time, in fact, up to the age of iron ships beginning in the latter part of the nineteenth century. A ship like the *Centurion*, which carried 400 seamen and 100 soldiers, was a floating fort, more compact than can be imagined now. All the duties of keeping watch, sailing the ship, cleaning, cooking, repairing, were done by those on board. She was a small self-contained world, a totalitarian state, if there ever was one. There were skilled craftsmen and laborers, all under the most rigid military discipline, for infractions of regulations were punished brutally in those days.

Even a century and a half after Anson's time, old wooden sailing men-of-war were not much different. I myself "slung" my hammock as a boy under the beams of the spar deck of the U. S. Sloop-of-war *St. Mary's*, then a school ship. Hammocks were depended from hooks in the beams, each having a billet number. The rows of hammocks were staggered so that they hung like a solid mat and swayed with the motion of the ship, the sleepers interlocked like sardines in a can. At "hammocks" in the morning watch, they were lashed with seven marling hitches and carried to the spar deck to be stowed in the "nettings" along the top of the bulwarks, then covered with tarpaulin flaps. The hammock nettings lifted the rail high and made an additional protection against shot and boarding. In the *Centurion* the over officers berthed on the quarter-deck, their temporary cabin bulkheads set up between the guns. When the ship cleared for action, the officer's quarters went overboard. Officers and men, in Anson's day, wore what they chose, and they often looked like a band of pirates rather than men of the King's Navy. It was a hard, desperate life, but there were men who loved it and went back for more. It did offer excitement.

At last the great ship approached an island. On June 9, 1741, nine months out of Spithead, the tough old *Centurion*, wallowing in the great Pacific swells, her high sterncastle swaying, her people deathly sick, came in sight of our old piratical rendezvous, Juan Fernandez. It was in the morning watch that they first descried the high peak of the main island. Chaplain Walter wrote: "It was to us a most agreeable sight, because at this place only could we hope to put a period to those terrible calamities we had so long struggled with, which had already swept away above half our crew, and which, had we continued a few days longer at sea, would inevitably have completed our destruction. For we were by this time reduced to so helpless a condition, that out of two hundred and odd men which remained alive, we could not, taking all our watches together, muster hands enough to work the ship in an emergency, though we included the officers, their servants, and the boys."

The wind coming northerly, they kept plying, that is, tacking, all day and the next night in order to approach the land. The scurvy had taken such toll of them after rounding the Horn that from a ship's company of 450, which had worked her through the Strait of Le Maire, the old barnacled *Centurion* could muster only 2 quartermasters and 6 sailors to watch.

They managed to sail in, fetching up in fifty-six fathoms, where they veered cable and were safe. A sail seen in the offing proved to be the *Tryal* sloop. Anson set some of his ablest men to board her. She was brought to an anchor between the *Centurion* and the land. Thirty-six aboard the *Tryal* had perished on the beat around the Horn, and, of the rest, only Captain Saunders, one lieutenant, and three men were able to tend the wheel and hand the sails. This was June 12, and Anson immediately took steps to transfer the sick ashore, erecting tents and huts, for the people in both ships were dying apace on board. The stench of the lower decks, the vermin, and the filth in which the sick men lay were nauseating. But, notwithstanding the dire necessity, it took them four days to send ashore canvas and prepare a place. Water had been brought out at once. During this time Commodore Anson, stripped to his shirt, worked with the men ashore and took his duty in the boats as they finally carried their remnant to the beach, slinging them in hammocks, since they were too weak to do more than lie. It was work of great fatigue. Deaths continued, and after the invalids were ashore the mortality kept up for nearly twenty days. For the first ten or twelve days they buried an average of six men each morning.

Anson carried on a survey of the anchorages, seeing Juan Fernandez as a valuable port of call for vessels coming into those seas. Had they been in possession of such information, between seventy and eighty men might have been saved through a more direct and expeditious contact with the land.

Anson supplied the ailing men " . . . out of his own stores, for, as his temperance had preserved his health, it now furnished him with the additional pleasure of supplying the sick with what another man would have spent at his table."

Gradually the climate, the fresh fruits and greens, and the newly killed meat that could be found, the abundance of sweet fresh water, the rest and freedom from the constant racking of the ship saved the lives of the survivors.

The *Centurion* and the *Tryal* swung at a precarious anchorage, always in alarm lest Spanish ships appear, indications ashore showing that ships, and probably men-of-war or pirates, had been there shortly before their own arrival. And with the crews of the British ships still not strong enough to fight, Anson was further concerned about the fate of his consorts. The rendezvous was definitely known. Both Juan Fernandez and the South Pacific held vast possibilities for disaster.

On June 21, ten days after their anchoring, some of Anson's people from an eminence, possibly Selkirk's lookout, descried a ship far to leeward, her courses even with the horizon. All else she carried was a main topsail. She disappeared in the night, and again on the twenty-sixth they saw a sail they took to be the same ship, off in the northeast quadrant. At one o'clock she approached so near that they could distinguish her as the *Gloucester*.

Commodore Anson sent his own boat to her assistance, carrying fresh water, fish, and vegetables. The more able-bodied men on the *Centurion* put out stoutly, coming up to their distressed consort in the dark of a terrible day. She had already thrown overboard two thirds of her complement.

Those capable of doing any duty were some officers and their servants, surviving only because of better rations than those furnished the crew. For a considerable time they had been on a pint of water a day, a slight "whack." They had so little left that if it had not been for the few casks brought by the boat all would soon have perished.

The *Gloucester*, foul with weeds and barnacles, plied within three miles of the bay. But, being so sluggish, she continued in the offing the next day. Anson sent out the *Tryal's* boat, manned again by Centurions, with a further supply of water and refreshments. Captain Mitchell was compelled to detain both boats so that the men could work the ship, for he had no longer any strength aboard. And in this extreme condition, the *Gloucester* continued to beat and be set back for nearly a fortnight. On July 9 they again saw her well to the eastward at a considerable distance, attempting to work to the southward of the island. Then she disappeared from sight for another week.

On July 16 the struggling death ship came near again, attempting to round the eastern point of the island, but the wind, still blowing directly from the bay, prevented her getting closer than four leagues from the land.

Captain Mitchell threw out signals of distress. Guns boomed. Anson dispatched the long boat with positive orders that she return, after delivering water and stores, for she could ill be spared. The situation, in the minds of those on the island, was desperate, but the actuality on board the *Gloucester* was extreme. The long boat made the ship but did not return. They feared her loss. On the third day they discerned her sails and sent out a cutter to help her. She had rescued six of the *Gloucester's* people, but two of them had died.

Without prompt relief by the boats all would certainly have perished aboard the consort. The conditions continued to be terrifying, apparently without remedy. The ship had already spent a month attempting to fetch the land. On July

23, having lost sight of her for several days, she opened the northwest point of the bay. All boats available were dispatched on board. In an hour's time they had her safely within the road. Out of her original complement of 350 men her people were reduced to less than 80.

With the people ashore, the three ships, especially the huge *Centurion*, were intolerably loathsome. They cleaned up and washed with vinegar, the great antiseptic of those days; they smoked the holds. The water butts were cleaned, coopered, and filled and the ships made ready in the greatest haste possible, always with an eye to Spanish cruisers that might suddenly appear. Great gusts of wind came in, once parting an anchor cable when the *Centurion* swung off to her best bower. The old hempen hawser stood the jerk, but they lost an anchor. Anson found it advisable "to *cackle* or *arm* the cables with an iron chain, or *rounding*, for five or six fathom from the anchor, to secure them from being rubbed by the foulness of the ground."

Captain Mitchell, of the *Gloucester*, had reported his thwarted attempt to make a landing at Massafuero (Más Afuera), and Anson planned to examine it, a high island lying twenty-two leagues to the westward of Juan Fernandez. He determined to send the sloop. "For this purpose, some of our best hands were sent aboard the *Tryal* . . . to overhaul and fix her rigging; and our long boat was employed in completing her water and whatever stores and necessaries she wanted were immediately supplied either from the *Centurion* or the *Gloucester*." She got off " . . . when having weighed, it soon after fell calm, and the tide set her very near the eastern shore. Captain Saunders hung out lights and fired several guns . . . upon which all the boats were sent to her relief, who towed the ship into the bay. . . . She anchored and got off again the next morning with a fair breeze. . . .

"And now we were employed in earnest in examining and

repairing our rigging, but in stripping our foremast, we were alarmed by discovering it sprung just above the partners of the upper deck. The spring was two inches in depth, and twelve in circumference; however the carpenters on inspecting it, gave it as their opinion that fishing it with two leaves of an anchorstock would render it as secure as ever."

The cordage and the blocks and ironwork had been poor when they sailed. "Besides this defect in our mast we had other difficulties in refitting, from the want of cordage and canvas; for though we had taken to sea much greater quantities of both than had ever been done before, yet the continued bad weather we met with had occasioned such consumption of these stores that we were driven to great straits, as after working up all our junk and old shrouds to make twice-laid cordage, we were at last obliged to unlay a cable to work into running rigging, and with all the canvas and remnants of old sails that could be mustered, we could only make up one complete suit."

(Walter referred to a suit of sails. "Twice-laid" rope is rope formed and laid of old yarns, taken from old cordage.)

They caught and rendered down sea lions and seals for oil to lubricate and burn for light. Forges were set up to repair and rework the old iron, chain plates, hooks, and the like. Still they were in dire need when, lo, a sail was sighted. It was their sturdy little victualer, come to the rendezvous, the brave historic *Anna*, pink. (A "pink" in those seagoing days of Anson did not refer to the color of a ship but to her shape. Pinks were smaller craft having sharp, or "pinked," sterns.) The stout little *Anna*, a chartered victualer, had kept on with the fleet after the *Industry* was discharged and sent home while they were still in the Atlantic. The *Anna* bested Cape Horn. Coming to the rendezvous two months after the *Centurion*, her master, Captain Gerard, and her people deserve all credit. Driving upon the coast of South America, in latitude 44 south, the pink, by a miraculous chance, her fore-topsail splitting, her anchors dragging as she closed with a high lee shore, drove to safety after her sixteen men and boys had given up hope. Here in Anna Pink bay, she lay for two months before venturing to sea. An Indian family appeared, was captured, and escaped. Fearing a general alarm of the tribes and being "well refreshed," the *Anna* put to sea, joining Anson at Juan Fernandez.

At once Anson set his people to unlading the pink. But . . . "we had the mortification to find that great quantities of our provisions, as bread, rice, grots, etc., were decayed, and unfit for use. This was owing to the water the pink had made by her working and straining in bad weather; for hereby several of her casks had rotted, and her bags were soaked through."

Anson was about to discharge the pink when her master, fearing a return around the Horn, asked for a survey. The carpenters reported: "The pink hath no less than fourteen knees and twelve beams broken and decayed; one breast hook is broken and another rotten; her waterways are open and decayed; two standards and several clamps are broken, besides others which are rotten; all her iron work is greatly decayed; her spirketing timbers are very rotten; and having ripped off part of her sheathing, we find her wales and outside planks extremely defective, and her bows and decks very leaky."

Aside from this, the *Anna* was in perfect shape. Anson condemned her, paid the owners £300 for her usable fittings; her master, men, and boys joined the weak handed fleet. Sending out a small ship, already rotten, was in keeping with the vile outfitting of Anson's fleet.

Careening as best they could, since much of the gear for heeling the fleet was in the *Wager*, still missing, the ships made rapid preparation for sea. The checkup on survivors shows a frightful mortality since they had left England a year before. Aboard the *Gloucester* every one of the Chelsea Hospital invalids perished, and out of forty-eight marine recruits only two survived. The *Centurion* had a somewhat similar experience, and the sailors, those who were seasoned, survived in larger numbers. Out of fifty invalids, four remained; out of seventy-nine marines, eleven remained, including four officers —a loss of over 65 per cent of their complements. But the voyage, the fighting, and the Pacific Ocean passage had only begun.

About eleven in the forenoon—Sept. 8, 1741, was the date —a cry lifted from Selkirk's lookout. "Sail, ho!" This stranger, which might and might not be one of the missing ships, approached until her courses lifted even with the horizon. A tremendous activity seized the camp. Anson ordered all hands aboard the *Centurion*, which was already in great forwardness. The people—ones who had far recovered—bent sail and hoisted with the greatest dispatch, then brought their anchor up. The stranger steered away to the eastward " . . . without haling in for the land!" There could be but one conclusion. She was a Spaniard or a pirate and might have seen the ships and tents from her mastheads.

Making all sail, they had but wind enough to get an offing of two or three leagues. It fell calm, and they hoisted out the boats, towing toward the chase. Night closed, and an anxious time it was. At daybreak nothing was in sight.

"As we were satisfied it was an enemy, and the first we had seen in these seas, we resolved not to give over the chace lightly." A small breeze sprang up. They got up the topgallant masts and yards, setting all sail, steering the eastward on a taut bowline, assuming the ship to have been bound for Valparaiso. All that day and the next they stood toward the land with no sign of the sail. At last they gave up the pursuit, " . . . haled up to the S.W.," standing back for Juan Fernandez. At daybreak of the twelfth, a fresh gale having sprung up in the midwatch, they made a sail on the weather bow. Then one of those strange happenings occurred, so

typical of the sea. "We immediately crowded all sail we could
. . . and soon perceived it not to be the same ship we originally gave chace to. She at first bore down upon us, shewing
Spanish colours, making a signal as to her consort."

The *Centurion* being unable to answer the Spaniard, " . . .
loofed close to the wind and stood to the southward." Anson
beat the crew to quarters—that is, they took stations, short-
handed as they were, to the beat of drums. "Our people were
now all in spirits, and put the ship about with great briskness."
The chase was a large ship, and they thought most probably
a man-of-war, possibly one of Pizarro's squadron, which they
supposed might still be following them. The greatest excitement prevailed. The small crew were fresh from their rest,
ready and waiting, expecting to meet stout resistance. "This
induced the Commodore to order all officers' cabins to be
knocked down and thrown overboard, with several casks of
water and provisions which stood between the guns, so that
we had a clear ship ready for an engagement."

But the sail was only a merchantman, called *Nuestra Señora
del Monte Carmelo*, as they soon discovered, having forereached
upon her, coming close. They fired four shot amongst her
riggings, at which she lowered her topsails in great confusion,
"their topgallant sails and staysails all fluttering in the wind."

And here Anson began the collection of his enormous booty.
Mr. Saumarez, first lieutenant of the *Centurion*, took command
of the prize. A cargo of blue Quito cloth, sugar, cotton, and
tobacco was negligible compared to "twenty-three serons of
dollars, each weighing upwards of 200 lb." The ship's burthen
was 450 tons. She was a thirty year old vessel and indifferently
rigged. Four six pounders taken out of the *Anna* were put
aboard her.

Anson's cruise up the coast of South America seemed almost
to follow a track first started by Drake. Over a century and a
half after the first raid the cities were again being sacked.

Englishmen and Dutchmen had fought in turn along the coast. At Payta, in Peru, Anson's men landed successfully. Some were killed among the English. And, incidentally, we read about an interesting item of an officer's attire during a landing party in those times: "Another of the company, the Honourable Mr. Kepple, son of the Earl of Albemarle, had a very narrow escape; for having on a jockey cap, one side of the peak was shaved off close to his temple by a ball, which however did him no further injury."

At Payta, as Anson's private journal notes: "1741, 12 November. I kept Posession of the Town three days and employed my Boats in plundering."

So they went northward, after traverses back and forth, mopping up the little Spanish settlements. Anson never burned any churches if he could avoid it, and he was kind to women and children captured. So he carried out his duty, and it was noted " . . . that the despoiling was no contemptible branch of that service in which we were now employed by our country."

At last Anson was to be done with the western shores of America. He, too, cruised with his ships, off and on before the old port of Acapulco, waiting for the Manila ship, but without success. On April 5, having been many months at sea and having but six days' water in the butts, they entered the harbor of Chequetan, thirty leagues to the westward of Acapulco. Two prizes brought north were set on fire and scuttled. The *Centurion*, her high poop lanterns burning in the night, bore off to the west, followed by but one ship, the *Gloucester*. Both were well laden with loot. It was May 6, 1742, when they left the coast of Mexico.

They held west, running before the trades in the latitudes of 13 and 14 degrees north. "Our two ships were by this time extremely crazy; and many days had not passed before we discovered a spring in the foremast of the *Centurion*, which rounded about twenty-six inches of its circumference and which we judged to be at least four inches deep. And no sooner had the carpenters secured this mast by fishing it, than the *Gloucester* made a signal of distress to inform us that she had a spring in her mainmast, twelve feet below the trussel trees; which appeared so dangerous she could not carry sail upon it. Our carpenters, on a strict examination of this mast, found it excessively rotten and decayed; it being judged necessary to cut it down as low as it was defective. It was by this means reduced to nothing but a stump, which served only as a step to the topmast. . . . "

Although the people had enjoyed good health since leaving Juan Fernandez, now the reverse was true, and scurvy once again began to make havoc. Fresh provisions were abundant, rains kept the water casks filled, yet the dread malady began to rage. "To what hath already been said in relation to this disease . . . it was resolved by the Commodore to try the success of two medicines, which, just before his departure from England, were the subject of much discourse. I mean the pill and drop of Mr. Ward. For however violent the operations of these medicines are said to have sometimes proved, yet in the present instance, where, without some remedy, destruction seemed inevitable, the experiment at least was thought advisable; and therefore, one or both of them at different times were administered to persons in every stage of the distemper. Out of the number who took them, one, soon after swallowing the pill, was seized with a violent bleeding at the nose. He was given over by the surgeon and lay almost at the point of death; but he immediately found himself much better, and continued to recover, tho' slowly, till we arrived on shore, which was near a fortnight after. A few others too were relieved for some days, but the disease returned again with as much virulence as ever. Though neither did these, nor the rest, who received no benefit, appear to be reduced to a worse condition than they would have been if they had taken nothing.

"The most remarkable property of these medicines, and what was obvious in almost every one that took them, was that those who were within two or three day of dying were scarcely affected; and as the patient was differently advanced in the disease, the operation was either gentle perspiration, and easy vomit, or a moderate purge; but if they were taken by one in full strength, they then produced all the aforementioned effects with considerable violence, which sometimes continued for six or eight hours together with little intermission."

A powerful potent this historic pill and drop of Mr. Ward.

On July 26, when they were about 300 leagues from the Ladrones, the steady trade wind, which had been under their quarters, swung around, and a stiff breeze blew in from the west. The two ships, hauling their bowlines, bobbing and sagging, began to ply off to sea, the head wind hammering them so that they made no appreciable way. This continued through four days of discouragement. Then the wind flattened to a calm, the ships rolling deep, the *Gloucester* splitting her fore-cap. Her fore-topmast went by the board, breaking her fore-yard in the slings. She lay a wreck upon the sea. Anson sent ten of his ablest and healthiest men to help clear away the wreck-age and get up a jury mast. Scarcely had the people got their job done, after ten days of continuous work, when a violent storm broke from the western board.

At once, in the laboring, the *Centurion* sprang a leak letting in so much water that all hands, officers included, labored constantly at the pumps to keep her afloat. Half-hourly the carpenter and his mates sounded the well, reporting to the First Lieutenant. The Commodore remained awake, anxiously scanning the sea. When dawn came, the *Gloucester* was seen, wallowing to leeward, her fore-topmast again gone, and, while they were viewing her with the greatest concern, the people in the flagship saw their consort's main topmast crash over her side. The *Gloucester's* men were so weak that they could not work. Anson sagged down ahead of the disabled ship, and Captain Mitchel brought to under the stern of the Commodore.

"We have seven feet of water in the well!" he called, his tones indicating despair as both ships drifted across the storm. He needed immediate and vigorous assistance. A boat was despatched to get the full report.

Those old British Navy sailors never abandoned a ship without certain ceremony. A survey report was sent the Commodore, signed by Captain Mitchel and his officers. Her defects were: a leak by the stern post, which was working loose, every roll of the ship opening the after hood ends; two beams amidship were broken in the orlop, no part of which could be repaired at sea. Officers and men had wrought at the backbreaking pumps, without intermission, for twenty-four hours. The water had then risen above the casks. The masts were all gone except the stumps standing forward and on the mizzen. A few rags of storm canvas held her hove to. The people on board, remaining alive, officers included, numbered seventy-seven men, eighteen boys, and two prisoners, of which only sixteen men and eleven boys were capable of keeping the deck.

Anson sent his own carpenter to make the strictest check. The *Centurion* herself was only kept afloat by continuous labor. The Commodore, being advised of the correctness of the damage list, ordered Captain Mitchel to abandon ship at once and to take out such stores as he could. Easier weather followed the gale. They roused out what stores they could, transferred her people, and carried over the prize money in the *Gloucester's* boats. It fell calm, and the work of abandonment went on. Seventy invalids were brought to the flagship, when, on Aug. 15, Captain Mitchel fired her, sent his officers over the side, and left his old ship roaring in smoke and flame.

In the *Centurion*, " . . . we immediately stood from the wreck, not without some apprehensions (as we had only a light breeze) that if she blew up the concussion of the air might damage our rigging; but she fortunately continued burning the whole night, so that her guns fired successively as the flames reached them, yet it was six in the morning, when we were about four leagues distant, before she blew up. The report she made upon this occasion was but small, although the blast produced an exceeding black pillar of smoke, which shot up into the air to a very considerable height.

"Thus perished his Majesty's ship the *Gloucester*."

So we find Commodore Anson with one ship remaining of his original squadron of six men-of-war and two tenders. His success in plundering had been considerable; his remaining ship was on the point of foundering far offshore; his reduced crew was ridden with scurvy. The winds were about to turn against him; he had been carried off 100 leagues more from the Ladrones. "The late storm, which had been so fatal to the *Gloucester*, had driven us to the northward of our intended course . . . we were in 17½° of north latitude, instead of being in 13½° which was the parallel we intended to keep in order to reach the island of Guam."

Longitude determinations in the era of Anson were more or less a matter of guesswork, of accumulative dead reckoning. "As it had been a perfect calm for some days since the cessation of the storm, and we were ignorant how near we were to the meridian of the Ladrones, though we supposed ourselves not to be far from it, we apprehended that we might be driven to the leeward of them by the current without discovering them. On this supposition, the only land we could make would be some of the eastern parts of Asia, where, if we could arrive, we should find the western monsoon in full force, so that it would be impossible for the strongest, best-manned ship to get in. Besides, this coast being four or five hundred leagues distant from us, we, in our languishing circumstances, could expect no other than to be destroyed by the scurvy long before the most favourable gale could enable us to complete so extensive a navigation. For our deaths were by this time extremely alarming, no day passing in which we did not bury eight or ten, and sometimes twelve of our men; and those who had as yet continued healthy began to fall down apace."

The current shifted to a southerly set, and on Aug. 23 the distressed *Centurion* sighted two islands on her western board. "At noon being not four leagues from the island of Anatacan, a boat was sent in to sound for an anchorage." Knowledge of the islands was extremely imperfect. Anatacan seemed to abound in coconuts, but they found no anchorage. The ship continued to ply toward the land, intending to send in boats for fresh fruit, but they were driven off so far to the southward that they could not attempt landing. Pasaros, the other island, appeared to be only a rock.

"Thus with the most gloomy persuasion of our approaching destruction, we stood from the island of Anatacan, having all of us the strongest apprehension (and those not ill grounded) either of dying of scurvy, or of being destroyed with the ship, which for want of hands to work her pumps, might in a short time be expected to founder."

By this time Commodore Anson was taken with scurvy, " . . . all hands being either completely incapacitated, or very much touched by the malady." A few were able to work, but only with the greatest pain.

Bad as things had been when Anson sighted Juan Fernandez, conditions aboard the huge *Centurion* were worse on Apr. 27, when, in the morning watch, three islands were discovered to the eastward. They afterward learned these islands were Saipan, Tinian, and Agiguan. Calms and light airs retarded them. The excessive heat bubbled old pitch from the seams of their decks. Long green grasses trailed from the bottom, the ship's sides were weathered white, the patched sails and fished masts made her appear some long lost galleon, come in like a ghost from the sea. Those on board were as decrepit as dead men arriving from a graveyard of the ocean. She was no longer a smart King's ship but a sole surviving wreck. The feeble clunk-clunk of her chain pumps sounded through the huge stinking hull like the clapping of a weak and breaking heart. Bloodshot eyes strained toward the islands. Their weak spying glasses searched the shore. They were then fourteen months older than when they had sighted Selkirk's island, but years of straining and abuse had passed over the crazy ship, and the crew, by the most reliable estimate, were reduced to less than 200, which included the survivors of the other ships. More than three fourths of them were desperately sick.

"About ten o'clock we perceived a proa under sail to the southward between Tinian and Agiguan. As we imagined from hence that these islands were inhabited, and knew that the Spaniards had always a force at Guam . . . we therefore mustered all our hands who were capable of standing to their arms, and loaded our upper and quarterdeck guns with grape shot; and that we might the more readily procure some intelligence of the state of these islands, we showed Spanish colours, and hoisted a red flag at the fore top-mast-head, hoping thereby to give our ship the appearance of the Manila galleon, and to decoy some of the inhabitants on board us."

Their cutter was hoisted and sent to sound an anchorage. A proa put off from the strand to meet the cutter and was promptly taken by the Englishmen, whereupon they sent their pinnace to take over the prize. A Spaniard and four Indians were captured. The Spaniard, a sergeant, reported the island uninhabited. He had only twenty-two Indians under his command, who had been employed in jerking the beef that was in the small bark. The *Centurion* let go her anchor in twenty-two fathoms. The bark, the only craft at Tinian, lay near and was promptly seized, and none of the men could escape.

The boats brought out some water and fruits. "When we had furled our sails, our people were allowed to repose themselves during the remainder of the night, to recover from the fatigue they had undergone." And with the day there opened up a prospect only possible in the great western fringe of the Pacific. The agreeable Spanish sergeant cheered them. "In particular he assured us that there was plenty of very good water; that there was an incredible number of cattle, hogs, and poultry running wild on the island, all of them excellent in their kind; that the woods afforded sweet and sour oranges, limes, lemons, and cocoanuts in great abundance, besides a fruit peculiar to these islands, which served instead of bread."

The stray Indians took to the hills as sick men were landed under the guns of their ship. The officers, headed by the Commodore, carried the invalids from the boats on their shoulders to a large hut found on the shore. So salutary was the climate, so fresh and invigorating the food, the fruits, and sparkling water that, though they buried twenty-one men on the first and the succeeding day, only ten more died during their two months on the island of Tinian. Paradise on the rim of the Pacific, as Walter described it: "The soil is everywhere dry and healthy, and being withal somewhat sandy, it is thereby the less disposed to a rank and overluxuriant vegetation; and hence the meadows and bottoms of the woods are much neater and smoother than is customary in hot climates. . . . These vallies and the gradual swellings of the ground which their different combinations gave rise to were most beautifully diversified by the mutual encroachments of woods and lawns, which coasted each other and traversed the island in large tracts. . . . Hence arose a number of the most entertaining prospects. . . . Nor were the allurements of Tinian confined to the landskipts only."

And so on, about fat kine, "lords of this happy soil," thousands feeding together in herds, all of them milk white, except for their ears, which were generally brown or black; the clamor of the frequent parading of domestic poultry; the cackling as they dropped their fresh eggs; and the porkers, willing volunteers to become the ham so much prized by sailors. They found large dogs in that place and used them in the running down of cattle. The choicest cuts of beef, rich puddings—well, those starved men grew stout. The woods yielded inconceivable quantities of coconuts "with the cabbages growing on the same trees." There were, besides, guavas, limes, sweet and sour oranges, as the Spanish sergeant had said, breadfruit " . . . so universally preferred that no ship's bread was expended."

But the anchorage was bedded in sharp coral. Their cables were rounded, as at Juan Fernandez, and the ship continued to leak. Immediate efforts were made to overcome this, lest she founder at her mooring. The leak was in the bow; so the guns were carried far aft, bringing the ship down by the stern. They ripped off what was left of the forward sheathing and caulked the seams on both sides of the cutwater, leaded them over and then renewed the sheathing as far down as they could. Returning the guns forward, they found the water rushing into the ship in the old place. Anson's anxiety was great. Again they hove her down by the stern; lifting the bow higher, they cleared the fore storeroom and sent 130 barrels of powder to the bark. Once again they did their job, but after putting the ship on an even keel they found to their amazement that the water burst into her again. "We durst not cut away the lining within board, lest a butt end or a plank start and we might go down immediately."

Then, by clinching and caulking within board, for the nonce, the leak was stopped. "But when the guns were all fixed in their ports and our stores were taken in, the water again forced its way through the stem where one of the bolts was driven in." So they contented themselves with pumping constantly, those capable of duty being sent back aboard ship. By that time Commodore Anson, too sick from scurvy to be of help, had to go ashore. He pitched a tent "near the well whence we got all our water, and (this) was indeed a most elegant spot."

From Sept. 18, when the new moon appeared, they awaited hard weather, " . . . but on the 22nd the wind blew from the eastward with such fury that we soon despaired of riding out the storm."

The greater part of the people were ashore with the Commodore. Communication with the land was impossible. A hurricane was blowing—momentarily they expected their cables to part. Chaplain Walter was aboard the ship: "Indeed we were not long expecting this dreadful event, for the small bower parted at five in the afternoon, and the ship swung off to the best bower; and as night came on the violence of the wind still increased, tho' notwithstanding its inexpressible fury, the tide ran with so much rapidity as to prevail over it; for the tide which set to the northward at the beginning of the hurricane, turned suddenly to the southward about six in the evening, forced the ship before it despite of the storm which blew upon the beam. The sea now broke most surprisingly all round us, and a large tumbling swell threatened to poop us, by which the long-boat at this time moored astern, was on a sudden canted so high that it broke the transom of the Commodore's gallery, whose cabin was on the quarterdeck, and would doubtless have risen as high as the tafferel had it not been for the stroke, which stove the boat all to pieces; and yet the poor boat-keeper, though extremely bruised, was saved almost by a miracle."

Their best bower parted, they cut the sheet anchor (their heaviest). But before it could bite, the huge *Centurion*, with Mr. Saumarez in command, was dragging out to sea, with a sketchy crew and water making into her old leak in the stem. Each moment they expected to be their last. Ashore, the horrified people saw the ship, as lightning flashed off to the east, swallowed in a cloud of spume and driving into the Pacific.

Here it seemed was the end of all. Almost any day the Governor of Guam would hear of the disaster. Deepest despair seized the camp. Fortunately, the carpenters taken from the *Gloucester* and the *Tryal* were ashore among the sick and had their tool chests with them. Anson began one of the most remarkable efforts of the history of the sea. He at once set about preparing the small bark to receive his people. They had no blocks or tackle for hauling her up; so, by digging, they con structed a dry dock into which they rolled her on logs. The bark was hauled up, and, two weeks after the blowing off of the *Centurion*, they began sawing her in halves. They cut trees and hewed planks and timbers for the lengthening of this little ship so that she could carry all their people.

They had no bellows, so they tanned hides with some lime they found, making a bellows, with the use of a gun barrel for a pipe. On every hand the greatest ingenuity was exercised, and the half recovered people worked like slaves, the Commodore in the forefront, swinging an adz. Even as the bark was enlarged, she was not over forty tons burthen and would have been close stowed with crew and provisions and most indifferently rigged. On Oct. 11, while this labor of Hercules was in progress and while all hands were expending their utmost efforts, one of the *Gloucester's* people, who happened to be on top of a hill at the middle of Tinian, descried a sail and recognized her as the *Centurion*, standing back toward the land.

So great was the Commodore's relief when he heard this news that " . . . he threw down an axe, with which he was then at work, and by his joy broke through for the first time, the equable and unvaried character which he had hitherto preserved."

Here was his greatest triumph. Had the *Centurion* foundered, laden with her plunder, Anson would have reached the Philippines in that heroic bark. There is no doubt that he would have captured a better craft, and such were his hopes and his plans.

The old *Centurion* had taken her pounding and returned. She was blown off a second time, but the Commodore was then on board, and only seventy men were ashore. However, they worked her back, completed their watering, and stood to the south.

Anson sailed by Guam, past Formosa, and to the Portuguese anchorage of Macao, across from the island of Hong Kong, at the mouth of the Chu-kiang. His dealings with the mandarins at Canton, his refitting, and his preparation for sea are no part of the story of the Pacific. But, where almost any other commander would have stood for home, thankful to have survived so far, George Anson did quite the opposite. At Macao he had the first word of his ships the *Severn* and the *Pearl*, driven eastward at Cape Horn, arriving at Rio de Janeiro. The *Severn*, in particular, had been extremely sickly, a fact they attributed to her being a new ship. The old *Centurion*, however, hove down and attended by Chinese caulkers, disclosed her bottom in remarkably sound condition. Her leak, found to be below the fifteen foot mark, was due to a defective bolt, and this was replaced and caulked.

Again on Apr. 19, at three in the afternoon, she stood to sea. Twenty-three extra men had been entered at Macao, the greater part of them Lascars, or Indian sailors, a few, Dutchmen. Word had been given out that Anson was bound for Batavia, but he shaped course for Cape Espíritu Santo, on the island of Samal (Samar), which was the usual landfall of the Acapulco ship. He had prevented one of the Manila bound galleons from putting to sea the previous year when his cruise off Lower California became known. Now he expected that one or more of the great treasure galleons would have been standing across the Pacific and should be about due in the Philippines.

So the *Centurion* sailed back across the China Sea, past Formosa and the Bashee Islands, and then south and southwest for Espíritu Santo. The Commodore called his people to the mast. He had but 227 in the crew, of which 30 were boys. He reminded them that the galleons were stout vessels, mounting 40 guns and carrying above 500 hands. They had their work cut out to take one of them. But he knew that his men would exert themselves to the utmost in view of the immense wealth that might be expected if they captured an Acapulco ship.

The speech of the Commodore was received by three hearty cheers. All vowed to succeed or perish. Gunnery drill was carried out constantly, and small arm shooting, usually delegated to the marines, was in constant exercise. "They were taught no more of the manual than the shortest method of loading with cartridges, and were constantly trained to fire at a mark, which was usually hung at the yard-arm, and where some small reward was given to the most expert. The whole crew, by this management, were rendered extremely skillful." Some became extraordinary marksmen and, as they stood, were a match for twice their number. The anxiety of the command is noted in a few extracts from the *Centurion's* log.

"May 31, (1743). Exercising our men at their quarters, in great expectation of meeting with the galeons very soon, this being the eleventh of June, their stile.

"June 3. Keeping in our stations, and looking out for the galeons.

"June 5. Begin now to be in great expectation, this being the middle of June, their stile.

"June 11. Begin to grow impatient at not seeing the galeons.

"June 13. The wind having blown fresh easterly for forty-eight hours past, gives us great expectations of seeing the galeons soon.

"June 15. Cruising on and off, and looking out strictly.

"June 19. This being the last day of June, N.S. (new style), the galeons, if they arrive at all, must appear soon."

On June 20, just a month after gaining their station, a sail was descried in the southeast quarter, lifting at sunrise. Great joy greeted this news, and the Commodore stood toward her under press of canvas. At seven o'clock the galleon fired a gun and took in her topgallant sails. "This was supposed to be a signal for her consort to hasten her up, and therefore the *Centurion* fired a gun to leeward to amuse her."

In fact, as afterward disclosed, the Spaniard knew the English ship was not her consort and actually continued to bear down on her with the intention of engaging. Anson had her cut off when the galleon "haled up her fore-sail and brought to under top-sails, with her head to the northward, hoisting Spanish colours, and having the standard of Spain flying at the top-gallant masthead." It was a brilliant day off to the eastward of Samar, the huge ships jockeying for position before coming within effective cannon shot. It was the custom of the Spaniards to lie flat on their decks when they saw the guns run out for a broadside from an enemy. Then, on receiving it, they sprang to their own pieces, fired or loaded, and prepared. But the *Centurion* was unable to fire in the orthodox way. Anson had no more than two men to a gun to swab and load while his full guns' crews moved from piece to piece, firing continuously as the guns were loaded.

At one o'clock, after noon, the *Centurion*, within gunshot of the enemy, hoisted her broad pennant and colors. The Spaniards began to clear their ship, throwing overboard cattle and lumber. Though his general directions had not been to fire until within pistol shot, Anson opened on them with his chase guns, to disturb them as much as possible. The galleon returned fire with two of her stern chases. The *Centurion* swung her spritsail yard fore and aft, to be clear for closing on the quarter and boarding. Anson held to the leeward, that is, to the west of the galleon to prevent her from putting up her helm and running before it for the port of Jalapay, only seven leagues distant.

The constant discharges of the *Centurion's* guns continued, to the amazement of the Spaniards, who were accustomed to broadside salvos. Anson came alongside and overreached the galleon. By the great wideness of his ports he could train aft and bring all his guns to bear, whereas the galleon could use only part of her broadside battery. The din was deafening. The shouts and the constant discharge of musketry were punctuated by a sheet of flame rising upward from the galleon's nettings. These had been stuffed by mats and hammocks, and a burning wad from the *Centurion*, lodged there, set the fire that rose to her tops. The Spaniards were thrown into the utmost terror. The fire also alarmed Anson, who feared the burning of his rich prize, for he felt certain the galleon would be his.

The Spaniards freed themselves by cutting away the netting, tumbling the whole burning mass into the sea. In the *Centurion* the topmen and sharpshooters cleared the deck of the enemy. Their first volley drove the Spaniards from their top platforms. The sailors made prodigious havoc with their small arms, killing or wounding every officer but one that appeared on the galleon's quarter-deck.

Wallowing in the blue sea, the water growing purple by a stream of blood down through her scuppers, the galleon, like a great bull being done to death in a ring, still continued to fire briskly. But great confusion reigned on board the Spaniard. The ships lay so near that officers of the galleon could be seen and heard above the firing, driving their people to the serving of the guns. Then, having given Anson a last salvo of six guns, " . . . they yielded up the contest."

Their ensign had been burned down, so they struck the standard at her main topgallant truck. The sailor detailed to this act was about to be shot when Anson, seeing his errand, gave orders to his marksmen to stop firing.

And no sooner had the galleon struck than word came to Anson that the *Centurion* was dangerously on fire near the powder room. All hope of escape by boarding the prize vanished as the ships locked, the galleon on the starboard quarter of the *Centurion*. If the magazine let go, both ships would sink together.

But the fire was quenched, and the galleon, commanded by

one of Anson's officers, sheered off. She was a shambles; sixty-seven had been killed in action and eighty-four wounded. Two of the *Centurion* had been killed and a lieutenant and sixteen wounded, one of whom died.

Their prize, the *Nuestra Señora de Covadonga*, was commanded by a Portuguese, General Don Jerônimo de Montero, most skilled of the commanders of the galleons of that time. She carried 550 men, mounted thirty-six guns, besides twenty-eight pedreros on her gunwales, her poops, and in her tops, each throwing a four pound ball.

So much for the last capture at sea of a galleon bound for Manila, laden with a great treasure. The Commodore, throughout the action, had remained on the quarter-deck with his sword drawn, giving directions with the greatest calmness. The cutter and long boat of the prize transferred 300 prisoners to the *Centurion*. Fifty English sailors went aboard the *Covadonga;* so the flagship had twice as many prisoners as she had crew.

Anson at once stood back for Macao, having learned that the second expected galleon had preceded the prize by some months and was safe in Manila. Captain Philip Saumarez saluted the Commodore with eleven guns, and three were returned, for Anson had that day commissioned him a post captain in the Royal Navy, as he was authorized to do, under the circumstances, by the regulations of the navy. With the courtesy of salutes came the tallying of treasure added to the large store of prize money aboard the flagship.

They had everything of value out of the prize, amounting in the whole to 1,313,843 pieces of eight, 35,683 ounces of plate and virgin silver.

The *Centurion* must ever take her place in the great annals of the Pacific as one of that ocean's greatest ships. Anson died on June 6, 1762, at his seat at Moorpark, in Herfordshire, laden with distinguished honors, one of the most stouthearted of the Pacific navigators.

Tahiti

AFTER Anson, many wondered if something more than plunder might not be found in the South Sea. The French missed their great chance in the appropriation of the East Indies, their French East Indies Company having been caught, and in a measure stopped, by the discovery and acquisition of the great island of Madagascar, which they still hold. So it was natural enough that savants of France should begin to speculate on the possibility of great discoveries and most valuable annexations in the South Pacific. More than a third of the globe still lay fallow. Here was a continent, as Beaglehole reports the imagining of Charles de Brosses, " . . . its center at the pole, projected far northward in capes and promontories that so many voyagers had seen. And within the bounds of these southern lands, what interest and profit? What peoples, customs and religions! What inconceivable variety of natural phenomena; what trade in gold and jewels, in medicines and spices, dye-woods and silks and skins, the liberal return for brandy, cheap looking glasses and iron."

De Brosses, president of the Parliament of Dijon, stirred the French with his *Historie des Navigations aux Terres Australis*, which appeared in 1756. The scientific age seemed to have dawned in the consciousness of men. Dampier, Woodes Rogers, and Anson, had been crude. A decade later John Callender published *Terra Australis Cognita*. The historian Beaglehole puts the finger on this latter author. "The British had deprived France of her colonial empire; now with as little scruple and considerably less trouble, a Scotchman appropriated De Brosses' work, and De Brosses' program. For Callender is little more than a free rendering of his predecessor." And in three large volumes.

Then came Alexander Dalrymple, a man of original talent and a student of accomplishment. He had been a servant of the East India Company, became its hydrographer and, later, the first hydrographer of the British Admiralty. His fame is preserved by Dalrymple Isle, in the southeastern seas near Papua and by a point bearing his name, marked by nun-buoys, thirty-three miles from Cape Upstart, somewhere off the coast of Queensland. And then there is Port Dalrymple, on the island of Tasmania. So we establish him as an authority in his time.

It was 1764 when Dalrymple published *An Account of the Discoveries Made in the South Pacific Ocean*, his most significant work. Three years later came a *Collection of Voyages to the South Seas*. All these matters are set down, for, from Mendaña and Quiros through to Schouten and the discoveries of Roggeveen, a great mystery surrounded the huge ocean that M. Malte-Brun proposed be named the Great Ocean. Happily, Magellan's christening has remained. So, after an enormous amount of guessing, of discussion, and of abortive planning, King George III, no less, impatient with all this French palaver and delay, signed a royal warrant for the first scientific expedition deliberately to set out on a voyage after knowledge, with the pious hope of valuable geographical discoveries. To this end the Admiralty fitted out two ships, the twenty gun sloop *Dolphin,* said to have been the first ship with a coppered bottom, and the smaller sixteen gun *Tamar.* The flagship carried a complement of 190 officers and men, the *Tamar,* 116. John Byron was in command of the small force, and Captain Mouat had command of the *Tamar.* This Byron was the same man as the young midshipman who had clung to and suffered with his captain after the wreck of the *Wager.*

The ships sailed from the Downs on June, 21, 1764, and, after their share of vicissitudes, entered the Pacific, via the Strait of Magellan, sailing northward to Massafuero, the westernmost island of the Juan Fernandez group.

Commodore Byron, more of a sailor than a scientist, was delighted with the *Dolphin.* Her bottom was smooth, for marine growths could not fasten on the copper, and even fishes seemed to avoid the gleaming, poisonous metal. She sailed like a witch, that tight little man-o'-war. A year after departing England, on June 7, 1765, having sailed to the westward in the Pacific southeast trades, Byron came upon a group of islands. His objective had been the Solomons " . . . if any such islands were there," and, if not, some new discovery. As usual, men were sick, but not with the desperate degree of incapacity experienced by Anson. Byron found no safe anchorage, and, when natives displayed hostility toward one of the small boats making soundings, he bore away, calling this group the Islands of Disappointment. He was on the northern fringe of the Tuamotus. In reprisals against hostile natives on two islands farther along, two or three natives were killed, " . . . one being pierced by three balls which went quite through his body. He took up a huge stone and died in the act of throwing it."

Still sailing to the west, Byron obtained several boatloads of coconuts and made the discovery of a carved rudderhead, belonging to a Dutch longboat, a relic, most likely, from the *African* galley of Roggeveen's fleet, wrecked on Schouten's Badwater Island in 1722. The latitude was between 15 and 16 degrees. "There were no venomous creatures," reported Byron, "but the flies were a continuous and intollerable torment." At another isle, to the westward, as they swept this distant ocean, one of those precocious wights, yes, a midshipman, swam ashore from a sounding boat, while the ship coasted along. The natives there seemed more friendly, he thought. But the adventurous middy was obliged to dive in again and swim back when the savages began to strip off his clothes. The people were after pearls. There being no anchorage, Byron named the isles after King George, a designation they still bear, together with his Disappointment Isles, on the northern fringe of the Tuamotu Archipelago.

He missed many considerable discoveries, however. He failed to sight the Marquesas, of Mendaña, and sailed largely on the course of Roggeveen. He sighted an island against which a surf was breaking. This he passed and named Prince of Wales Island. Heading farther to the north, in latitude 10 degrees and 15 minutes south, he fell in with another group, " . . . fertile and beautiful, and swarming with people, but defended in every direction by rocks and breakers." He called these the Islands of Danger.

Byron lost faith in the mythical Solomons, noting that only Quiros had seen them. But Mendaña had also sighted those rich and elusive shores.

One sweet atoll, Byron's Island he called it, was " . . . low and flat, green and delightful in appearance and like so many others, without anchorage." The copper-colored people, their smooth bodies flashing in the sun, came off in hundreds, cheerful, chattering and crying greetings, stark naked except for strings of shells. "Some of them were unarmed," noted the Commodore, "but others had one of the most dangerous weapons I have ever seen; it was a kind of spear, very broad at the end, and stuck full of shark's teeth, for about three feet of its length."

These people had thievish tendencies, and the ships sailed on for Anson's lush paradise of Tinian, hoping to recuperate at that delightful island of the Ladrones. They had broiled under a vertical sun, riding a blistering sea, and not a man was free from scurvy. Time, even in those days, worked its changes, always, it seemed, for the worse. They remained nine weeks on Tinian and got greens and fresh meat enough to recruit their crews, but every time they spoke they inhaled a mouthful of flies. The meadows were covered with stubborn reeds, higher than their heads, that cut their legs like whipcord. Centipedes bit them, and scorpions bled them. They located the *Centurion's* well and found brackish water, full of worms. "The heat was suffocating, being only nine degrees less than blood at the heart."

As for the fat and lovely kine of Anson's visit, only two decades before, these were gone. "It took six men three days and three nights to capture and kill a bullock, whose flesh when dragged to the tents proved fly-blown and useless."

The *Dolphin* anchored over the mooring of the *Centurion*, a depth of twenty-four fathoms (144 feet), floating in water so clear they could see the anchor lying on the bottom. Great fish swam below them as if seen through the glass of a mighty aquarium, an uncanny thing, as sailors know.

Byron left Tinian for Batavia and so went home by the usual round the world route. He had demonstrated, after a two year voyage, that copper sheathing would keep a ship's bottom from fouling. He came to London, reporting to the Admiralty as to the safety of his ships, the loss of only six men in each ship. "An' damme, sir, more of 'em would had died had the people remained at home and ashore."

Commodore Byron was severely criticised by the Royal Society for "his dearth of scientific results." True, he was not exactly a savant; his genius lay in his loins, for one of his sons begot a grandson, George Gordon, sixth Lord Byron.

Bluff, red-faced, forthright "Foulweather Jack," a stout sailor, rose to the rank of admiral, commanding a squadron in the West Indies during George III's war against his rebellious colonies.

The Royal Society, the world's most distinguished scientific body, lost no time, after the return of Byron, in petitioning the King. And soon H.M.S. *Dolphin*, sound as a new plank, and H.M.S. *Swallow*, were fitted out for another swing around the world, with special reference to the Pacific, for Commodore Byron, it seems, had pretty thoroughly ignored his orders.

Captain Samuel Wallis, R.N., a handsome officer, was given senior command in the *Dolphin*, and Philip Carteret, who had served as first lieutenant of both the *Tamar* and, later, the *Dolphin*, a resourceful and determined officer, was given command of the *Swallow*, a ship that proved almost unmanageable at times. She separated from her consort in a storm just west of the Magellan Strait, and they never met again.

Carteret's discoveries were of high interest. Westward of our Juan Fernandez, toward nightfall, on July 2, 1767, land was descried. On the morning, having kept the crazy little *Swallow* hove to, Captain Carteret bore up to it, a small island rising out of the sea like a great rock, crowned by a growth of trees, a rich green chaplet; at one side a silver stream of dropping water cascaded into the dark blue sea. Guns were discharged, the echoes bouncing back as if this island were a King's ship returning the salute or, more appropriately, a pirate firing a hostile broadside. Frenzied screams from flocks of wild birds rose from cliffs and trees, their white wings winking in the sunlit sky. But there were no people to be seen. They were certain that the high island was uninhabited. It lay in

25 degrees 3 minutes south latitude. A rumbling surf beating against black rocks, rising in a succession of lacy veils as it ran along the steep shore, prevented a landing.

This island was named after the young gentleman who first sighted it, a middy, a son of Major Pitcairn, of the Royal Marines—Pitcairn Island.

Tempestuous weather prevailed. Carteret stood to the northwestward. In longitude 165 degrees west three small green islands were seen, uninhabited. Their English names became those of various placid and forgotten royal dukes. Scurvy appeared among the sailors, leaks opened. Gear was wearing out, the usual thing. They were in the old historic path of Quiros. Their Queen Charlotte Islands were most probably Quiros's Santa Cruz. Carteret sighted New Britain and sailed into a bay called St. George by Dampier. Here he nailed a leaden plate on a high tree. The *Swallow* returned to England after three years, less two days.

Although the discovery of Pitcairn Island was the most memorable event of Carteret's voyage, the veteran coppered *Dolphin*, a smart ship, commanded by a brilliant skipper, after various minor discoveries was coming to the old island of Sagittaria, of Quiros. Arriving on June 19, 1767, at Tahiti, Carteret, believing it a primary discovery, called this magnificent find King George III Island.

Coming in close under shortened sails, a boat sounding for an anchorage, the *Dolphin* was surrounded by a multitude of canoes carrying at least 800 natives. They were friendly, contenting themselves with petty thefts as they clambered on board like a band of children out of school. One of the naked natives, standing near the ship's gangway, looking outward, became a perfect target for the *Dolphin's* pet ram. The beast charged, with head down, and the terrified Tahitian shot overboard with a yell, all natives on board jumping in the sea at sight of the ferocious goat, the tars, the while, roaring with laughter. The boat, sounding ahead into the Bay of Matavia, signaling the depth, was seen surrounded by canoes. The *Dolphin* sent a nine pound shot over them, splashing in the bay, at which a skirmish followed in which several were wounded on both sides. The island was aroused, 2,000 warriors in 300 canoes, led by a Chief, came from around the island. They attacked the King's ship with a hail of stones. Repulsed by musket fire, they twice returned bravely to the attack, hurling stones from slings, missiles weighing two pounds. The people on board bent below the nettings; the ship was becoming pock-marked by this silly barrage. Officers were struck, a distinct violation of the Articles of War. So Captain Wallis ordered a great gun discharged at the chief, and the cannon ball cut the canoe in two, causing these childish islanders to retreat in precipitate haste.

The Captain and his first lieutenant being anything but well, Second Lieutenant Tobias Furneaux landed with the marines, turned a sod, and hoisted the Cross of St. George, taking possession of the island in the name of the King.

Again the natives chose to make a demonstration after the ship had anchored. Wallis cleared the coast with his guns and sent his carpenters ashore to destroy their abandoned canoes, some fifty feet in length. These measures brought the natives to terms, and they became friendly. Tents were erected ashore in which the Englishmen lived sumptuously on poultry, fruits, and the native vegetables. They made love, and trafficked in the delights of Eros, nails being the principal medium of exchange. Soon, so the pursers found, there grew up a depreciation of their currency. Some of the Tahitians produced large spikes, which were the sort of nail they then wanted. The sailors, it seemed, having no nails of their own, and great hungers, began to draw out hammock pins and took the spikes from cleats. One seaman, Francis Pinckney, was caught drawing the spikes from a mainsheet cleat. It was too much. Captain Wallis, though still ill from a touch of scurvy, mustered the crew of the *Dolphin*. "Men, you are wrecking my ship," he thundered. "And for what, I ask you, for what?"

The grins were quickly wiped off when Pinckney was flogged with nettles while running the gauntlet three times around the deck, the worst spike stealers lashing him the harder lest they be given the same. And so things settled down to a more pleasant routine at Tahiti.

On July 11 the midshipman on watch reported the approach of a large ceremonial canoe. Officers were called. The Captain hastily donned his best uniform, his epaulets, cocked hat, and sword, wearing his faultless white doeskin breeks and tassled polished leather boots.

Queen Oberea, sovereign of Tahiti, was announced coming alongside. The officer of the deck helped her on board and conducted her to the cabin, explaining, as best he could, that Captain Wallis had been ill. At once, on receiving the welcome of the skipper, Oberea invited him, by signs and smiles, to come to the friendly shore and perfect his convalescence.

The officers, sailors, marines, and servants of H.M.S. *Dolphin* were more or less guilty of lechery. The log book had to be signed by the Captain (according to the King's regulations), and few would dispute the will or the way of the commander of a Royal ship in full commission, off on far waters in the Pacific. Hence the very discreet recordings of old logs and narratives must be read as they were set down, within the shadow of the Thirty-six Articles of War.

Captain Samuel Wallis returned the royal visit, as he was in duty bound to do, by courtesy and regulation. With him as aide, most likely followed by a few marines, came the surgeon of the *Dolphin*. The air was balmy, scented, and tropical amid coconut palms and mallows. They approached the royal lodge, under cool shadows within a high thatch lifted upon pillars. The dark gradually disclosed a half nude figure, shamelessly perfect, even if somewhat oversized. The dancing girls, also naked to their navels, their firm breasts pointed pink, garlanded with flowers, their grass skirts swaying, were lined in rows, narrowing to the throne. Drums beat; strange instruments made haunting music. Smoke from censers filled the audience lodge with aromatic perfumes. Low, sweet voices lifted in chanting song.

> "*Havai'i, fanaura's fenua.*
> *Havai'i, the birthplace of lands.*"

Captain Wallis bowed. The girls performed in sarabands. The heavy scent, the cackling of scurrying poultry, the closeness of a warrior guard, the vision of the Queen, who arose before him, all this—and the sea weary commander seemed to swoon. The surgeon was at his side. But the regal Oberea, her tones resonant with command and assurance, caused the withdrawal of the guard, the vanishing of the dancing girls. As she stepped from the dais, a pallet of mats was quickly moved into the cleared space of the royal lodge. Grass screens were drawn, wide open eaves were lifted, letting in a fragrant ocean wind. Quickly the Queen spoke her commands. Captain Wallis was lifted to the pallet. Four girls pulled off his boots and stockings and gently chafed his feet and ankles. A basin of cool water was brought. Oberea loosened his high stock and laved his forehead, his face. And, as he came to consciousness, her eyes were close as she bent over him, murmuring words of unmistakable affection and concern.

The surgeon knew he could do no more than was being done unless he sent aboard for the leeches and bled his Captain. But of course these Tahitians used no such remedies. It was hot, and he lifted his wig and put it on a stool.

At once there was consternation. The girls twittered. The Queen seemed amazed, and Wallis, quite recovered, laughed aloud.

"They could not have been more amazed," said Wallis, "had they discovered that the surgeon's limbs had been screwed on to his trunk."

The whole company stood motionless, in silent astonishment, cringing at a withering look from Oberea. The hut was cleared. The surgeon, clapping on his wig, went out to where the marines and the purser stood on guard. The Queen bent over Captain Wallis; he was very weak. He was to return on board, for the afternoon had been exhausting. On their way to the boat, and quite naturally, Oberea helped her distinguished guest.

The next morning the royal barge was at the *Dolphin* gangway long before breakfast, the Queen impatiently waiting after a long night.

"I would advise, sir," the surgeon spoke to the captain with professional restraint, "a sojourn ashore, sir. It will do you great good, sir, to leave the ship for a few days."

The idyl of King George III's Island keeps simmering on in the ever renewing fires of time. Oberea wanted Captain Wallis to remain in the islands for not less than twenty days. He lived amid the glowing discovery of timeless emotions. She tied wreaths of plaited hair around his chapeaux, giving him to understand that the hair was her own, the working of it her delight. She sent out many things to the ship, sows, big with young, and baskets of ripe coconuts. Many of the officers and tars came ashore for refreshment. But these avoided the royal lodge.

Tahiti tossed up its peak 7,300 feet above the blue ocean, seemingly higher because of the low margin of seacoast. It could be seen forty-five miles at sea and commanded the land with its companion peaks, Pito Hiti and Vaoria, sometimes called the Diadem. There were places, in the time of Wallis, where fumaroles smoked in the fissures. Wild things abounded.

And there were purple nights, when time seemed to sleep under the marching stars, and there was a moon, warmer and larger than in England. Scurvy departed from the mariners. Great lassitudes sometimes descended upon them. The smart little ship, safe in Matavia Bay, looked like a picture painted by a Chinaman, every spar and rope correct—as apparently unreal as nature always is in its true clarity.

After seven days and six nights Captain Samuel Wallis came on board. Something told him he had better sail. Oberea followed him to the ship. She burst into tears and was only partly pacified. She knew the decision was final—they would weigh anchor on the morrow. The Queen then threw herself on an arms chest, in full view of officers and men, and wept passionately. The old account says, "She was with difficulty got over the side into her canoe, where she sat the picture of helpless, unutterable woe."

Presents were tossed down to her, caught by her servants, articles of use and ornament. She silently accepted, without looking at the insulting gifts.

That night, after a sickening interval of indecision, Captain Wallis, R.N., ordered away his gig. He landed and bade the Queen adieu more privately ashore.

His coxswain and a midshipman were waiting with the boat, early in the dawn. Their Captain, pale, stern, was rowed out silently to the *Dolphin*. Her cable was at short stay, a breeze sprang up with the morning, and H.M.S.*Dolphin* stood out to sea on July 27, 1767, nevermore to return.

There is little more to tell of Wallis in the Pacific. On the way to Anson's Tinian he discovered an island, Wallis Island. The report of the world-round voyage was delivered to the Admiralty and the Royal Society, in May, 1778, in time to help the learned society prepare more complete instructions for the guidance of Captain James Cook, whom we shall soon meet. But another navigator of fame was shortly to touch at Tahiti.

Chevalier Louis Antoine de Bougainville, born in Paris in 1729, long famous as author of *Un Voyage autour du Monde*, was not strictly a sailor but a gallant colonel in the French army, a polished gentleman and a philosopher. He took two and a half years to circle the world in the smart new frigate *La Boudeuse*, accompanied by the storeship *Étoile*. Aboard the flagship were 11 officers, 3 volunteers, and 200 men. Among the supernumeraries, the volunteers, were M. Verron, a young astronomer, and M. Commerçon, a distinguished naturalist. The young astronomer was charged with making observations that should determine the longitude at sea, a problem that occupied most of his time during the voyage.

M. Commerçon, who was accompanied by his faithful servant Baré, was a scientist not too keen of perception, except in matters strictly botanical. He it was, no doubt, who gave the name to that exotic bloom the bougainvillaea, discovered in the tropical parts of South America on this sometimes brilliant voyage.

Also among the distinguished passengers was that lofty personage—and a good shipmate, too—the youngish Prince of Nassau-Singhen, who passed up an opportunity to found a grand Pacific dynasty. But we horse ahead on our cable, even before coming to an anchorage off the Island of Tahiti, on Apr. 4, 1768, roughly a year after the departure of the *Dolphin*.

Two days before this they had sighted the high peaks of the Diadem and in that time were plying off and on, attempting to make the land. The ship moored safely in a good bay, *La Boudeuse* having far outsailed her supply ship. She sent down light yards and struck her topmasts.

So thick were the canoes from the island that they had a hard time to warp in to the anchorage, and the presence of swarms of lovely girls, naked as Eve, gay, unspoiled creatures of superb beauty, made it difficult to keep the sailors at their work.

These men, like so many others, had undergone great privations. On entering the Pacific, the matelots complained of sore throats, which the surgeons attributed to the drinking of snow water in the Strait of Magellan. They cured this condition among the men by putting a pint of vinegar into the daily water butt and plunging therein a dozen red hot musket balls. Scurvy was kept under control by the issue of lemonade prepared from a concentrated powder of the dried fruit. Fresh water was obtained, a barrel of it each night, by means of a very scientific apparatus, a still. Their bread, however, was kneaded in salt water "dipped up from the sea."

After passing some low "half drowned" islands, one of which, because of its shape, de Bougainville named Harp Island, they sighted the high peaks of Tahiti and, as they approached, saw fires burning during the night over a wide extent of coast.

Now, as these sex starved, salted, and sea weary mariners brought their ship into the bay, a Chief named Ereti came out, a man with a prodigious growth of hair standing on his head like bristles. A huge cluster of golden ripe bananas was offered to the arriving Frenchmen—an olive branch of friendship. Twelve naked men paddled the chief's canoe. Presents were exchanged and friendship sealed.

The visitors found themselves in the midst of a fragrant paradise, the mountains covered with gleaming foliage to their summits and the lush lowlands of a fresher green, with meadows and plantations of tropical fruits, lying amid a cobalt shadowed ocean. Flowers bloomed in this enchantment, and thatched huts were seen along the shore. Boats laden with fish were sailing in from the sea. All was animation; luring cries and laughter of girls were heard. De Bougainville gallantly recorded, "These natives are not inferior for agreeable features to most European women."

To impress the chief properly, and as a matter of courtesy, de Bougainville went ashore the next day to return the royal visit, attended by a group of officers, all in their formal dress. Perhaps a bit of extra vanity was shown by the younger members, with their ruffs and velvet collars and their gilt buttons and polished boots. They were received with the greatest cordiality.

Only one venerable man, " . . . whose thoughtful and

suspicious air seemed to show that he feared the arrival of a new race of men would trouble those happy days which he had spent in peace," was less than happy at the arrival of a second European ship. But the girls and women had no such aversion to the sunburned sailors.

The ship landed her empty water casks, and preparations were made for the pitching of an armed camp near a little brook. The sick were being conveyed ashore. Then Ereti and his council made objection; the visitors were welcome to all the island afforded in presents and peaceful trade; they might come ashore as much as they pleased, spending all the day, but not the night.

De Bougainville said they would give the populace an entertainment, making stars and music—besides, his men were sick; many of them needed rest. That night the French sailors made a display of skyrockets and witch quills and many other pyrotechnics. The musicians played, the huskier sailors danced hornpipes, whirled around the girls, and merriment, which those simple people accepted, won the day and night. Moreover, the ships would remain only eighteen days—so the gay, suave commander made known by drawing marks in the sand.

Ereti, learning that the Prince of Nassau-Singhen was of royal blood, offered him a wife of equal lineage. The Princess seemed a trifle advanced in years, and correspondingly mature, but undoubtedly sound and willing. The Prince diplomatically conveyed the idea that he was already happily married, even though he had sailed away from his French bride; so the great French-Pacific match failed to be consummated. But numerous less formal unions took place. De Bougainville named the island Nouvelle Cythère.

The Frenchmen heard of the *Dolphin's* visit, their own anchorage being on a side of the island away from Papeete. Nothing was seen of Oberea.

Like Wallis, de Bougainville added to the abundance of the island by planting grains, wheat, barley, potherbs, and onions, and he made Ereti presents of a pair of turkeys and some ducks and drakes. Some natives were slain by the Frenchmen in a dispute growing out of Eros, and de Bougainville had four suspected soldiers flogged and put in irons. He distributed cloth and tools and made every gesture he could to hold the friendship of the Tahitians.

His departure was hastened by a great storm. Four anchors were lost on the parting of the flagship's cables in a great swell and rain, followed by a hurricane. Only sterling seamanship saved *La Boudeuse*. Having survived the tempest, the commander determined to complete watering, move his sick, who had mostly recovered, back on board, and, foregoing surveys he had planned, proceed to sea. Something else may also have moved him, for resentment seemed to have been growing among the natives.

But one of them, the adventurous Aotourou, the first Tahitian to go to Europe, had become so fond of his brothers aboard the ships that he begged to be taken along. He gave his young wife the pearls he had in his ears, leaving her flat, and, in time, after many adventures, reached the great city of Paris.

La Boudeuse, by watering all night, was ready, and, to take possession of the island, the French carved the names of their ships and dates on an oaken plank, which, with a bottle containing the names of the officers, was buried at the camp site. They put to sea on Apr. 14. The *Étoile* got out beyond the reef. The good Chief Ereti wept and brought gifts, and many wives and maidens cried. The whole populace came to see off the brave Aotourou (whom, after a year in France, Chevalier de Bougainville sent back to his home, "much polished by his year in Paris").

Narrowly escaping the reef when the wind fell, being towed off by the boats at the last moment, brave *La Boudeuse* got clear, and the Diadem peaks sank in the blue.

The ships sailed westward, sailed through the islands of

Samoa, which de Bougainville named the Archipelago of the Navigators. Admiral Krusenstern, a great Russian navigator and Pacific authority, identifies these islands with those named the Bauman Islands, discovered by Roggeveen in 1721. Chevalier de Bougainville deserved the honor of their discovery. Samoa they are today, and we shall visit them later. But now, as the frigate and her tender arrived at these Navigator Islands and passed on to the Grandes Cyclades, the word came to de Bougainville that the self-centered botanist, M. Commerçon, was, indeed, either a clever rascal or a saintly dunce. For, with the coming of warmer weather, the natives, with the keen intuition of savages, had paid Baré (his servant) the attentions due a lady, exclaiming in their native tongue, "It is a woman."

De Bougainville, and possibly the Prince of Nassau-Singhen, who was a recognized authority on such matters, went on board the *Étoile*, which contained M. Commerçon and his servant.

Baré was taken to the cabin and confronted with the gossip.

"Will M. Baré submit to examination by the surgeon? Or will Mlle. Baré confess?" the Chevalier asked, smiling. She saw at once there was no punishment in the mind of the gallant chevalier.

"It is true, your honor, I am a woman. And that, I think, is no crime. I am an orphan, monsieur, and have used men's clothes, for it is safer for a young girl. I saw your ships and talked with M. Commerçon. He did not suspect. He has never suspected. I have been faithful, I have been discreet."

And Chevalier de Bougainville honors her by recording her as always acting with the most scrupulous modesty. This daring Frenchwoman was the first of her sex ever to encircle the world.

De Bougainville made many rediscoveries, and we leave him to sail out of our Pacific, carrying the charming Baré and the good botanist, M. Commerçon. When you see the exotic bougainvillaea, think of Baré, her master, the savant, and the gallant officer after whom that bloom is named.

Captain James Cook: Explorer Extraordinary

THE year 1769 was made memorable by the transit of Venus over the disk of the sun: " . . . a phenomenon of the greatest importance to astronomy, geography and navigation," the ancient Royal Society of London said in its memorial to His Majesty King George III. The society set forth many advantages to be derived from accurate observations of this transit between the 140th and 180th degrees of longitude, west from the Royal Observatory at Greenwich. The motions of the spheres, the inevitable culmination of this great astronomical event, were to reach their fullest effect out in the Pacific.

King George III directed his Admiralty to provide a proper vessel, and the *Endeavour* bark was fitted for the distant southern voyage. Her command was entrusted to Lieutenant James Cook, of the Royal Navy, who had already demonstrated unusual knowledge of astronomy. He was also a commander of boldness, of calculated caution, free from prejudice and humane, as that quality was evaluated in the later years of the eighteenth century at sea. He stood over six feet tall, was clean shaven, and wore his hair combed back to a twist. His features were strong, eyes direct, large nose, and firm mouth and chin, and, although affable by nature, he was also short tempered at times and direct of speech. His determination verged on obstinacy. He spared himself not at all when duty was before him, nor did he spare his people in tasks demanded by their employment.

The *Endeavour* sailed from Deptford, on the Thames, on July 30, and we board her in the Pacific after her passage around Cape Horn. The logbook entries are of as Apr. 4, 1769, nine months out of England, when Peter Briscoe, servant of Mr. Banks, of the scientific staff, discovered land to the south, three or four leagues distant. Captain Cook immediately hauled for it, closing with an atoll, an island of oval form, with a lake in its center. When within a mile, they cast their lead 130 fathoms down, finding no bottom. Since they could meet with no anchorage, they again filled away to the northward. "There were several natives on shore; they seemed tall, with remarkably large heads, probably increased by their headdress; their hair black, and their complexions copper colored. Some that were abreast of the ship, had in their hands pikes or poles twice the height of themselves."

This was Captain Cook's first sight of the Polynesians, and his first Pacific island.

On Apr. 10, they arrived at Otaheiti, for the name given the island by Wallis quickly lost its grip. When the natives were asked the name of their paradise, they cried "O-Tahiti," or, "It is Tahiti." So it was set down as Otaheiti by Cook and his people. Here, for the sake of uniformity, Tahiti is the name.

The expedition arrived a month and three weeks in advance of the astronomical rendezvous. An observatory site was carefully chosen on the north end of Tahiti, at what is now called Venus Point, a name having, some think, a double meaning connecting it with the Nouvelle Cythère of the gallant de Bougainville. Guns of the ship covered the spot, for nothing was to stop the scientific enterprise, even if a taboo were declared. However, only the most amiable relations prevailed; the local chief even donated the roof of a house as his contribution to science.

As the tight little man-of-war lay at her moorings, light yards sent down, topgallant masts struck, and gun ports squared to a hair, she presented a pretty sight. She had been in the coastal collier trade before, a cat-built bark—that is, a craft with round bluff bows, deep waist, and a tapering stern. When refitted she made an ideal vessel for the expedition. At Cook's suggestion she was sheathed with wood rather than copper, making repairs easier in case of bottom damage. Ninety-four comprised her complement.

Whereas de Bougainville had anchored in a harbor opposite that used by Wallis and seemed not to have met the great Queen Oberea, Captain Cook fetched up in Matavia Bay, the same spot, the observatory being made on the eastern point. Oberea seemed, in the short interval of two years, to have fallen some from her high estate. A youth who was carried on a man's back and treated with great reverence was pointed out as king of the whole island.

Tahiti has a perimeter of at least 100 miles. The axis lies roughly in a northwest and southeast direction, and its outline is not unlike that of a lady's hand mirror, the handle off to the southeast. Nouvelle Cythère in every way kept its romantic implications.

During this period of preparation for the mysterious transit, " . . . there was the usual commerce between the sailors and the native women." How many Tahitians of this day are descendants of the sailors and officers of the ships of Wallis, de Bougainville, and Cook must be left to a more competent calculation—not a few, it seems, the old Europoids having met the whole world round.

Captain Cook had most to do with two chieftains nick-named by one of his followers, Lycurgus and Hercules. The Tahitians, having been given English names, themselves named the navigators. Captain Cook was Toote; Lieutenant Hicks, Hete; Lieutenant Gore, Toura; Dr. Solander, Tolano; Joseph Banks, Esq., was Opane; astronomer Green, Treene, etc., down the line, all names more or less descriptive of the looks and actions of the English.

Toote, the Captain's Tahitian name, described a severe, serious man in pursuit of the planet Venus, nothing else, much mindful of his secret orders from the Admiralty to make diligent search in attempting "discovery of the Southern Continent so often mentioned." And this advice was on his mind while he prepared for the great astronomical phenom-enon predicted by the astronomers.

On Apr. 13, when the *Endeavour* entered Port Royal Harbor, a great number of natives came off in South Sea style, barter-ing their commodities for beads and trinkets. An elderly fellow named Owhaw, who was known to Mr. Gore and others who had been there in the *Dolphin*, came on board and acted as a mentor in matters Tahitian. Captain Cook drew up some necessary rules of conduct and ordered that they be strictly observed.

When the ship was made safe, the Captain, Mr. Banks, and Dr. Solander (the two latter, scientists attached to the expedi-tion) with a party under arms, guided by old Owhaw, went ashore to be met by several hundred natives. So awestruck were the Tahitians that the first of them crept almost on his stomach when presenting branches of trees as a token of peace. The Englishmen received these branches with demonstrations of satisfaction and friendship. The landing party was then conducted to the place where the *Dolphin* had watered, this place being cleared. The chiefs of the natives threw down their branches. Captain Cook and his companions followed the gesture. The marines were paraded and, with precision, dropped their boughs on top of the heap. Captain Cook was granted this site for a camp.

Ground was marked out for a small fort while the Tahitians looked on, behaving in the most peaceful manner. While Mr. Banks and others, accompanied by natives, went shooting in the woods, they set a guard over their tent. Almost immediately they heard the discharge of two pieces and hurried back. A Tahitian had snatched away one of the sentinel's muskets. The young midshipman in command ordered the marines to fire, and they did. Several natives were wounded; but the criminal did not fall. The midshipman, dirk in hand, led the guard in chase, and they shot the Tahitian dead.

Mr. Banks was greatly displeased and, through the medita- tion of an old man, prevailed on many of the natives to come over to him. They did so, bearing planting trees and clapping their hands on their breasts, crying "Tyau! tyau!"

Few came aboard next morning, and old Owhaw foresook them. Captain Cook warped the ship nearer the shore, moor- ing broadside to the beach. But in the evening he again landed with some marines, and the natives again trafficked peace- fully. But the Britons took no chances, throwing up entrench- ments, some cutting fascines and pickets, which the Tahitians cheerfully assisted in bringing from the woods. Breadfruit and coconuts were offered in such large quantities that it was necessary to reject these gifts and ask that no more be brought for two days. Beads were eagerly taken in exchange. It was just no use; the Tahitians were friendly and nothing else. A Dr. Monkhouse, taking his evening stroll, saw the body of the native who had been shot, " . . . the corpse placed on a frame of wood, with a matted bottom, supported by posts five feet high. The copper colored criminal was covered with a mat, overlaid by a white cloth; by his side lay a wooden mace, and toward the head two cocoanut shells; toward the feet was a bunch of green leaves and small dried boughs, tied together and stuck in the ground, near which was a stone the size of a cocoanut; here also was placed a small plantain tree and a stone axe." The Tahitians seemed displeased at the doctor's curiosity.

On Apr. 26, six swivel guns were mounted upon the fort. This caused some fishermen living near by to remove farther off, imagining they were to be fired upon. But the next day Chief Tubora Tumdida (Lycurgus), with a friend and three of his women, dined at the fort. He returned after this visit, complaining that the ship's butcher had threatened to cut his wife's throat because she had refused to sell him, for the price of one nail, a stone hatchet that had taken his fancy.

The people aboard the *Dolphin*, during all this time, had kept their weather eyes lifting for a sight of Queen Oberea. A number of the officers and men had been aboard the *Endeavour* with Wallis. Were their stories true?

The master, Mr. Molineux, who was among those in the *Dolphin*, was first to recognize and point out the Queen. News spread through the ship. She was soon conducted on board the *Endeavour*, being received with great ceremony, all officers in their best uniforms, with side arms, the marines drawn up in files, the crew at their stations. Young Mr. Banks looked as if he had just stepped out of Piccadilly, his valets having dressed and trimmed him. A salute was fired, trumpets blared, and there was a ruffle on the drums. Overhead the Royal Standard of Britain folded out in the breeze. Aft was the Cross of St. George.

The Queen came aboard with some of her retinue, and many presents were made to her, including a child's doll that seemed most to engross her attention. But she was no longer in the full bloom of her flaming beauty, then being over the horizon of forty. Yet she had great expression in her eyes. Her skin was white and her figure large, but she was tall and well proportioned. The men-of-war's men had to admit that she must have been superbly handsome, and indeed she was still far from unattractive.

Captain Cook accompanied her ashore, where her suite brought him a hog and some plantains. These presents were carried to the fort; Oberea and Captain Cook brought up the rear of the procession. They were met by Tootahah, who, though not a king, seemed at that time to have sovereign authority. He immediately grew jealous of the doll given Oberea; so a similar one was sent for and presented to him.

On May 1 one of the chiefs came aboard by himself, having made a previous visit with some of his harem, who had fed him. On his solitary visit he sat in great dignity but did not partake of food until one of the ship's servants fed him, for it was taboo for him to feed himself.

There was never a dull moment in Tahiti, day or night. Huge double canoes with their great vertical spritsails slipped by the little man-of-war. Visits were constantly in progress between the shore and ship and to the fort. What these Englishmen were after was a mystery. Something to do with a visit to the sun by a god named Venus. Their own medicine men knew—but such things were not for common knowledge, and only the head men of the ship knew.

And all these ceremonial tributes were duly repaid by the Europeans. On May 5 the Captain and Dr. Solander, accompanied by Mr. Banks, set out in the pinnace to visit Tootahah's lodge at Eparre, a few miles west of the tents. Here they found him surrounded by wise old men. The natives shouted, "Taio Tootahah [Tootahah is your friend]." There were exchanges of presents, and a great wrestling match was staged for the entertainment of the guests.

On Tuesday, the ninth, Oberea paid them a visit, accompanied by her favorite paramour, Obadee. She brought a hog and breadfruit. A great many ceremonies continued.

On May 27, as the time of transit approached, a sort of farewell party took the principal officers to Atahourou, where Tootahah had removed his lodge. Captain Cook and Dr. Solander went in the ship's pinnace, but young Mr. Banks left his companions, having accepted a place in Oberea's canoe, where he retired to rest.

"Notwithstanding the care Oberea took of his clothes, having them in her own custody, they were stolen, with his pistols, powder horn, and many other things that were in his waistcoat pockets. The alarm was given to Tootahah, who slept in the next canoe, and who went with Oberea in search of the thief, leaving Mr. Banks in the morning with only his breeches on, and his musket uncharged."

The long and the short of it, as told in the gun room of the ship, was that Captain Cook and Dr. Solander, who slept in a hut ashore, had only lost their stockings and jackets. Years later, when Mr. Banks became Sir Joseph Banks, at many a very special dinner, lingering over the second or third bottle of port, he may have been importuned by his intimates. "Damme, Sir Joseph, tell us again how they took everything but your breeks, and how you saved 'em, and what a woman that Oberea was?"

So much of history is hidden under dusty old taboos, especially in the far Pacific!

Astronomical phenomena wait for no man. If the savant is not ready, well, it's just too bad. Captain Cook was a man to be ready, "Aye, ready!" From instructions given by the Royal Society, Captain Cook took no chances on a drift of cloud at the fateful time. On June 1 he dispatched the long boat to the neighboring island of Moorea, looming from Tahiti like a gigantic medieval castle, with battlements and spires. This isle, named Duke of York Island by Wallis, lies about ten miles from Tahiti, and there they picked a second observation spot some fifteen miles away from Venus Point. Lieutenant Gore was in charge, with Dr. Monkhouse and Mr. Sporing, of Mr. Banks' staff. These secondary scientists were supplied with the necessary instruments, men, and a few Tahitians. Since it looked like an adventure, Mr. Banks accompanied this party to that isle standing bluish green off to the west.

Rowing the best part of the night, they located their observatory upon a rock. Time was getting short, and Mr. Banks, early in the morning of the fateful day, went ashore to Moorea for fresh provisions, returning with Tarrao, King of the island, and his sister, Princess Nuna. These were at the observatory when the great event took place. Mr. Banks presented His Majesty with an adz and a shirt and gave some bright beads to the lovely Nuna. Then the comely woman of Moorea saw Venus, a little black dot, transit the sun.

With a marine guard about the observatory and sailors at stations aboard the *Endeavour*, guns shotted and in battery lest some untoward circumstance occur, Captain Cook made certain of guarding against every intrusion but that of clouds. The day was hot, rising to 119 degrees Fahrenheit; the waiting was intensely dramatic. Three telescopes of different magnifying powers stood in place in the main observatory. The natives, some distance off, watched the magic with due solemnity, expecting almost anything, such as the landing on their island of the goddess "Wenus," for several of the sailors and marines had solemnly assured them this event would take place.

The silence grew ominous. Some of the chiefs, looking through smoked glass, saw, to their utter amazement, the little pill of black enter the disk of the sun. Although this was not what they had expected, at least it was something. There was real voodoo in Captain Cook, their Toote.

That day the astronomers entered figures on their tablets. Here is the score, as given to the world by Mr. Green:

Elements of the Transit of Venus
June 3rd. 1769
At the Island of Otaheite.

Morning

The first external contact, or appearance of Venus on the sun, was
9 hours, 25 minutes, 4 seconds.
The first internal contact, or total immersion, was
9 hours, 44 minutes, 4 seconds.

Afternoon

The second internal contact, or beginning immersion was
3 hours, 14 minutes, 8 seconds.
The second external contact, or total immersion was
3 hours, 32 minutes, 10 seconds.

Latitude of the Observatory, 17° 15′ 29″ S.
Longitude, 149° 31′ 30″ W. of Greenwich.

Captain Cook noted, "The day proved as favorable to our purpose as we could wish; not a cloud was to be seen the whole day, and the air was perfectly clear: so that we had every advantage in observing the whole of the passage of the planet Venus over the sun's disc. We very distinctly saw an atmosphere, or dusky shade, round the body of the planet, which very much disturbed the times of the contact, particularly the two internal ones. It was nearly calm the whole day, and the thermometer, exposed to the sun about the middle of the day, rose to a degree of heat we have not before met with."

It may be of interest to set down the position of Venus Point Light, on Tahiti, as given in the *Table of Maritime Positions*, Bowditch, issue of 1934.

Latitude   17° 29′ 10″ S.
Longitude 149° 29′ 00″ W.

The remarkable accuracy of the longitude determined by Cook differing only 3 degrees and 30 seconds from the most modern determinations, may be due to a cancellation of errors. Cook's latitude differs 3 minutes and 41 seconds, being too far north. But this may have been an error in their tables of declination rather than in their observations or instruments.

Captain Cook carried no chronometer, even though John Harrison's successful timekeeper had won £10,000 of the reward offered by Parliament in 1765 for a chronometer capable of accurate longitude demonstration. Also, it is interesting that the first publication of the *Nautical Almanac* appeared in 1767 and that Cook therefore had the third and some succeeding issues from which to take his declinations and right ascensions of the heavenly bodies.

Longitudes, years before and after Cook, were determined by observations of the moon known to early navigators as lunars, that is, the measurement of angular distances of sun and stars from the moon, involving laborious calculations and extreme accuracy of observation.

Even as late as 1904, lunar distances were being observed at sea on a long Pacific voyage in the S.S. *Texan*. The old "Lunarian" was Captain George D. Morrison, under whom this writer served as second mate, or navigating officer. The operation was not far from archaic, judged by the quick navigation of today. Three of us, two officers and the skipper, stood on the bridge with our sextants; another officer or quartermaster stood by to record readings. The Old Man, with his huge sextant, took the angle between the sun or a star and the clear limb of the moon. When he called out, "Mark," his officers measured the altitudes of the bodies being observed, moon and sun or star. These were duly recorded, with the chronometer time of observation as a check.

The calculation of "clearing the distance" is no idle mathematical exercise. This lunar computation, if all the measurements are accurate, gives the Greenwich time at ship at the moment of obseŗvation. That is, without chronometers, working an ordinary time sight for local time, the navigator can determine his longitude. How very accurate this can be is attested to by many of the results obtained by the late

Captain Morrison, one of the most finished navigators at sea in his day.

Captain Cook was a master of these difficult determinations and, with astronomer Green, reached an astonishing measure of accuracy.

After completing these observations, Captain Cook prepared to celebrate the thirty-first birthday of his sovereign, King George III, falling so happily on June 4. A banquet was readied in the fort, to which all the chiefs of the island, their wives, and their courtiers were bidden, up to the capacity of the place. Naturally the party ran on into the dark, the scene about lighted by the native dooe dooe nuts, sputtering dimly like great, smoky fireflies. Inside the fort, ship's lamps added to the grand effect. Outside, the wharra trees, the coconut palms, and plantains moved in the trade wind, and songs and cheers and dances enlivened the affair. The *Endeavour* had stopped at Madeira on her way to the Pacific, and the mild but deceptive wine of that distant sister island worked its spell.

Casks of porter were broached for the men, and there was, of course, the expected accident. Tubora Tumaida, no less, doubled up with excruciating stomach pains. Word flashed about that he had been poisoned. Good Dr. Monkhouse plied him with copious drafts of coconut milk. The result—complete recovery. Tubora, it seemed, had been given a large sailor's quid of chewing tobacco, which he proceeded to eat, following the example set by the hospitable tar. Swallowing the stuff was his mistake.

Tubora Tumaida's disaster ended. They toasted King George III. "Kilnargo!" the Tahitians cried with enthusiasm. This *was* a night in old Tahiti.

On a long voyage such as that made by the *Endeavour* into lawless countries and distant seas, amid simple people, the strictest sort of underlying order had to be maintained. Often enough this was broken, for the sailors and marines of that time were a rough lot, largely untutored except in the arts of their calling. The Thirty-six Articles of War, for the regulation of His Majesty's Navy, were not a mere code of ethics but hard biting actualities, as many sailors found out. Article 1 stated that captains, etc., "shall cause" public worship according to the liturgy of the Church of England, to be performed in their ships, and that "chaplains in holy orders" perform these rites "diligently." The Lord's day was to be observed according to law. So out on the Pacific or in the luscious, perfumed ports, there was no nonsense about Sunday worship.

A dozen or so offenses and crimes called for death. And another dozen were left to courts-martial to determine what punishment best fitted the crime. All robbery was punishable either by death or by a severe flogging.

Flogging was common in those days, but Cook's memory is honored for his moderate use of the cat. He never had recourse to the lash except in cases of marked necessity. His logs, in the archives of the Admiralty, show that even in the grossest cases of disobedience he never sanctioned more than a dozen lashes. Once he meted punishment because a sailor would not eat fresh provisions, preferring salted beef. One entry refers to a seaman sentenced to twelve lashes " . . . for refusing to come on deck when all hands were called, and afterward refusing to comply with the orders of his officers." Another was given " . . . twelve for getting drunk, grossly assaulting the officer of the watch, and beating some of the sick."

Having completed their main mission, they now found other matters that needed attention. They circumnavigated Tahiti, made soundings and mapped the shore line. They were dined on roasted dog, a rare delicacy, for the dogs there were vegetarians. "It was deemed a very good dish." Hatchets were exchanged for hogs, nails were in circulation again.

This "coin" was stolen, but the ship's fittings were not pulled apart as were those aboard the *Dolphin*.

Oberea again appears in the records. "Many of the natives brought various kinds of presents to the party at the fort. Among the party was Oamo, a chief of several districts on the island, who they had never before seen, and who brought with him a hog. The Chief was treated with great respect by the natives, and was accompanied by a boy and a young woman. The boy, though able to walk, was carried on a man's back. Oberea, and some other of the Tahitians, went out of the fort to meet them, their heads and bodies being first uncovered as low as the waist. . . . The curiosity of Mr. Banks, and the other gentlemen, being excited from these circumstances . . . they were informed that Oamo was Oberea's husband, but that by mutual consent they had been for a considerable time separated; and that the youth and girl were their offspring. The boy was named Terridiri, and was heir apparent to the sovereignty of the island; and was to espouse his sister as soon as he had attained the proper age."

Whether this report of intended incest was correct may be in some doubt, as are many of the phonetic spellings, the curious understandings, and the strange reports, for the Englishmen as well as the Tahitians had only the sketchiest ideas of what they were observing and being told.

The indefatigable Mr. Banks planted watermelon, oranges, lemons, and limes. He also gave seeds in great plenty to the natives; some of the melon seeds sown on their arrival were already producing plants in a very flourishing state. There was a bit more robbery and some mayhem on both sides, but a matter that had to be settled was the desertion of two marines, Webb and Gibson. These lads had gone ashore and fallen in love with two Tahitian maidens, the native marriage ceremony having been performed. Instead of leaving these honorable men behind, Captain Cook had them captured and returned on board, much to their discomfort and that of their wives. Of course, if Captain Cook had winked at this, his whole complement, officers and men, might have settled in Tahiti.

A few days later, on July 13, they were ready to sail. Following the indulgence granted by de Bougainville, Cook allowed a Tahitian named Tupia, who had been prime minister of Oberea when she was at the pinnacle of her power and who was also a principal priest among the people, to come aboard with his son, Tayota, aged twelve, and his servant, Taiyota. Tupia later died in Batavia.

As the ship stood out, her guns boomed in salute. The ceremonial canoes, great double boats carrying the chiefs and Oberea, clustered about. Many wept, regretted the going, but some were glad. Chants and gongs and garlands filled the bay of Matavai, the Diadems crowned all. The anchor had been catted and fished, and as the smoke lifted amid the sails Cook lifted his chapeau in a gesture of farewell.

Cook then discovered the archipelago to which he gave the name (Royal) Society Islands. One of the chiefs, Oree, on the island of Huahine, made a proposal to exchange names with Cook that was readily assented to. Captain Cook presented the King, among other things, with a small pewter plate bearing the inscription:

HIS BRITANNIC MAJESTY'S SHIP
Endeavour, Lieutenant Cook Commander, 16th, July, 1769.

On Aug. 15, they celebrated their first anniversary since leaving Plymouth by broaching a large Cheshire cheese and tapping a cask of porter " . . . which prooved to be as good as any they had ever drank in England." On the twenty-eighth the boatswain's mate died, his death occasioned by the boatswain, John Gathray, who gave his mate part of a large bottle of rum. "He was found to be very much in liquor that night," and Cook noted "as this was no more than what was common with him when he could get any, no further notice was taken of him. . . . About eight o'clock he was found speechless and past recovery." These matters, perhaps of no scientific moment, fill the logbook. The narrative of the Pacific is a very human one.

As the ship worked through that maze, south from the Society Islands between the 150th and 160th meridians west of Greenwich, they discovered the Cook Islands. At one of these Tayota, old Tupia's young son, was kidnaped. Muskets were fired, one of the knaves was wounded, and the lad, who had been held in the bottom of the canoe, leaped overboard and swam to the ship. Cook named the point Cape Kidnappers and the bight beyond, Kidnappers Bay, its shore resembling the high down of England. In these islands they met with parrots and parakeets. They also discovered an island they named the Mayor, and a number of islets lying contiguous they called the Court of Aldermen. Here Captain Cook judged it expedient to chastise the natives, who had attempted to board and take the ship. He gave them a few volleys of musket balls. Also at this place on Nov. 9, 1769, they observed the transit of Mercury and called the place Mercury Bay.

As they neared New Zealand, they met natives who anointed their hair with oil, melted from the fat of fish and birds and marked their bodies with black stains they called Amoco.

Cook had sailed to 40 degrees 22 minutes south, searching for Davis Land, or the great Pacific continent, without seeing it. On the way back the *Endeavour* struck on a reef, was carried over a ledge, and struck again. Their best chance of escaping seemed to be by lightening her. They instantly started the water casks in the hold and pumped it up. The decayed stores, oil-jars, casks, ballast and six of their guns were hove overboard. Their situation grew desperate. Their leak was stemmed by pumping but they could not discover it. Here

Midshipman Markhouse made the classic suggestion that they fother her, as he had once seen this done. An old studding sail was bridled; oakum and wool, chopped small, was lightly tacked on with sail twine in bunches. The dung of their sheep and other filth, was spread over it, and the sail was hauled under the ship's bottom by ropes, till it came to the leaks, where the fibres were sucked into the open seams. "This succeeded so well that instead of three pumps working, one kept her free."

They found a place to refit at Hope Island, and we have them out of the Pacific.

So outstanding were the results of Cook's great voyage that the Admiralty readily assented to his being sent on another attempt into the Pacific, especially to " . . . complete the discovery of the Southern Hemisphere, which for ages had been considered by some of the ablest geographers, as containing another continent."

And was Captain Cook famous! How much he went around is not recorded, but his shipmate Joseph Banks got about a bit in Royal Society circles, and, although the Navy, especially the aristocratic officers, may have looked at James Cook as a man from the lower deck, yet no one ever failed to give him the greatest credit both as scientist and sailor.

The voyage, coming in the wake of those of Byron, Wallis, and Carteret, and the great de Bougainville, stirred things up mightily on both sides of the Channel. In 1771, both Kergulen and Marion de Fresne, French commanders, sailed in search of the land of de Gonneville, in the far south Atlantic. The Spanish, ever since Balboa and Magellan, had felt a proprietary right in the Pacific and resented the English "voyages of curiosity." After all, these Britons were merely renaming the far earlier discoveries of Mendaña, Quiros, and Torres. The Dons formally annexed Easter Island, a Dutch discovery, as we know. They sent Catholic missionaries to Tahiti—and God knows they needed them—and fumed with indignation at the way the English and French had filtered through the vast Pacific cloud of islands, the mighty Polynesian triangle, except that its apex was still unknown.

Lieutenant Cook was promoted to the rank of Commander, R.N. While he remained a year in England, most of his time was employed in collating the results of his voyage and in planning the one to come. The enrichment of the ethnological collection of the British Museum was notable, and the sixty-first volume of the *Philosophical Transactions* is devoted to Cook's scientific findings. The greatest enthusiasm attended preparation for the second voyage. Young Joseph Banks planned to visit the South Sea again, lavishing expense on his own equipment, engaging Dr. Solander to again accompany Cook, and arranging for Zoffany, the portrait painter, to join the party. England, he hoped, would see that those beautiful Tahitians were not the figment of travelers' tales. He made the arrangements for a train of others—scientists, draughtsmen, and servants—a total of twelve besides himself.

The *Resolution*, of 462 tons burthen, the flagship selected, was hardly able to hold such a company in addition to the officers needed to work her and the commander, with his servant or two. Banks favored the employment of a large, commodious Indiaman, but Cook knew what he needed among the atolls and dangerous reefs of the Pacific and the heavy ice he hoped to penetrate in the Antarctic. He needed a vessel of convenient size for handling, of not too great draught, one strong enough to be laid ashore without serious damage. A North Country ship, of heavy scantling and handy rig, altered to his purpose, was the best. The *Adventure*, which he chose for a consort, was also such a ship, being of 336 tons, and her command was given to Lieutenant Tobias Furneaux, who had sailed with Wallis in the *Dolphin*.

These craft were fitted with unusual completeness, and

there was great eagerness among sailors to make the voyage; several of the old officers volunteered. Alterations had been made in the *Resolution* to accommodate the large scientific staff—so many that Cook and his principal officers considered her unsafe. She was therefore restored to her original seaworthy condition. Joseph Banks, Esq., considering the accommodation impossible for himself, and, in spite of having spent £5,000, gave up the expedition and took his party to Iceland to cool off.

Although the friendship of Cook and Banks remained firm, the scientific staff that was finally assigned was not happy. John Reinhold Forster, a German naturalist, and his son, John George Adam, proved difficult shipmates, the father being a bit on the querulous side. The Board of Longitude appointed two astronomers, one to each ship, Mr. Wales going with Cook. Four of the new chronometers were sent on the voyage. These "watch machines," however, were not of much service, because no one understood their use. The astronomers still clung to the moon, to the measurement of lunar distances.

On July 13, 1772, the little ships put out from Plymouth, 112 persons aboard the *Resolution* and 81 in the *Adventure*. Cook sailed around the world to the eastward, the easiest way. He thoroughly combed the Southern ocean, going well below the Antarctic Circle in the Atlantic and in the Pacific, but he missed seeing Wilkes' Land, later to be discovered. He did prove there was no continental body of land in the temperate South Pacific, as Quiros had believed.

Cook made great advances in the preservation of health on long voyages. The horrors of scurvy experienced by earlier voyagers and felt by his own people were carefully studied, and remedies were taken along. At the outset of this second voyage he made three puncheons of beer, " . . . of the inspissated juice of malt. The proportion was about ten of water to one of juice." This was regarded as a sovereign specific against many ills.

Cook's course on this second voyage carried him around the world, eastward, whereas his first voyage had taken him around sailing to the west. His progress over an uncharted ocean, among many islands and reefs, through unknown currents in a sailing craft, would give the modern seaman something to think about. The daylight hours were fairly safe, always with masthead lookouts scanning the sea for white water. But at night, in pitch black darkness, the ship snugged down, with extra lookouts posted, always on the *qui vive* for the dreaded cry, "*Breakers ahead!*"

Many of Captain Cook's observations were later on modified by subsequent explorers who followed the great Pacific discoverer. But his visit to the Tonga Islands, among many others, stands forth in its idyllic beauty.

In January, 1643, Abel Janszoon Tasman, in the *Zeehaen* flute, a long, narrow ship of small burthen carrying less than fifty men, had anchored on the northwest side of Tonga Tabu, to which he gave the name of Amsterdam. To Eooa he attached the good Dutch label of Middleburg, and Namuka became Rotterdam. He had friendly relations with the islanders, and this tradition still prevailed when Captain Cook's ships came to anchor at Tonga in 1773, 130 years after Tasman. Cook was the second European to visit that group lying to the east of the middle meridian in the Pacific, in the mean latitude of 20 degrees south. Now we know them as three groups, Vavau to the north northeast, Haabai in the middle, and Tonga Tabu to the south southwest, just below 21 degrees south.

The *Resolution* came to anchor off Tasman's old holding ground in October. Two canoes paddled by three men came boldly alongside. In one of these was the chief, Tioony, who was given a new hatchet and five nails. Cook landed, accompanied by Tioony, who pointed out a little sheltered creek lined with luxuriant foliage, the land perfumed with flowers. Tioony held up the branch of a tree of peace and pointed toward a large group of islanders, who welcomed the Englishmen with loud exclamations of joy. Not one of them carried a weapon. They closed in on the boat so that it was difficult to land. They were eager to give rather than receive. Many threw fruits and bales of cloth into the boat as their offering.

Tioony conducted the visitors to his lodge in the midst of a noble plantation, beneath the shade of shaddock trees. The floor was spread with mats. Bananas and sweet coconuts were set before them. The chief clapped his hands, and a large gourd was brought in. A ring of Tonga people sat around industriously chewing pieces of aromatic root, masticating and grinning and spitting into the bowl. The native maidens held cups made of green leaves, sylvan beakers holding at least a pint, old women strained the liquor into the cups, and these were offered to the visitors, the guests, and the high men of Tonga.

All the natives lifted their cups and drank, and so did Captain Cook. But his staff, his English officers, gagged at the concoction, turning white and sick. After all, a captain must lead; let others follow him who can.

Their proas were ingenious. By merely turning the sail, held in a fork at the masthead, the stern became the prow. They could stop promptly and reverse without using a paddle or a rudder, sailing with great speed in either direction.

Captain Cook "had the satisfaction of beholding a feast of human flesh." A portion of a young man of twenty years was broiled and eaten with evident relish by one Gobiah. Several of the ship's crew were rendered sick by the sight.

In his circling and traversing the South Pacific, making three enormous irregular loops, Cook met waterspouts and whales and visited most of the known islands and discovered many others. He discovered the large island of New Caledonia and mentions its inhabitants as "possessing an excellent character." Navigators to follow found them to be cannibals, and of a lower strain. Perhaps they were of different origin from the Tahitians. Cook touched at Roggeveen's Easter Island and made note of a curious condition prevailing there in 1774. They counted 700 men and only 30 women—no old maids there at that time.

At Malecolo, in the New Hebrides, which old Quiros had called Australia del Espíritu Santo in its northern part and which de Bougainville had named the Cyclades, Cook explored more thoroughly. He it was who called these islands the New Hebrides. He found there great volcanoes that belched. One, " . . . which was about four miles to the west, vomited up vast quantities of fire and smoke, as it had done the night before when the flames were seen to rise above the hill which lay between. At one eruption it made a long rumbling noise, like that of thunder, or the blowing up of large mines. A heavy shower of rain, which fell at this time, seemed to increase it; and the wind blowing from the same quarter, the air was loaded with ashes. It was a kind of fine sand or stone, ground or burnt to a powder, and was exceedingly troublesome to the eyes."

This was the island called Tana.

On the last long crossing in the high parallel of 56 south, the *Resolution* veered eastward and south. Parted from the *Adventure*, she sailed along from New Zealand in the teeth of the howling westerlies and, rolling before mighty following seas, across a hitherto unexplored ocean. Cook "ran his easting down," as seamen call it. Every dark hour of those nights, roaring into an unknown sea, was living on the edge of disaster. Shorten sail as they might, they were driving east. Storm petrels screamed across their wake, and great fulmar gulls soared over their mastheads. The sailors saw the mighty albatross, great air king of the lonely, stormy Southern Pacific. Ice loomed close by. There were signs of land, but far, far to the south. Cook noted, "I will not say it was impossible anywhere to get farther to the south." But he was fulfilling his mission and had erased for all time the myth of a large land body in the South Sea, between the Antarctic Circle and the line. Of islands, there were thousands, but there was no continental land between the meridian of New Zealand and Cape Horn.

So ended the work of the years 1772, 1773, 1774 of Captain Cook's second voyage. His fame grew to the greatest proportions. His contribution of knowledge surpassed anything expected. The *Resolution* anchored at Spithead on July 30, 1775, having been away three years and eighteen days, sailing between 60,000 and 70,000 miles, and having lost only four men, one by disease. Not a single one of his people died of scurvy.

In spite of the beginning of the American rebellion and the public attention drawn to this traitorous war, Cook's return created an immense stir, especially in scientific and naval circles. He was promoted to the rank of post captain, that is, a seagoing naval captain commanding a ship. George III honored him by a long conversation, for the unhappy monarch longed to escape to the South Seas. All Cook's officers were elevated in rank.

Finally, in February, 1776, Captain Cook was called in consultation by the Admiralty. He was in a snug billet at Greenwich, but when new duty on further exploration was offered him he accepted with alacrity. His old ship, the *Resolution*, was sound; tried shipmates were eager to again go with him, officers and men. Some new shipmates were selected after the most careful scrutiny of their records and abilities. Among them was William Bligh, who sailed as master in the *Resolution*. In place of the *Adventure*, which had returned, they chose the *Discovery*, another Whitby ship, of

300 tons. Omai, the Tahitian, was to return with Cook to his native island.

No scientists were taken, since Captain Cook qualified in all these matters himself. His first lieutenant was John Gore, who had sailed with Wallis in the *Dolphin*. The command of the *Discovery* was given to Charles Clerke, who had been with Cook in the *Endeavour* as master's mate and as second lieutenant in the *Resolution*. James Burney was second in command under Clerke, having sailed as a lieutenant with Captain Furneaux, in the *Adventure*. These officers on Cook's last voyage were a well seasoned lot. And we must mention that on the *Resolution* was Midshipman George Vancouver, then nineteen, whose name was later made famous on the northwest coast of North America.

Investigating a North American passage between the Pacific and the Atlantic was the great task assigned to the navigator. North of the equator, the Pacific was practically unknown, and he was to penetrate that void. True, many navigators had sailed across this ocean, following in the wake of the galleons, but none had ventured into its mighty middle. Cook himself, in all his searching for the continent Pacifica, had kept below the line. So here was a virgin ocean for his keels.

Although Britain was on the verge of losing the greater and most valuable part of her American colonies, she went ahead to explore a passage around them, to make mighty discoveries, and to gain little or nothing by this bold enterprise except an undying fame.

Cook looped around through the maze of islands, the Cook group, then northward to Tahiti, where he landed Omai. Omai had been cherished by Cook, painted by Reynolds and apostrophized by Cowper, yet this distinguished Tahitian was unhappy. Cook set him up in a house constructed by the ships' carpenters on the neighboring island of Huahine, advising the natives that if Omai, his brother, was disturbed in the possession of his European goods and comforts, all hell would break loose in the form of cast-iron cannon balls. One rascal who stole from Omai and also lifted a sextant belonging to Cook had his head shaved, and, for good measure, the incensed Captain had them crop off his ears.

While in the Royal Society Isles, Captain Cook, like so many men turning the age of fifty, leaned toward the reform side. He induced his red faced sailors to give up their grog and use the mild milk of the coconut instead. But, to put over this reform on the pragmatic men-o'-war's men, he submitted the undoubted fact that, by drinking their spirits in that warm latitude, they might have none left when the voyage took them into colder climes, when cordials would be most needed. "So why not dispense with your grog now, my men," he said, "when we have so excellent a liquor as that of coconuts to substitute for it?" All agreed, and grog was stopped except on Saturday nights, when the toast, "Our many sweethearts and wives!" resounded along the lower decks and in the gun rooms.

Some found that if they kept their coconut milk in a deck bucket hidden under a gun for several days, it acquired a terrific wallop. In that bland, expanding atmosphere, Pigafetta had noted something similar centuries earlier.

After the *Resolution* and the *Discovery* left Huahine they were soon plowing a virgin sea. Magellan had sailed by hundreds of islands without sighting them, passing many most probably at night, and Captain Cook, curiously enough, missed islands now known as Flint, Vostok, Starbuck, and Malden, and passed only a few miles from dangerous little Jarvis Island, which stretches a mile and a half, east and west, and only rises ten or twelve feet from the sea, a perfect place to wreck a ship at night. Such matters were constantly on the minds of the commanders and their officers. The day before

Christmas, 1777, they were three weeks away from Bolabola, as Cook called it, or Bora-Bora, western isle of the Society group. That day they had crossed the line for the first time in the Pacific. They had been seventeen months out from England, and many among them were thinking of Christmas and of home.

In the afternoon land was descried, low, green land, showing a few coconut palms. It stretched some thirty-five miles across their course. "It had a very barren appearance." They stood off and on during the Christmas Eve. "At daybreak I sent in boats to search for a landing place." Two were sent to angle, bringing back several hundredweight of fish. They anchored, and on the twenty-sixth and the twenty-seventh caught great numbers of turtle. An eclipse of the sun was approaching, due on Dec. 30. This event was observed. Three hundred green turtles were taken, "weighing, one with another, about ninety or a hundred pounds."

The place abounded in cavalla, small snappers, and rock fish. "There was not the smallest trace of any human being having ever been here before us. . . . As we kept our Christmas here, I called this discovery Christmas Island."

They sailed the day after New Year, standing to the north. Christmas Island, by the way, lay but 2 degrees north of the line. On Jan. 18, at daybreak, " . . . a high island made its appearance, and soon we saw more land, entirely detached from the former.

"On the 19th [January, 1778], at sunrise, the island first seen bore east several leagues distant. This being to windward which prevented our getting near it, I stood for the other, and not long after discovered a third island in the direction of west-north-west, as far distant as land could be seen."

Here, in a few terse words, is the discovery of the greatest group of mid-Pacific Islands.

The ships were to leeward, that is, to westward of the islands. The second island to open out as they increased their northing, standing close hauled with starboard tacks on board, was Oahu, and the third land seen to the west northwest was Kauai.

The magnificent proportions of the group gave the great navigator some idea of the importance of his discovery. The ships neared shore, beating up against the trade wind over a brilliant ocean, the mountains looming bluish gray.

Their first contact with Hawaiians is described by Cook: "Soon after [on the sighting of land at sunrise, Jan. 19, 1778], we saw some canoes coming off from the shore toward the ships. I immediately brought to, to give them time to join us. They had from three to six men each, and on their approach we were agreeably surprised to find that they spoke the language of Otaheite, and of the other islands we had lately visited."

Since Hawaii lies 2,300 miles northward from Tahiti (Honolulu to Papeete, 2,381 miles), the recognition of language, in which Cook and his people had become reasonably familiar, gives a hint of distant voyages, either to or via Hawaii, in the great settlement of the Polynesian Triangle, of which they now had seen the peak.

To go on with Cook: "It required but very little address to get them to come alongside, but no entreaties could prevail upon any of them to come on board. I tied some brass medals to a rope, and gave them to those in one of the canoes, who, in return, tied some small mackerel to the rope, as an equivalent. This was repeated, and some small nails, or bits of iron, which they valued more than any other articles, were given them.

"These people were of a brown color, and though of the common size, were stoutly made. There was very little difference in the casts of their color, but a considerable variation in their features—*some of their visages not being very unlike those of Europeans.*" The italics in the quotations from Captain Cook are mine.

The Hawaiians were friendly, "mild," Cook called them, though the first canoes had brought out stones, presumably as missiles. Finding these were not needed, the natives hove them overboard. When the ships made sail, standing back to the southeast, the canoes left, but others came out. What the scene was on the highlands and along the shores may be imagined. Ships may have been seen before; the reputed "discovery" of the islands by Juan Gaetano in 1555, its records, lost or hidden in the great archives of the Indies, and the tradition of a wreck, one of Álvaro de Saavedra's squadron, a half century before Gaetano, may have persisted. But if these things were facts, two centuries and more might have wiped them out of memory. The natives, as reported by Cook, were utterly astounded at the sight of his ships. A multitude must have watched them, and signal fires, runners, swift canoes, and the like must have carried the news of their appearance along the coasts and inland.

On the morning of Jan. 20, " . . . we stood in for the land and were met by several canoes filled with people, some of whom took courage and ventured on board.

"In the course of my several voyages I never before met with the natives of any place so much astonished as these people were upon entering a ship. Their eyes were continually flying from object to object—the wildness of their looks and gestures fully expressing their entire ignorance about everything they saw, *and strongly marking to us that till now they had never been visited by Europeans,* nor been acquainted with any of our commodities *except iron, which, however, it was plain they had only heard of, or had known it in some small quantity, brought to them at some distant period.*"

The islanders asked for iron under the name of "hamaite," probably, as Cook surmised, "referring to some instrument, in the making of which iron could be usefully employed. For the same reason they frequently called iron by the name of 'toe,' which, in their language, signifies a hatchet, or rather a kind of adz. When we shewed them some beads, they asked first what they were, and then whether they could eat them. But on being told that they were to be hung in their ears, they returned them as useless. They were equally indifferent to a looking-glass which was offered them, and returned it for the same reason, but sufficiently expressed their desire for hamaite and toe, which they wished might be very large. They were in some respect naturally well-bred, or at least fearful of giving offense, asking where they should sit down, (Where is the toilet?), and whether they might spit upon the deck, and the like. Some of them repeated a long prayer before they came on board, and others afterward sung and made motions with their hands, such as we had been accustomed to see in the dances of the islands we had lately visited."

Captain Cook noted another resemblance between the Hawaiians and the more southern Polynesians. "At first on their entering the ship they endeavored to steal everything they came near, *or rather to take it openly.*" The sailors and marines soon convinced them of their mistaken idea as to property, keeping a watchful eye over them.

To Third Lieutenant John Williamson, of the *Resolution*, belongs the dubious credit of having caused the death of the first native of these islands at the hands of Europeans.

"At nine o'clock (Jan. 20th) being pretty near the shore of the second island Atoui or Kauii, I sent three armed boats, under the command of Lieutenant Williamson, to look for a landing-place and for fresh water. I ordered him that if he should find it necessary to land in search of the latter, not to suffer more than one man to go with him out of the boats."

As always, in the case of sailing craft on an uncharted coast, the ships stood off and on, that is, tacked back and forth under topsails, keeping ranges on the mountains and, of course, making those observations of survey that Cook so rigorously carried out. This job of plotting the ship, constantly keeping the Captain informed, was largely under the charge of Master

William Bligh. The water was deep, more than 1,000 fathoms, close to the shore. "At about noon Mr. Williamson came back, and reported that he had seen a large pond near one of the villages which contained fresh water. He also reported that he had attempted to land in another place, but was prevented by the natives, who, coming down to the boats in great numbers, attempted to take away the oars, muskets, and in short everything that they could lay hold of, and pressed so thick upon him that he was obliged to fire, by which one man was killed."

Cook makes an appended remark showing that Lieutenant Williamson was fearful of his unfortunate experience and that it was not immediately reported. "But this unhappy circumstance I did not know till after we had left the island, so that all my measures were directed as if nothing of the kind had happened." What the rigorous Captain Cook said to his third lieutenant when the killing was finally confessed must be left to the imagination.

Unaware of the killing, Cook landed. "Between three and four o'clock I went ashore with three armed boats to examine the water, and to try the disposition of the inhabitants, several hundreds of whom were assembled on the beach.

"The very instant I leaped on shore the collected body of the natives all fell flat upon their faces, and remained in that very humble posture till, by expressive signs, I prevailed upon them to rise. They then brought a great many small pigs which they presented to me, with plantain trees, using much the same ceremonies that we had seen practiced on such occasions at the Society and other islands; and a long prayer being spoken by a single person, in which others of the assembly sometimes joined, I expressed my acceptance of their proffered friendship by giving them in return such presents as I had brought with me from the ship."

Returning on board, he gave orders for sending in the casks in the morning, when he again went ashore with the watering party. They met with no obstruction, the natives assisting in rolling the casks to and from the pool. They also started a lively trade in hogs and taro (potatoes, Cook calls them), giving the natives nails and pieces of iron suitable for making chisels.

Captain Cook made an excursion into the country, accompanied by Mr. Anderson, the surgeon, and Mr. Webber, an artist, and followed by a numerous train of natives. One native, most active in keeping the rest in order, was chosen as a guide. "As we ranged down the coast from the east in the ships we had observed at every village one or more elevated white objects, like pyramids, or rather obelisks; and one of these, which I guessed to be at least fifty feet high, was very conspicuous from the ship's anchoring station, and seemed to be at no great distance up this valley. The moment we got to it we saw that it stood in a burying ground or morai."

At noon Captain Cook returned on board the *Resolution.* There was a conference of officers in the great cabin, Captain Clerke coming over for dinner with the squadron commander. Roast pig and yams were of that feast and a bottle or two of Madeira. Cook says here, "These people merited our best commendations, never once attempting to cheat us, either ashore or alongside the ships."

"One of our visitors, who offered some bone fish hooks for sale, was observed to have a very small parcel tied to the string of one of them, which he separated with great care and reserved for himself when he parted with the hook. Being asked what it was, he pointed to his belly. It struck us that it might be human flesh. The question being put to him, he answered that the flesh was part of a man. Another of his countrymen who stood by him, was then asked whether it was their custom to eat those killed in battle, and he immediately answered in the affirmative."

On going ashore again, Cook reports: "The ground through which I passed was in a state of nature, very stony and the soil seemed poor. It was, however, covered with shrubs and plants, some of which perfumed the air with more delicious fragrancy than I had met with at any other of the islands in this ocean. The habitations of the natives were thinly scattered about, and it is supposed that there could not be more than five hundred people upon the island. Our people had an opportunity of observing the method of living amongst the natives, and it appeared to be decent and cleanly. They did not see any instance of the men and women eating together, and the latter seemed generally associated in companies by themselves. It was found that they burnt here the oily nuts of the dooe dooe for lights in the night, as at Otaheite, and that they baked their hogs in ovens. A particular veneration seemed to be paid here to owls, which they have very tame; and it was observed to be a pretty general practice amongst them to pull out one of their teeth, for which odd custom, when asked the reason, the only answer that could be got was, that it was *teeha*."

Captain Cook spent from Jan. 20 to Feb. 1, inclusive, in the northern Hawaiian Islands. His intention, of course, was to return there for a thorough examination. His instructions were to proceed to Drake's coast of New Albion and sail it, in the hope of finding a northwest passage from the Atlantic into the Pacific. By this route, if he found it, Cook was to sail home, presumably out of Davis Strait, back to England. This accounts, in large part, for the short time spent at the scene of his historic major discovery, which he named the Sandwich Islands, in honor of the Earl of Sandwich, First Lord of the Admiralty.

On Feb. 2, 1778, the small squadron of exploring ships was outbound from their anchorage at Niihau. Cook, a year and a half away from home, like most supreme commanders, had drawn much into himself. With him were some officers of extraordinary ability and loyalty, and these either were ill, worn out by the rigors of the service, or were of subordinate rank, such as Midshipman Vancouver, or of the lower grade of commissions, such as Master William Bligh. A few, as in the case of Lieutenant Williamson, were not too reliable. Cook knew all this, of course. For Captain James Cook was one of the greatest of all modern discoverers and undoubtedly the first scientific overseas explorer. His ships demanded that he be a skillful sailor, and this he proved on many occasions. He was also a man given to quick emotions, being harsh—too harsh on some occasions and on others, too lenient—but in the main his character struck a balance on the side of sanity and fairness.

Cook's party, their blood thinned by nearly two years' steaming in the tropics, was to feel an abrupt drop in temperature when they reached 43 degrees north.

Where Drake turned back to the south, Cook, after making Nova Albion on Mar. 7, 1778, on the shore of our state of Oregon, turned toward the north, his ships skirting the dread American coast while he made a running survey of extraordinary accuracy. Stormy weather prevailed. Great sky-reaching, snow capped mountains loomed to the east. His sketchy Spanish charts showed the "straits" of Martin de Aguilar and Juan de Fuca. He found the coast inhabited, as had Drake and others. He writes of the people: "Their colour we could never positively determine, as their bodies were incrusted with paint and dirt . . . when these were well rubbed off, the whiteness of the skin appeared almost to equal that of Europeans."

Cook's progress northward, during which he examined every inlet in the hope of finding it a passage across the continent, brought him up the considerable water of Cook's Inlet, at the eastern start of the long Alaska peninsula. Here, at the head, emptied the river Susitna, flowing from the foothills of Mount McKinley. So he turned back, his ships skirting the shore, on the Pacific side, then north past Unalaska, and, always searching for an opening, up through the strait of Vitus Bering into the Arctic Ocean.

The terrific battle against ice and the stormiest of weather, alternated by polar day, with no night, at times calm and surpassingly beautiful, is not part of our Pacific story. The stout sloops-of-war *Resolution* and *Discovery* made a heroic effort. Cook did come to the start of a northwest passage, figuring it from Europe or, rather, the end of it, but this was impenetrable to him or any other sailing ships, at least from the west. As the season closed, his people exhausted, his ships having been hard used by the ice, he bore out past the Aleutians and sailed due south.

It was Oct. 26, 1778; he had been on this quest for nine months. "My intention was now to proceed to the Sandwich Islands, there to spend a few of the winter months, in case we should meet with the necessary refreshments, and then to direct our course to Kamchatka, so as to be there by the middle of May of the ensuing summer."

The last month spent at sea by Captain Cook, each day dropping the latitude, the North Star lowering over his taffrail, the weather growing warmer, must have been of a prophetic nature. His drive into the far north, like his drive into the Antarctic, had been a work of negative discovery. He had erased from the maps of the world that old "Strait of Anian." And although such voyages of disillusion are grand, his mighty positive discovery of the Hawaiian islands was to mark the high point in his career. Up to the time of Cook the whole North Pacific had been a blank. Not by the wildest guess had geographers or cartographers ever placed a great archipelago, volcanic, fruitful, between the northern and the southern routes of the ancient galleons.

Captain Cook had received the highest consideration from the scientific world. He had been elevated to post rank in the Royal Navy, he was a Fellow of the Royal Society, his friends and country were both powerful and appreciative. He might have dreamed that Lord Sandwich and others would grant him high naval rank, that of vice-admiral at least, and then an honorable retirement to the bosom of his family in Yorkshire. He may even have imagined himself Admiral Sir James Cook, G.C.B., the highest Order of the Bath. Men had been given peerages for lesser services than the discovery of a great group of magnificent islands midway in the vast Pacific. Such things may have gone through the mind of Cook as he collated notes, supervised the plotting of surveys, the proper ordering of the immense amount of data, specimens, and observations.

He wrote of this time, being too busy to do otherwise, "Nothing remarkable happened during our course." And that meant no land sighted as they sailed southward along the 160th meridian.

When Cook first sighted the islands, he fetched them near their western middle part, counting five, and ending at one of the least of them, Niihau. On making them again, sailing down from the north, he records the landfall. "At daybreak on the 26th of November, land was seen extending from the south south-east to west. We were now satisfied that the group of the Sandwich Islands had been only imperfectly discovered, as those which we had visited in our progress northward all lie to the leeward [westward] of our present station.

"I bore up and ranged along the coast of the westward." That is, he kept on the windward side, being in the trades, and had a lee shore on his starboard hand.

Canoes came off for the usual traffic in nails and hogs. "I kept plying all night." That is, he close hauled and held off-shore for safety. " . . . and in the morning stood close in shore. . . . In the afternoon of the 30th, being off the north-east end of the island, several canoes came off to the ship. Most of these belonged to a chief named Terreeoboo, who came in one of them."

A double hulled sailing canoe came out to attend on the chief, and Cook towed her all night. "In the evening we discovered another island to windward, which the natives call Owhyhee [Hawaii]."

They had been off the coast of Maui, in sight of its mighty Haleakala—the House of the Sun, greatest extinct crater on this earth. They sailed across the thirty mile Alenuihaha Channel. It was Dec. 1. "At eight in the morning, finding that we could fetch Owhyhee, I stood for it; and our visitors from another island, called Mowee [Maui], not choosing to accompany us, embarked in their canoe, and went ashore.

"Next morning we were surprised to see the summits of the mountains on Owhyhee covered with snow." Natives came out, shy at first, but later more friendly. They brought aboard a quantity of sugar cane. Cook, ever on the side of procuring healthful specifics, notes in the midst of his epic coasting that he made a beverage of this sweet sugar cane. "Finding a strong concoction of it produced a very palatable beer, I ordered some more to be brewed for our general use. But when the cask was now broached, not one of my crew would even so much as taste it. I myself and the officers continued to make use of it whenever we could get materials for brewing it. A few hops, of which we had some on board, improved it much. It had the taste of new malt beer; and I believe no one will doubt of its being very wholesome." This great hearted man must have been much aggrieved amid his moments of extraordinary discovery, for he wrote in his journal, after this plea for his sugar beer, "Yet my inconsiderate crew alleged that it was injurious to their health."

And now one more paragraph, which shows how Cook fought the great enemy of the old deep water voyages. "Every innovation whatever on board ship, though ever so much to the advantage of seamen, is sure to meet with their highest disapprobation. Both portable soup and sour kraut were at first condemned as stuff unfit for human beings.

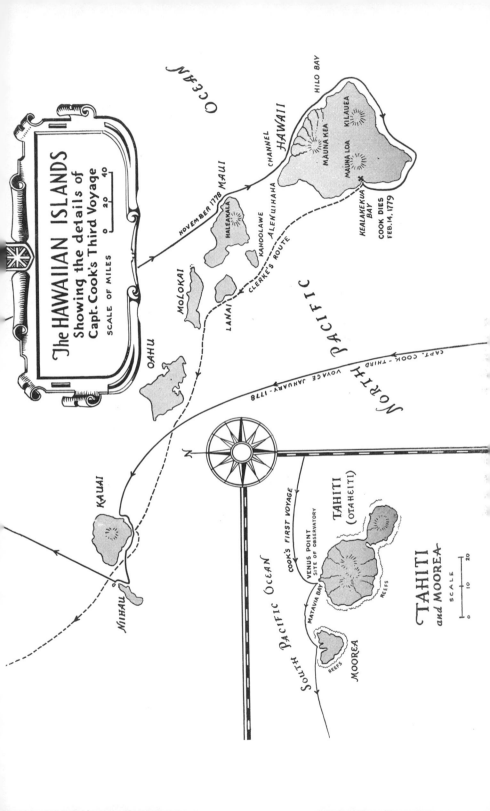

" . . . Few commanders," he wrote with pride, "have introduced into their ships more novelties, as useful varieties of food and drink, than I have done. It has, however, been in a great measure owing to various little deviations from established practice that I have been able to preserve my people, generally speaking, from that dreadful distemper, the scurvy, which has perhaps destroyed more of our sailors in their peaceful voyages than have fallen by the enemy in military expeditions."

The *Resolution* returned to sea, that is, stood off, and, when daybreak came on Dec. 14, they found themselves close to the high cliffs of Hawaii, " . . . a dreadful surf breaking upon the shore." Great rivers ran to the sea, but not as rivers do in European lands. These came to the edge and dashed down in roaring cataracts, one by the side of another, plunging into the Pacific, their source the slopes of Mauna Kea, lifting two and a half miles out of the sea. As they tacked to the southward with hopes of weathering this island, Mauna Loa rose to the west, and Kilauea, like a gigantic censer, expelled a cloud of smoke. Canoes followed them, and they again closed. At midnight, being in close company with the *Discovery*, Cook tacked, stretching to the north, as day broke on Dec. 24. He supposed Captain Clerke would see him go about so omitted the signal. In consequence, the ships separated. Christmas Day was spent off the dangerous coast, plying offshore constantly to avoid rocks. On the thirtieth, being in great want of fresh provisions, the foul and hard wracked ships hailed some canoes, receiving fruits and roots and three small pigs. On New Year's Day of the fateful year 1779, the " . . . atmosphere was again loaded with heavy clouds; and the new year was ushered in with very hard rain." They crossed Hilo Bay and for three days ran down the southeast side of the island. On the fifth they were rejoined by the *Discovery*.

One of the islanders who had been taken aboard Captain Clerke's ship refused to leave, acting for them as a pilot. "For several days [being around the south point] we kept standing off and on with occasional visits from the natives. At daybreak on the 16th, seeing the appearance of a bay, I sent Mr. Bligh with a boat from each ship to examine it, being at this time three leagues off." Again canoes clustered around, and one native clambering aboard the *Resolution* stole a boat's rudder. Cook fired muskets and two or three four pounders over the absconding canoe. In the evening "Mr. Bligh returned, and reported that he had found a bay, in which was good anchorage and fresh water."

Cook determined to carry his ships in the next day to refit. They were in dire need of attention, following their buffeting in Bering Sea; his people were sea weary; he himself must have been exhausted after a constant beat, off and down the shores of Maui and Hawaii, through waters never sailed before by European seamen. Nov. 26, 1778, to Jan. 16, 1779, are the dates in the logbooks. Fifty-one days!

Before invoking the final scene, let us glance over the shoulder of Captain Cook as he enters remarks in his journal on the evening of Jan. 17.

"At eleven o'clock in the forenoon we anchored in the bay which is called by the natives Karakakooa [Kealakekua Bay]. The ships continued to be much crowded with natives, and were surrounded by a multitude of canoes. I had nowhere, in the course of my voyages, seen so numerous a body of people assembled at one place. For besides those in the canoes, all the shore was covered with spectators, and many hundreds were swimming round the ships like shoals of fish. We could not but be struck with the singularity of this scene; few now lamented our having failed in our endeavors to find a northern passage homeward last summer. To this disappointment we owed our having it in our power to revisit the Sandwich Islands, and to enrich our voyage with a discovery which, though the last, seemed in many respects to be the most important that had hitherto been made by Europeans throughout the extent of the Pacific Ocean."

James Cook put down his pen. He was to write more details during the three weeks and some days to follow, but his last great entry had been made in the journal. He was weary— too tired, it seemed, for a man just turned fifty-one. The King's ships, on far and hazardous service, were no place for longevity. The dreadful cold and wet had already touched poor Clerke in the *Discovery*, his lungs being none too robust. Twinges of rheumatism gripped Cook. In Tahiti he was seized by a severe attack and cured, native fashion, by being beaten from head to foot; a heroic remedy but, for the time, successful. He was weary as only shipmasters get when some grilling voyage has come to a safe anchorage.

A quality of hushed expectancy, of impending destiny, overhung the ships lying in the bay against the western shore of old Hawaii. Already work was going forward to land and refit. An ancient native named Touahah came aboard. He was of the priesthood, known as Kooa. He arrived with solemn ceremony and, on the quarter-deck of the *Resolution*, covered James Cook with the red cloth of the gods.

The priests had recognized Captain Cook as their god, Orono, deity of the New Year, who had left Hawaii many ages before, prophesying his return in a great ship bearing a small forest of trees.

He had come twice in the New Year, once to receive the adoration of his people of the north in Kauai. Then he mysteriously left, the islands ringing with speculation as to his visit. The second time he appeared at Hawaii, coming from the north.

He spoke their language, not as they understood it but as the gods deliver it. He came with his court, his great forested ships with huge arms and wings and with great instruments of fire, with thunders and many strange beings out of the heavens.

Every mark of adoration was shown him. He was a large man, as a god should be, serious, obeyed by his many minor gods and servants quickly, without question. He brought great stores of iron, of haimaite and toe, the precious metals.

When Captain Cook went ashore in his barge, accompanied by his minor priests, guarded by his invincible men, fearless, and stern, he landed amid ceremonies of the most elaborate kind. His own thoughts must have lifted him to exalted heights. Always in his contacts with native votaries of the South Sea, Cook had respected and conformed to the taboos. As a god, he could not touch food with his anointed hands, nor could he masticate it. He was ceremoniously fed, as a symbol, with kava and with hog meat, the food already chewed for himself and Lieutenant King, who came ashore as his aide.

They ascended a scaffold, and ten men bearing the sacred red cloth prostrated themselves before the god Orono. Before Captain Cook retired to his ship they went to the *marai* and were seated between the sacred images.

When a refitting site was asked for, a part of the Bay of Kealakekua was set aside for them and made taboo. Toward the end of the month the King of Hawaii was about to return from Maui, and preparations were made to receive him in his magnificence aboard the *Resolution*.

Everything had been offered to Orono. The countryside had become depleted by its votive gifts, filling the ships with provisions. On the great ceremonial visit, Taraiopu, the King, with many richly clad chiefs, in three canoes, paddled around the ships. Kooa and his priests chanted their solemn rituals.

Captain Cook called away his barge, leading the dignitaries to the observatory, where Lieutenant King turned out the guard of Royal Marines. Here Taraiopu invested Captain Cook in his own magnificent feather cloak and helmet. At this the King of Hawaii went to the ship and was in turn given a fine linen shirt, and Cook "girt his own hanger around him."

During these ceremonies no common canoes were seen in the bay, the inhabitants being in their houses or lying prostrate on the ground. A few days later, when a seaman died from a stroke of paralysis—a strange, unexplainable death— he was interred in the *marai* by special order of Taraiopu, his funeral followed by three nights of ceremony, with sacrifices and chanting by the priests.

By now the ships were refitted, and the countryside had been stripped of pigs and vegetables. So intense was the adoration that Cook grew alarmed. On Feb. 4 the ships of trees spread their wings and sailed to the north. That night a howling gale swept across the Pacific, sails were split, the vessels bore down before the blasts. The following night the actual gods of the seas again lashed the imposters. The foremast of the *Resolution* was sprung; the storm had driven them off the Bay of Kealakekua, whipping them back to the scene of their exalted triumph, not as victors but as vanquished gods.

On Feb. 11 they came to moorings in the familiar bay, strangely empty. Taraiopu had gone away, placing the district under taboo.

Now they were in a port of distress. Captain Cook, no longer Orono but a ship commander of the Royal Navy, acted with decision. His mast was unstepped and sent ashore to be fixed. Since they would be there two or three days and since science was always demanding, the instruments—their magic—were sent ashore to the observatory. Here, so the priests said, they talked with the gods. Again they occupied the sacred *marai*, the minor priests being benevolently inclined. After all, Orono must know what he wanted. But the common natives were less believing.

Some thefts occurred. A watering party was molested; there were expostulations and some stone throwing by the natives, the rabble. Cook resolved to use force. All natives were expelled from the ships; sentries about the observatory were doubled. And then came the unpardonable thing. The *Discovery's* cutter was stolen—and later found on the beach, broken up for the sake of her nails.

Cook should have embarked his people and sailed at once. Instead, as was his custom when moral issues arose, boats were stationed at each wing of the great bay to prevent the escape of canoes. A landing party of marines went ashore to seize hostages as security for the return of the cutter. This stratagem had succeeded before in other islands. If the boat was not returned (Cook was then unaware of its demolition), he threatened to destroy the canoes.

Before colors at eight in the morning of Feb. 14, Captain Cook in the pinnace, accompanied by Lieutenant Molesworth, Philips, and nine marines, landed and marched to the village of Kaawaloa, where Taraiopu was. But the King could not be too concerned about so petty a theft as that of a boat. He was willing, he said, to go on board the *Resolution* with his two young sons. At this his wife and some of the chiefs remonstrated and held him back. Cook had abandoned his plan of taking the King as a hostage when shots were heard on the other side of the bay. As some canoes were about to leave, the guard had fired, killing an important and friendly chief called Kalinau.

The last few minutes had arrived.

Cook, accompanied by Philips, followed by a mob, walked toward the beach to board the pinnace. The killing of Kalinau had aroused the natives. One man threatened Cook with a large stone. Cook ordered him to desist. He flourished a *pahooa*, a long iron pike, and, since he persisted in his insolence, Orono, the god of the New Year, fired his pistol, the barrel charged with small shot. The pellets rattled on the native's mat. The apparent ineffectiveness of the firearm encouraged the shouting and the revolt. Stones were hurled at the Royal Marines, and one of the earees tried to stab

Mr. Philips with his *pahooa*, receiving a blow from the butt end of his musket.

Captain Cook, seeing that something definite must be done, because the yelling natives were closing around, fired his second barrel, loaded with ball, and killed the foremost of the mad mob. But it was not the native who had attacked Philips. The sergeant of marines told Cook he had killed the wrong man.

A general attack immediately followed, with the hurling of more stones, killing four marines and wounding the others. Philips was stabbed but immediately shot his assailant. Then the boats, coming off the beach, fired into this scene of utmost horror and confusion.

Captain Cook, towering over his surroundings, reached the water's edge, facing the natives. He was still a god, erect and unharmed. But the gods never turn, and he did. He ordered his boats to cease firing and come in. At this moment the inshore boat was crowded with fugitives from the shore. The offshore boat, in charge of Lieutenant Williamson, failed to respond, lying at a safe distance.

James Cook's last moment had come. He was struck on the head by a stone and stabbed from behind, falling seaward, with his face in the water. A moment later an uproarious shout arose, and, while Philips and his surviving marines struggled out to the boats, Captain Cook, their Orono, was dragged ashore in triumph.

When Cook fell Williamson did not even dash in to rescue his commander. Instead, the craven boat parties returned posthaste to the ships. Cook was never seen alive again.

That night a priest came off to the flagship with a mat bundle containing some parts of Cook's body. On the twentieth and twenty-first, what were said to be his bones were brought to Captain Clerke, the new commander of the squadron. At sunset, amid the firing of minute guns, these mortal relics of the great navigator were given to the Pacific.

Sealers and Whalers

THE sealers, whalers, and merchantmen that sailed the Pacific in the latter part of the eighteenth century and the early decades of the nineteenth were the most ubiquitous sea rovers the world has ever known. They were of several nationalities, but the Yankees of New England led all the rest in numbers and were far ahead in discovery, for much that we know of that vast ocean is due to the dollar-chasing skippers who put out in bluff-nosed barks or full-rigged ships to hunt for sperm oil for the lamps of the United States, England, and France, and skins and sandalwood and *bêche la mer* for mandarins of China. They were the real wanderers of the Pacific, going where the wind listeth, hunting for fabulous islands, making their reckoning by-guess-and-by-God, filled with the curiosity of a pioneering and acquisitive people.

There are homes in New England where yet can be found relics of the days from shortly after the Revolution until just before the Civil War, the years when the China trade and whaling were at their best, when captains of Nantucket, New Bedford, Stonington, and Sag Harbor sailed the seven seas in their quest for treasure. Their ships dotted the North and South Atlantic, the tea clippers rounded the Cape of Good Hope, their sealers penetrated far below Cape Horn to the fringes of the Antarctic continent; but when New England maritime commerce was at its height it was the Pacific that the traders and whalers and sealers crossed most frequently.

The sperm whale was a rover, too, and as life became precarious for it in the Atlantic it sought the Pacific as a refuge, and the whalers followed; and, as the sealers decimated the herds in the South Shetlands and other sub-Antarctic islands in the South Atlantic, they also pushed into the Pacific in search of more skins.

The ships that made these voyages have vanished; their bones are strewn on every coast from Patagonia to Bering Strait and from Chile to Canton. But the descendants of the hardy sailors who shoved their noses into every corner of the Pacific still retain things that great-grandfather or great-uncle Swain or Starbuck or Jones or Coffin or Macy brought back. Many a story is hidden in a Japanese crystal ball on a New England mantlepiece or a sandalwood glove box, carved in delicate figures or dainty Chinese paintings on rice paper or an inlaid tea caddy that is still in use. They came back through gale and typhoon, through wreck and tragedy, or in ships riding low with their precious freight of tea and silk and chinaware. Those were the days that John Masefield might have sung about in his poem *Cargoes*, cargoes rich in perfume and value—although the whalers, despite their precious freight, did not smell so good.

But it is the sealers and the whalers with which we are most concerned in this era, because they were the wanderers, the adventurers, whose keels ploughed the Pacific in their trackless crossings. The sealers were the merchantmen; the whalers were the hunters. Both were manned by hardy men, and both have left their mark, famous and infamous, on the ocean that called to them. Perhaps the sealers were the better of the two, for they robbed their rookeries in the early days when men before the mast bore as famous names as those who walked the quarter-deck, whereas in the later days of whaling, not in the beginning, the ships were often manned by the scum of the earth. What some of them did in the South Seas is fortunately concealed in the nebulous past, but one can find the record if one seeks it, and it is not a pleasant one. But, on the other hand, there were among them men of intelligence and probity, with the instincts of the explorer as well as those of the hunter, who sailed well, did brave deeds, and who, when they perished, did so nobly. But of all the scarred, battered, and bitter annals of the sea, some of the worst came out of the whaling voyages.

Let us first look at the sealers, those men who combined hunting with commerce, although the logs of both sealers and whalers overlap in the Pacific. It was the practice in those days to hunt for seals in the South Atlantic and later the South Pacific and then to take the skins back to New York or Stonington or to Canton, where they commanded high prices. If they did not have a good catch, they might pick up a little sandalwood or *bêche la mer*, the latter being a delicate wormlike thing, found on the coral reefs, that the Chinese highly esteemed in soup and stew. It was either black, yellow, or white, but the black variety brought the best prices. It must have been a strange delicacy, for if it was left in the sun it would evaporate, dry up like a jellyfish on a hot rock. But if it was carefully disemboweled—and it was a worm, remember— dried in the shade, salted, and then packed in barrels, it was worth much money at the Canton factories. Godowns, they call them now; here we call them warehouses. After disposing of these odoriferous cargoes, the sealers would then take aboard their tea and silk and chinaware and sail around Good Hope to New York or Boston.

One of the most famous of these early traders was Captain Edmund Fanning. He is known largely because he is one of the very few of these early seal hunters and traders who left intelligent accounts of their voyages. The sealers did not seek publicity any more than do the modern Norwegian whalers who keep the knowledge of their Antarctic hunting grounds a secret between themselves and their owners. If a sealer was fortunate enough to find an island alive with seals, he made a cryptic note in his log that only he could understand, or he put down the latitude and longitude and stowed the rest of his information in his cranium. Much of the ambiguity that attaches to early sealing and whaling voyages, particularly international disputes as to who discovered what, is due to this desire for secrecy. As long ago as 1836, J. N. Reynolds, an optimistic member of Congress who had been on a sealing voyage to the Antarctic for the fun of it and who was largely responsible for the first United States government exploring expedition to the Antarctic and Pacific—that headed by Lieutenant Charles Wilkes—noted this tendency to secrecy.

"In the history of the seal trade," he said in a speech in the House of Representatives, "secrecy in what they know has been deemed a part, and a very important part, too, of their capital."

So it can be readily understood why the unique narrative of Fanning has come to be of so much importance in maritime history.

He came from Stonington, Connecticut, the greatest of all sealing ports. Fanning was an odd person. He was a remarkably good navigator, an excellent observer, and a good seaman. He sailed for the South Atlantic in 1792 for sealskins and for the next twenty-five years made voyages to the Pacific and around the world. Fanning's Island, in the Pacific, which he discovered, is named for him. He had an important part in sending the sealing expedition under Captains Benjamin Pendleton and Nathaniel B. Palmer to the Antarctic, which led to the American claim that Palmer discovered that part of the Antarctic continent south of Cape Horn that is named for him. He also had a good deal to do with the promotion of Lieutenant Wilkes's expedition. He either commanded or acted as agent for more than seventy voyages to the South Seas and China.

But he was odd. He would not permit any of his crew to swear. He told them that he would do the swearing and they would do the work, that no officer would be permitted to swear at them; and he adds that he never knew a crew that did better work by reason of abuse. This was before the days of the tough Atlantic packet boats, noted for their bucko mates, but swearing was not an infrequent occurrence on shipboard. He was kind to the natives, and rather than fire on them when he thought his ship might be in danger he would set sail and put to sea. He seems to have been a God-fearing and kindly man. When he returned in one of his ships after a China voyage, a trip on which he had several wooden guns made to imitate the iron guns—for all Pacific traders were armed merchantmen in those days—guns that so closely resembled the real ones that they could not easily be distinguished one from the other, he sold the vessel. He was rather proud of the deceptive appearance of those wooden guns, for he says in his narrative—and here steps out the Yankee trader:

"This may be better conceived from the fact, that when sold with the ship on her return to New York, the purchaser, although he had been on board daily, while the cargo was being discharged, and had stood upon them very frequently, bought them all as so many iron guns, but when discovered to him, came with a complaint, asserting that he had been imposed upon; he looked as we seamen say, 'like one struck all aback,' when informed that the inventory merely stated, armed with carriage guns, without specifying the exact number."

Shades of Connecticut wooden nutmegs! Captain Fanning didn't swear. But such peccadillos in a race bred to Spartan living may well be overlooked. His other virtues far overbalanced his thriftiness, if one wants to call it that.

Fanning sailed from New York on June 13, 1797, on the first voyage of an American ship, manned by American sailors, around the world from that port. A long way from Magellan. The ships were better, and there were better instruments, but the voyage was nevertheless one of adventure. Stonington is now a sleepy town on Long Island Sound, but it retains its charm. Its beautiful old elms were probably young when Fanning sailed, and some of its churches were not yet built, but it has the flavor of a New England village that played a part in world affairs in its day.

They were a great breed of seamen, those Stonington mariners. They sailed tiny ships around the Horn more nonchalantly than members of the Larchmont Yacht Club put out on a Saturday afternoon. When they left port they expected to be gone for from two to three years; and they never knew what unknown reef would trip them on their venturesome voyages. Fanning was of the best of this breed, as were Palmer and Pendleton and many others. He had been reading of Drake, Byron, Anson, and Cook and set out in " . . . the hope of being able to add some new discoveries to the knowledge already in possession of man relating to those seas, and the no less flattering hope of realizing a fortune, if the enterprise were well conducted, and successful in its termination, were sufficient to bind me to exert myself in bringing about this desired voyage."

True, Fanning was above the average seaman who set out for the South Seas, but it might be said of the best of them that this was their credo, to learn, to discover, and to make money. And of these, the least was not money.

The ship in which he put out from New York, the brig *Betsey*, was of a little less than 100 tons, less than the tonnage of most ferryboats. But she was a good sea boat and had been built for a Charleston packet. Her rigging was refitted, and the stores, consisting of provisions, beads, cutlery, looking glasses, buttons, needles, and other things for trading with the natives, were put on board. She sailed with twenty-seven men, among them Jonathan, a Green Mountains boy. Jonathan was one of those simple lads who so often make good on difficult voyages because of their kindness and willingness to do something for others. When they got off the coast of Patagonia, Jonathan approached Fanning with great diffidence and asked for a tub, some molasses, and rum, with which to catch a Patagonian "giant." He had heard these giants were so big there was more than a foot between their eyes, but he was sure that with the molasses and rum, with which he had caught bears in Vermont, he could make any giant helpless, bring him aboard, and tie him to ring bolts in the deck until he could be tamed. And what a fortune Jonathan was going to make when he got the Patagonian giant back to the United States! He was a premature P. T. Barnum. His ideas were all right, but there were no Patagonian giants, and the ship did not touch at Patagonia. But everybody aboard came to love Jonathan.

Then there was the lad of fourteen who fell overboard about 16 degrees south of the equator while he was drawing a bucket of water at the fore chains. As he went past the stern, Fanning called to him to float and not be scared, that he would be picked up. An officer was sent aloft to keep him in sight, and a boat was lowered. When they picked up the boy sometime later, the officer in the boat asked him if he was not scared while waiting so long.

But little Henry said, "No, sir. For as I passed by the stern, the captain told me to keep still, only to try to float and not to be frightened and that he would send a boat for me; so that I was not scared."

And, as Fanning added, "This was uttered with the most innocent composure and cheerfulness." Pretty good stock, these Stonington folk, even at fourteen—and also a side light on Captain Edmund Fanning, who did not permit swearing but appreciated bravery in others.

Now it must not be supposed that Captain Fanning's first voyage around the world was typical of all American voyages in those days, for it was supremely successful, but it does show what the average New England skipper tried to do in the seal trade. Later Fanning met with reversals in which he lost ships. But the *Betsey* was fortunate. At the Falklands he fell in with the whaler *Olive Branch*, of Nantucket—one could find a Nantucketer then almost anywhere in the Atlantic—and was told by her captain, O. Paddock, that at the island of Massafuero in the South Pacific he could find many fine fur seals and could land safely. This was contradictory to what Fanning had heard before, but he knew Paddock and believed him. It was perfectly possible for a whaling captain to pass along information to a friend hunting seals or for a sealer to tell a friendly whaler of a good fishing ground, but no sealer would ever tell another, friend or not, where seals could be found. Business was business. So Fanning set out for Massafuero.

It was an island on which it was supposed to be impossible to land; or, if one could land, the surf was so bad that fur sealskins, which must be kept dry, could not be got out to the ship. But there had been little sealing at the Falklands; so Fanning put off for the island with the strange name. When they got there Fanning sent off two boats, warning the officers in each not to attempt a landing if the surf seemed difficult, because he was sure that would abate and they could then get ashore easily. But when the boats got near the island, those in them saw between 300,000 and 400,000 seals, and the temptation was too much for the second officer. He tried to beach his boat, was wrecked, and the men were washed up on the rocks, battered but still alive.

The next day a boat was sent near the island, and a good swimmer in the crew guided a cask of water and one of bread through the surf. Now shows the determination of these Yankee sealers. A boat's crew was marooned ashore, but in another twenty-four hours another boat had been sent toward the rocky beach and landed not only food but also sealing weapons. They also brought off the bruised members of the first boat's crew. So they killed and skinned seals while the ship stood on and off the island and in ten weeks filled their ship so full that not only the hold but also the cabin and forecastle were nearly filled, leaving room merely for members of the crew to move about. Even so, they left 4,000 skins on the island, with a boatswain and a boat's company to take charge of them until another vessel from the owners came to take them off. And it is significant of the readiness of these sealers to put up with discomfort that so little was thought of leaving members of the crew behind on a rocky little island in the South Pacific that Fanning does not even mention whether they were ever brought home.

When Fanning left Massafuero, he estimated that there were between 500,000 and 700,000 fur seals there and several thousand wild goats, and he also said that after his visit at least 1,000,000 skins were taken from the island. So, of course, the men left behind were rescued. And all these skins were taken to Canton and there exchanged for tea and silk and other goods that could be disposed of in the United States. It sounds like a tremendous business, and it was then; but when the *Betsey* got back to New York, after many adventures, the cargo brought the sum of $52,300. That doesn't seem an awful lot nowadays for a two years' voyage, but Captain Edmund Fanning was vastly pleased with it and comments that the amount paid into the United States Treasury as duties was more than three times the cost of the ship and her outfitting. As a matter of fact, Captain Fanning frequently referred to the amount paid into the Federal Treasury, seemingly as a matter of pride. Nowadays he would probably roar like a sea lion and say that the voyage was entirely unprofitable because of the strangling hold of taxes on the China trade. But taxes were light in those days.

After Fanning the merchant and sealer had filled his ship with sealskins, Fanning the questing Yankee started westward, hoping that on the way to the Canton factories he might find some new islands. It is typical that this merchant explorer should devote much more space to his descriptions of the South Sea Islands and his brushes with the natives and Malayan pirates than he does to his sealing or trading. Seldom have there been a more fortunate group of seamen than these early sealers, for they combined business with pleasure; they became rich while carrying out the dominant pioneering instincts of the Yankee breed. They were the maritime contemporaries of Daniel Boone and David Crockett. The distant and unknown horizon beckoned to them—after they had a hull full of skins—just as the wilderness beyond the Appalachians called to Leatherstocking. It is only by realizing this that we can catch the dual personality of these hard-living descendants of Puritans, men who would pass the collection plate at home but who would drive a bargain that would make David Harum look like an innocent.

So when Captain Fanning turned the *Betsey's* bow toward China he had high hopes of adventure, and he found it. But first he did something that shows the type of seaman that manned those New England vessels. The standing rigging of the ship was not in good shape. He did not know when he would encounter a gale, and typhoons must always be expected in the western Pacific and China Sea. So, running before the gentle trades, he stripped the foremast, " . . . securing it well by purchases and tackles at the hounds, before letting up on the lower rigging, afterwards putting up the new suit on the lower mast, topmast, etc., and then setting all taught up, preparatory to spreading sail upon it." Then they tackled the mainmast, the mizzen having been rerigged at the Cape Verde Islands. Captain Fanning was quite proud of this achievement, as he may well have been. "As nothing of the kind had ever been performed before this, or if it had, never to our knowledge, it must of course be considered as an American precedent." And he was also proud of the fact that it didn't cost the owners a cent. Besides, it kept the sailors busy at a time when they hardly had to start a sheet for days. The ship was in better condition than when it left home except for bottom fouling.

It was not long before Fanning ran into the Marquesas, to be met by war canoes filled with apparently friendly but impatient natives. They wanted the white men to run into harbor, anchor, and go ashore to exchange metal and odds and ends for food. While they were standing on and off, waiting for a favorable wind, a canoe came alongside with two natives, apparently, in it. One of them called out: "Sir, I am an Englishman, and now call upon, as I have come to you, to preserve my life." When he came aboard he said, "I am a missionary," sank back in a chair, and bowed his head in prayer. After a time he told them that he was the Reverend William Pascoe Crook, sent out from London by the missionary ship *Duff* to save souls. But not long after he got there an Italian escaped from a ship that touched at the islands and proceeded to convince the chiefs that they could capture ships that put into shore, massacre their crews, and, with the weapons captured, become the richest and most powerful community in the islands. Crook had escaped with the assistance of a friendly chief to warn Fanning; so the Stonington captain promptly put to sea. When the chief dropped over the side into his canoe, he promised to warn other ships, but he said that if Crook didn't come back in a few moons he would probably not be alive.

And so, after later discovering Fanning Island, after nearly running on a reef in the night, being saved only by a somnambulistic instinct that caused him to order the ship hove to until morning, Captain Fanning came to Canton and disposed of his cargo. In the story of the Pacific, Fanning is an American sailor of whom we can all be proud. He helps to raise the record above the depravity to which some other seamen tried to sink it.

Sealing, as a means of opening unknown lands, of building bridges across the seas, was far antedated by whaling, which began in Europe 1,000 years ago and spread first to Spitzbergen and Greenland. Both sealers and whalers began to go into the South Atlantic toward the middle of the eighteenth century, and it was natural that at about the same time they should round the Horn and enter the Pacific. As a matter of fact, the whalers probably slightly preceded the sealers into this little known ocean, for long before Captain Fanning went there—and he was not the first sealer—the ship *Amelia*, Captain Shields, an English vessel manned largely by Nantucketers, sailed for the Pacific from London in 1787. Her first mate, Archelus Hammond, is credited with killing the first sperm whale taken west of the Horn.

A clipper ship flying across the Pacific, her stu'n's'ls set, used to look with scorn on the stubby little whalers she met in her passage. Wandering aimlessly, looking for whales, taking in sail at night, the whalers were unmistakable. There were the lookouts at the mastheads searching the sea for spouts, the graceful whaleboats swung out on the davits waiting to be lowered, the grimy and sea beaten hull, the stubby masts and spars, all the things that portrayed that this was a vessel not built for speed but for her own peculiar purpose. There were probably no more ungraceful or lumbering ships ever outfitted in this country, for New England was then famous for its swift ships of smooth line that could carry sail and hurl the ocean behind them. But the whaler had its own job to do. It had to remain at sea for from two to three and a half years, to meet every demand upon it by weather, and it was broad enough in the beam to stand up under a sixty ton whale lashed to its side, which was broad indeed. It used to be said in

New Bedford that whalers were "built by the mile and cut off as you want 'em." That was a slander on the bluff-bowed, thick-sided wooden craft, but it was about the way they looked, and anyone who can remember a whaler tied up at a dock as a curiosity of the past will recall the wonder that such ships could get anywhere at all. Their average speed, except in a gale, when they were generally snugged down, was about four miles an hour. They didn't need to go any faster.

We think of those days as the great days of whaling. It was an imposing industry; it formed a large part of our maritime activities, and there were not many large industries in the United States. The golden age of the whaling industry was from 1830 to 1860. Elmo Paul Hohman in his interesting book *The American Whaleman*, which, however, deals almost entirely with economic and social aspects of the business and almost overlooks the importance of whalers in the history of exploration, says that:

"By January 1, 1844, the fleet had increased to 644 vessels, and its value had risen to $19,430,000—a rate of growth which averaged $675,000 per year. Together with the catchings at sea, the value of the whole was placed at $27,784,000. These 644 whalers, of 200,484 tons burden, were manned by 17,500 officers and men, who consumed annually $3,845,500 worth of commodities. The annual yields of oil and whalebone were sold in the crude state, for about $7,000,000; and when manufactured for $8,000,000 to $9,000,000."

Not all this whaling, of course, was in the Pacific, but the largest part of it was. The ships themselves came from many ports. In 1836 when there were 460 ships, averaging 375 tons each, hunting whales, one tenth of the total tonnage of American shipping, they came from the following towns:

New Bedford	154	Bristol	17
Nantucket	71	New London	29
Lynn	5	Norwich	1
Gloucester	1	New York	6

Portsmouth	4	Newburgh	3
Warren, R. I.	15	Wilmington	3
Providence	2	Dartmouth, Mass.	4
Mystic	3	Wareham	1
Greenport	3	Edgartown	8
Hudson	11	Plymouth	4
Newark	1	Salem	9
West Port	3	Provincetown	1
Rochester	4	Wiscasset	1
Falmouth	4	Newport	9
Fall River	3	Stonington	3
Dorchester	4	Sag Harbor	24
Newburyport	4	Poughkeepsie	4
Portland	1	Bridgeport	2

After that list it may seem strange that there is more whaling done now—at least there was until 1939—than in those halcyon days of picturesque hunting of the sperm, right and humpback whales. But the fact is that the big blue whale of the Antarctic that weighs from 80 to more than 100 tons, the largest mammal that has ever lived, has provided a much larger whaling industry. These whales are much too large and powerful to be taken with the old-fashioned harpoon; they are hunted with a harpoon gun that explodes what amounts to a shrapnel shell in the poor whale, a charge that releases inside him a harpoon that looks like a grappling iron. These modern whaling factories run as high as 21,000 tons and bring back as much as 78,000 barrels of oil from a single voyage, of which only four months are spent on the whaling grounds; and the value of only a few such cargoes would be more than the total of all the hundreds of ships engaged in whaling in a year in the good old days. Some of these modern whalers have also contributed their bit to exploration.

But they have not the romantic appeal of the old whalers, whose fires under try pots lighted up the Pacific at night and sent a smudge and a smell over it by day. The life of the modern whaler is luxurious compared with life on a whaler in the first half of the last century. Living conditions in the stuffy forecastle were vile. Air entered only through the companionway leading down from the deck, and men lived and ate in the accumulated filth of months in an atmosphere thick with the smell of unclean bodies, sweaty clothing, greasy boots, and blubber. The food was abominable—salt meat years old, biscuits filled with maggots, and other things so repulsive that plum duff, that heavy, hard pudding of the forecastle, was looked upon as a luxury. Scurvy was a constant disease, dissipated at times when the ship managed to get some fresh meat or fruit from shore. Reynolds, that incorrigible optimist, speaks of the use of tea, coffee, and chocolate as antiscorbutics, but they did not exist in the captain's cabin on most whalers. And the whaler, working on shares, seldom came back with enough money to last him for more than a short time ashore. It was a hard, bitter life, often marked by mutiny and desertion.

But these tough men made history on the Pacific, and many an island was found and named by them—at least 400, it has been estimated. Most of these islands were located with considerable accuracy, but many were not. Whalers did not bother to take many observations. They didn't care much where they were so long as they knew they were near the whale grounds. As Reynolds says:

"When, however, we reflect on the disadvantages under which they labor; unprovided with instruments of improved construction; often computing their progress by the run of the log alone, without allowance for the influence of the currents, the force and direction of which they do not stop to investigate; it must be conceded that information they have imparted is more correct and explicit than we could reasonably anticipate."

It is probable that Reynolds underestimated their knowledge of the currents, for Maury, in his famous book on ocean currents, shows that he was constantly in touch with whaling captains because of their valuable observations. However, one can look through their logbooks page by page without finding anything but laconic remarks about the weather and whales. Take this typical extract from the log of the ship *Hopewell*, out of Warren, Rhode Island, a day to which any energetic writer could have devoted reams of paper. But the captain wasn't interested in details.

"Commences with strong breezes and a Heavy sea, with some fog at 3 saw a Whale. Lowered. The Larboard Boat struck had been fast But a short time when he stove her. the Bow Boat struck him and he ran very quick to windward without stoping at all had to cut Saw 2 more Whales But could not strike. Latter part fine weather until 11 A.M. then it began to rain at 5 A.M. saw A R (right) Whale going Quick to windward. Carpenter employed in mending the Boat. so ends."

There are several interesting things about that entry. Mr. Whale is always endowed with a capital W. He was the most important thing with which the *Hopewell* had to deal. There is no entry of latitude and longitude—indeed, they seldom bother with longitude anyway. And the stove boat is dismissed as a mere incident in the day's work. How the men got back to the ship, how badly the boat was smashed, whether anyone was hurt—all that was not worth putting down. A few days later a man fell out of the fore-topmast crosstrees, and this was worth several lines but not the smashed boat.

Sperm whales were often pugnacious creatures. They are a square headed whale, whose blubber produces the best oil. In the head is a cistern that yields barrels of pure oil and a spongy substance known as spermaceti, used in the old days for the finest candles. A sperm whale, unlike the right and other baleen whales, has teeth, and it sometimes turns on its hunters and tries either to catch the boat in its huge jaw or to smash it with its bony head. So powerful are sperm whales that there are instances of their having sunk ships.

One of the classic instances of a whale's sinking a ship is

told by Alexander Starbuck in his book on Nantucket whaling. Starbuck is a name to conjure with in anybody's Nantucket history. (Melville made it famous.) He tells of the *Essex*, of Nantucket, which was after whales on a November day in 1819 in latitude 40 south and longitude 119 west in the South Pacific:

"Whales were discovered, and all three boats were lowered in pursuit, the ship being brought to the wind, and lying with her maintop-sail hove aback waiting the issue of the contest. The mate's boat soon struck a whale, but a blow of his tail opening a bad hole in the boat, they were obliged to cut from him, and devote their entire attention to keeping afloat. By stuffing jackets in the hole, and keeping one man constantly bailing, they were enabled to check the flow of water and reach the ship in safety. In the meantime the captain's and second mate's boats had fastened to another whale, and the mate, heading the ship for them, set about overhauling the boat preparatory to lowering again. While doing this he observed a large sperm whale [In the account given by the mate, Mr. Owen Chase, the length of this whale is estimated at about eighty five feet] break water about twenty rods from the ship. After lying there for a few moments he disappeared, but immediately came up again about a ship's length off, and made directly for the vessel, going at a velocity of about three miles an hour, and the *Essex* advancing at about the same rate of speed. Scarcely had the mate ordered the boy at the helm to put it hard up, when the whale with a greatly accelerated speed struck the ship with his head just forward of the fore-chains. 'The ship,' says the mate, from whose account this is condensed, 'brought up as suddenly and violently as if she had struck a rock, and trembled for a few seconds like a leaf.' The whale passed under the vessel, scraping her keel as he went, came up on the leeward side of her, and lay on the surface of the water, apparently stunned, for about a moment; he then started suddenly off to leeward.

"Mr. Chase immediately had the pumps rigged and set going. At the time the vessel was beginning to settle at the head, and the whale, about 100 yards off, was thrashing the water violently with his tail, and opening and closing his jaws with great fury. Signals had been set for the return of the other boats, for the ship had already settled quite rapidly, and Mr. Chase had given her up as lost.

" 'I, however,' writes he, 'ordered the pumps to be kept constantly going, and endeavored to collect my thoughts for the occasion. I turned to the boats, two of which we then had with the ship, with an intention of clearing them away, and getting all things ready to embark in them, if there should be no other resource left; and while my attention was thus engaged for a moment, I was aroused with the cry of a man at the hatchway, "Here he is—he is making for us again." I turned around and saw him about 100 rods directly ahead of us, coming down apparently with twice his ordinary speed, and to me at that moment it appeared with tenfold fury and vengeance in his aspect.'

"A line of foam about a rod in width, made with his tail, which he continually thrashed from side to side, marked his oncoming. Mr. Chase hoped, by putting the helm hard up, the vessel might cross the line of the whale's approach, and the second shock be avoided, and instantly gave orders to that effect; but scarcely had the course of the ship, already somewhat waterlogged probably, been changed a single point, when the head of the whale crashed into her bows, staving them completely in directly under the cathead. The speed of the whale at this time was about six miles an hour, the *Essex* moving at about one half of that rate. After the second assault the whale passed under the ship as before, and out of sight to the leeward.

"Whatever was to be done now, must be done with the utmost dispatch. They were in mid-ocean, more than a thousand miles from the nearest land, their ship rapidly settling beneath them, and nothing to save them but frail open boats, each of which must of necessity be heavily loaded. The lashings of the spare boat were cut, and she was carried from the quarter-deck to the waist; two quadrants, two practical navigators, and the captain's and mate's trunks had been hurriedly secured from below by the steward; and the mate had saved the binnacle compasses. Then, as the ship fell over on her beam-end, the boat, into which these articles had been placed, was launched. No more than two minutes had elapsed since the whale had first attacked the ship, and now she lay full of water, her deck scarcely above the surface of the waves, and her crew abroad on the ocean. As the captain and second mate came up in their boats, their amazement and horror on seeing the condition of their late home cannot be described. By order of Captain Pollard the masters were cut away and the decks were scuttled, and about 600 pounds of bread, some 200 gallons of water, a musket and a small cannister of powder, two files, two rasps, two pounds of boat nails, and some turtle were secured. Each boat was fitted with two masts, and a flying-jib and two sprit-sails constructed for each out of the lighter canvas of the ship. The boats were also strengthened and built up about six inches above the gunwales as an additional measure for safety. These preparations occupied the larger portion of three days. The ship was now rapidly breaking up, and the captain called a council of the officers to determine what should be done. By an observation taken at noon on the 22nd of November they found they were in latitude 0° 13′ North, longitude 120′ West. The nearest land was the Marquesas Islands, next to them the Society Islands, but at this time the Pacific was but little explored, and these islands were presumably inhabited by savages than whom the very elements were more kind and hospitable. The final conclusion then was to make for the coast of Chili or Peru. The men were accordingly apportioned among the boats; the mate's boat being the weakest, having been stove several times and being old and patched, was assigned six, while the other two carried seven each."

They then started off on a long and sad voyage. Part of the bread was damaged by water, the boats were battered by the sea, and Captain Pollard's boat was nearly wrecked by "some kind of a fish." They landed on Dec. 20 at Ducie Island and left three men there who did not want to go any farther. Then they started on the 2,500 mile trip to Juan Fernandez Island, the island made famous by Robinson Crusoe. On Jan. 10, the second mate, Matthew P. Joy, died and was buried, if tossing him overboard can be accounted a burial. On Jan. 12, the boats were separated. The second man in the mate's crew to die was eaten. The three survivors of the crew of that boat were picked up by the English brig, *Indian*, Captain William Crozier, on Feb. 17. The Captain's and second mate's boats kept together until Jan. 29, 1820. Four men died in the two boats and were eaten. The men drew lots in the captain's boat to see who would be killed for food. On Feb. 23, three months after the ship sank, Captain Pollard and Charles Ramsdell were picked up by the ship *Dauphin* of Nantucket, Captain Zimri Coffin. The third boat was never heard from.

A grim story but not an unusual one in the Pacific whaling trade. There was seldom a more hazardous occupation or one in which the men were more poorly rewarded. But they made history.

Wilkes: America's Captain Cook

IT IS strange that the name of Lieutenant Charles Wilkes, who retired from the navy, after a stormy career, with the rank of rear admiral, is not better known to his countrymen. There may be a few who know that during the Civil War he nearly caused Great Britain to side actively with the Confederacy because of his precipitate action in removing the Confederate commissioners Slidell and Mason from a ship near Bermuda while they were on their way to England. The Union government apologized, and the commissioners were released.

But that startling episode was the least of the accomplishments of this impetuous man. From 1838 to 1842 he led the first exploring expedition by sea ever sent out by the United States government, was one of the first to sight the Antarctic continent—which also became a matter of controversy—and the tracks of his ships across the Pacific covered so much area that they look like a cobweb. As a matter of fact, in miles traveled by his various ships and islands visited, the voyages of Wilkes in the Pacific possibly equal Cook's. He had the same passion for detail, the same scientific enthusiasm, the same technical training, and he brought back a mass of information, much of it corroboratory and much of it new and original discovery. The instructions to his officers as to what they should observe during the day at sea and on shore, his insistence on recording the most minute matters that might aid any branch of science and navigation are sufficient evidence of the thoroughness with which he prosecuted his task. Wilkes had many faults, but lack of vigor and constant application to the work entrusted to him were not among them. Yet who knows about him in this day when exploration is so popular as almost to have become a racket?

Wilkes put out with his squadron of six ships on Aug. 18, 1838, from Norfolk. His flagship was the *Vincennes*, a sloop-of-war of 780 tons. Originally she was single-decked, but for the cruise a light deck had been built, making her a sort of frigate. His second ship was the *Peacock*, 650 tons, which, although built in 1828, was a most unsatisfactory vessel. Her upper works were rotten, her spars not too strong. And her survival until wrecked on the bar off the mouth of the Columbia River was due to good luck and the skill of her commander, Lieutenant William L. Hudson, who slightly ranked Wilkes and was with difficulty persuaded to make the voyage for this reason. He justified his selection. Then there were the *Porpoise*, a brig of 230 tons, not too well suited, because of her accommodations, for the trip, the slow supply ship *Relief*, eventually sent home, and two pilot boats, the *Sea Gull*, of 110 tons, and the *Flying Fish*, of 96 tons. They were far from being perfectly outfitted, for although Congress had authorized enough money for every possible need, mismanagement and jealousies among naval officers who had charge of maintenance and supplies led to serious defects. The pumps of the *Peacock* were so badly rusted and rotten that they were practically useless until repaired in South America. But, despite all these defects, Wilkes determined to put out to sea and disappear from the derisive grins of those who had watched and commented on the stupidity and slowness with which the squadron had been organized before he took command. That he was not too sanguine as to the result is obvious in the first pages of his journal, where he remarks on the first day out:

"I shall never forget the impressions that crowded on me during that day in the hours of (divine) service. It required all the hope I could muster to outweigh the intense feeling of responsibility that hung over me. I may compare it to that of one doomed to destruction. We were admonished in the discourse to repose confidence in the aid and protection of Him whom all hands had been called to worship, and the admonition was well calculated to do us good."

But, although many slighting remarks have been made about the equipment and condition of the vessels, particularly by explorers of other nations, the squadron, with the exception of the *Peacock*, was composed of sound ships. Commentators have referred to it as entirely worm eaten and unseaworthy, but such was not the case. The ships could never have made their remarkable journeys if that had been true. But it is due to Wilkes and Hudson and some of his energetic and enthusiastic lieutenants that they succeeded in weathering their difficulties.

With their voyage in the Atlantic and to the Antarctic we are not now concerned. By the time they had reached the west coast of South America they knew the qualities of their ships and had made many repairs. The *Sea Gull* was lost in May, somewhere in the Antarctic; how is not known, but she may have rammed an iceberg. No trace of her was ever found. On his way up the South American coast, in Chile and Peru, Wilkes shows that avid attention to details that marked Cook's work. Everything he could learn about the countries he visited, their form of government, their army and navy, the habits and customs of the people, he noted. One gets a good picture of Latin America of those days from his journal.

It was on this expedition that the custom was inaugurated, since common among many American explorers, particularly Peary, who discovered the North Pole, of having every officer in the party make voluminous notes and then turn them over to the head of the expedition. This was done by Wilkes, as by other explorers before him, because it was a government expedition, and whatever of value was observed was deemed to be of benefit for the United States, inasmuch as the expedition was intended largely to aid in the whale fishery and to chart islands and shoals and currents for the benefit of American skippers. Since that time it has been done to protect the leader of an expedition against articles or books that might compete with, or dispute, his own account; or to protect his source of income. Both motives are undoubtedly praiseworthy, but Wilkes's objective appears more laudable. He was, after all, an active member of the naval service and therefore subject to military orders.

It was while at Callao, Peru, that the first of those incidents that led to his court-martial took place. Stores were discharged from the *Relief* at another port, and the marines placed on guard over the spirit room, with six men detailed to move whiskey, bestowed more of it on themselves than was necessary. They all got drunk, and the entire crew of the *Relief* went on a riotous spree. Wilkes did not want to take time to court-martial, and to let the matter pass, as he says, with merely twelve lashes, would have been to mitigate the offense. Those were the days when flogging was still common in the navy. So he gave each of the offenders twenty-four lashes, except the two ringleaders, who got thirty-six and forty-one. Wilkes mentions that he did this merely to preserve discipline and that it was for the good of the service and adds:

"I should not have mentioned this statement, had it not been that this was the sole charge, out of eleven, spread out into thirty-six specifications, on which a court of thirteen members, after an investigation of three weeks, could find that I had transgressed the laws of the navy in the smallest degree."

Wilkes determined first to visit the islands of the Tuamotu group, because the famous Russian admiral and explorer Krusenstern had recommended that much good work could be done there. From Callao he headed for one of the most eastern of the group, and some idea of his precision and his thoroughness may be obtained from a short statement of his own.

"I deemed this to be the most interesting point at which to begin our surveys, and the researches of our naturalists, particularly as it was inhabited, and would thus enable us to trace the inhabitants from one end of Polynesia to the other, across the Pacific. At the same time, it afforded a very desirable point for magnetic observations, and a visit to it would also enable me to settle a dispute between the two distinguished English and French navigators, Captains Beechey and Duperrey relative to its geographical position.

"On the 14th we found the current setting to the northwest-by-west three quarters of a mile per hour.

"The 15th, at one hundred and twenty miles from the land, we had changed the temperature of the surface water to 67° being a difference of 7°. At three hundred fathoms depth, it was found to be 51°. This day the current was found setting south-half-east, half a mile per hour."

It was in this way that records were kept.

Wilkes's examination of the natives, or the observation made by those under his command, was far more careful than was usual in those days. Not only did he note their appearance, their customs, religion, resources, temperament, and manner of living, but his assistants measured their heads. His expedition was one of the first, if not the first, to carry out such a program in the Pacific, and it has since been found that this is the most accurate way of tracing the migration of races and

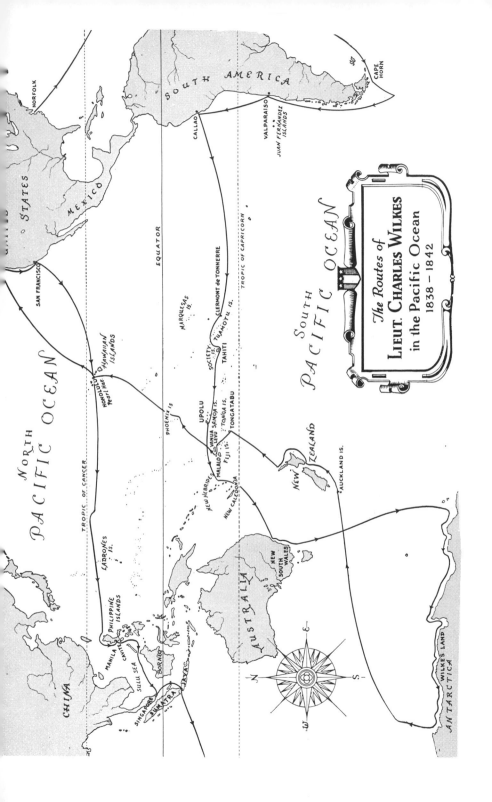

The Routes of
LIEUT. CHARLES WILKES
in the Pacific Ocean
1838 - 1842

tribes from island to island. And his observations on the temperatures and currents produced the first fairly accurate map of the Pacific Ocean movements from the Japanese coast to California, from the Aleutians to the Antarctic. It must be remembered that one of his principal objects was to learn everything possible for the benefit of the whalers, an industry then one of the most flourishing in the country, for the sails of whalers, in his own words, then whitened the waters of the Pacific.

It can be imagined with what interest the crews of the exploring ships came upon the tiny atoll of Clermont de Tonnerre in the Tuamotus on Aug. 13 at five o'clock on a sunny afternoon. The palm trees first rose up out of the water and then sank again like the masts of a fleet, and, as the vessels drew nearer, they could see the white beach rising out of the ocean, the surf breaking on the reefs, and the smooth lagoon of a deep blue color. It was their first coral island.

But the natives had a far different aspect than the smiling hospitality of their home. Some of them were apparently cannibals. They brandished spears and yelled defiance from the beach and the bushes, and all they said to the interpreter was, "Go to your own land; this belongs to us, and we do not want to have anything to do with you." The interpreter, a native of New Zealand, was annoyed that the islanders received the gifts thrown to them without even returning thanks and brandished a boat hook to such effect that his " . . . animated attitudes and gestures were the admiration of us all." They were not received so fiercely at all islands, however. At one, the natives laughingly offered an explanation of the white man's coming: " . . . as they lived on an island without women, they had come for some." Wilkes comments laconically that no answer was made to that. One island in the group had apparently never been inhabited, and the sharks around it were so ravenous that they bit at the oars. There were armies of pirate crabs and quantities of snakes and eels and spiders. They were glad to leave that island. It was also on one of the Tuamotu islands that the natives saluted by raising their arms with the palm of the hand outward, a purely North American Indian, Roman, and Nordic gesture, of course, although neither Mussolini nor Hitler had yet been born.

When Wilkes reached Tahiti he didn't think much of the beautiful outlines of the island that had been praised by so many other mariners. But he did discover that washing clothes was the prerogative of the queens and chiefs and only avoided having his clothes washed by the queen because she was *enceinte*.

Wilkes comes stoutly to the defense of the Tahitians on the subject of licentiousness and gives the women a better standing than women in other, more civilized communities. He is also one of the rare defenders as well as critics of the early missionaries. The missionaries had done some good, but he sagely argues that if they had spent less time in teaching the Scriptures and more in helping the Tahitians to employ their idle time, there would have been less licentiousness. The women, for instance, had an industry of weaving tapa cloth, but when the missionaries persuaded them that long cotton dresses (Mother Hubbards, they were called in Hawaii) were desirable, the women then had time for other interests and found means of obtaining the foreign cloth that they had been taught was valuable. Neither had the missionaries taught the men the art of agriculture, so as to provide them with more supplies, although agriculture is rather a bore on a tropical island where food is to be had on every other tree. Nor did the missionaries have a physician, although many diseases, including venereal, had been introduced by the whites, and it should have been the duty of those seeking the native's salvation to provide medical aid.

He was also shocked to find that in the schools for the children of missionaries and other whites the children of white fathers and native mothers were excluded, thus bringing about a feeling of superiority among the very people they wished to wean to their own principles of ethical, if not religious, democracy. Altogether, Lieutenant Wilkes's observations on Tahiti, although not particularly valuable otherwise, show him to be a man of tolerance and good judgment.

Since Wilkes's instructions from the Navy Department were to protect the rights of American seamen and to uphold the dignity of the flag, he had to constitute himself a sort of roving Pacific policeman. Indeed, one cannot help comparing the duties of his expedition with those of the Northwest Mounted Police, who try cases among the Eskimos and keep order in high latitudes where only their word is law. Wilkes had a regard for the flag that is inherent in every conscientious American naval officer. It often carried him to extremes, but he had a good example in Decatur. An unfair injury to an American sailor was to him an affront to Washington. So whenever he came upon a case of cruelty or murder, in which a citizen of the United States was the victim, he acted firmly and sometimes ruthlessly, but never with cruelty. One of those cases now confronted him.

A native named Tuvai had killed an American whaler on the island of Upolu in the Samoan group, part of which is still under the American flag. Captain Hudson had preceded him there, had heard of the crime, had arrested the murderer, and was in the midst of the trial when Wilkes arrived. Tuvai admitted he had killed the man for his clothes and knife. The chiefs defended him, saying that he was a poor man, of no account, and that, being a heathen, he did not know that murder of a white man was such a heinous offense. The chief defender, Pea, said that many offenses on natives had been committed by white men, and he wanted to know whether the Christian religion sanctioned execution. Hudson quoted the Scriptures to the natives, the old doctrine of blood for blood, which did not seem so Christian, perhaps, to the darkened heathen. They insisted that this was a new law, that in Samoa the relatives of the criminal made a present to the injured family, and made obeisance by knocking their heads on the ground. This seemed unusually cruel to the Samoans, but they finally agreed that the man must die if the white men said so. But they didn't want him executed on shore; if he must be killed, let him be taken to one of the ships and executed there. This rather put Captain Hudson in a spot; his principles were backing up on him. At this point Wilkes arrived, and he finally compromised by getting the chiefs to agree that the criminal should be transported to another island, far from his people, where he would never have the opportunity of killing another white man. And so Wilkes saved the face of everybody involved without the necessity of hanging Tuvai from a yardarm.

Then the Samoans took up some of their complaints against American whalers. Some of the latter had evaded their port charges and refused to pay for provisions. It is probable that Wilkes was somewhat embarrassed by the proceedings, for he immediately agreed to indemnify them for all losses caused by the whalers and consented to take the natives' word for the amount. The chiefs were impressed by his point of view, as Wilkes had probably been by the chiefs', and refused any indemnity. Whereupon Wilkes told them that they would be paid the port charges for the squadron; the prisoner was sent aboard a ship, and everybody was quite satisfied. There may be more amusing instances than this of the contacts between the Americans and the South Sea Islanders, but memory does not furnish them, and faintly one can imagine Lieutenant Charles Wilkes, of the United States Navy, feeling that he may not have had the best of the argument. Whalers did some very cruel things to the natives in those days.

From Samoa, Wilkes went to Australia, where he made a survey of part of New South Wales, and then continued his explorations in the Antarctic, where he discovered Wilkes

Land. After great danger and much hardship his ships found their way to New Zealand and then to the Tonga Islands. Here Wilkes acted as policeman again, for he heard of an attack on the American brig *Charles Doggett*, which had resulted in the killing of a boat's crew. Inasmuch as the mate of the *Doggett* had gone on shore, at the invitation of the natives, with medicine for a young chief, Wilkes determined to capture the ringleader, a chief named Vendovi. He was at Rewa, and when Wilkes arrived there he invited the King, Queen, and their retinue on board and then told them that they could not leave until Vendovi was captured. They were only too glad to have him removed, for he was feared and hated, and a rival, Ngarananigiou, was sent after the fugitive. Both returned the next day, and Vendovi calmly admitted causing the murder of part of the crew of the *Doggett*. In fact, he admitted holding the mate in his arms while the mate was brained with clubs. The King agreed that Vendovi should be punished, that he might be taken away, and added that he would like to go to the United States himself, since he had been well treated by Wilkes and was eager to see the country from which the ships came. But Vendovi alone was taken to New York and died there.

While Wilkes was at Somu-Somu, in the Fiji group, he heard from a group of missionaries of a cannibal feast they had been forced to witness. Inasmuch as much has been said about cannibalism and little is authoritatively known about it, this description of what was not uncommon in those days among the South Sea Islanders may be gruesomely interesting. Somu-Somu is on what is now known as the island of Vanua Levu, in the Fijis. In February, 1840, a Mr. and Mrs. Hunt and Mr. and Mrs. Lythe, missionaries, were living there, having arrived about seven months before. They heard that the king had sent for two dead men from a near-by town, but eleven men were brought in. Let Wilkes tell it:

"On the day of the feast the shutters of their houses (the missionaries houses) were closed, in order to keep out the disgusting smell that would ensue, but Mr. Hunt took his station just outside his fence, and witnessed the whole that follows. The victims were dragged along the ground with ropes around their necks, by these merciless cannibals, and laid, as a present to the king, in front of the missionaries' house, which is directly opposite the king's square, or public place of the town. The cause of the massacre was, that the people of Lauthala (a nearby town) had killed a man belonging to the king's household, who was doing some business for the King.

"The utmost order was preserved on this occasion, as at their other feasts, the people approaching the residence of the king with every mark of respect and reverence, at the beat of the drum. When human bodies are to be shared, the king himself makes a speech, as he did on this occasion. In it he presented the dead to his son, and intimated that the gods of Feejee should be propitiated, that they might have rain etc. . . . The son then rose and publicly accepted the gift, after which the herald pronounced aloud the names of the chiefs who were to have the bodies. The different chiefs take the bodies allotted to them away to be devoured.

"The chief of Lauthala was given to their principal god, whose temple is near the missionaries' house. He was cut up and cooked two or three yards from their fence, and Mr. Hunt stood in his yard and saw the operation. He was much struck with the skill and dispatch with which these practised cannibals performed their work. While it was going on, the old priest was sitting in the door of his temple giving orders, and anxiously looking for his share. All this, Mr. Hunt said, was done with the most perfect insensibility. He could not perceive the least sign of revenge on the part of those who ate them, and only one body was given to the injured party. Some of those who joined in the feast acknowledged that the people of Lauthala were their relations, and he fully believes that they cooked and ate them, because they were commanded to do so.

The coolness, Mr. Hunt further remarked, with which all this was done proved to him that there was a total want of feeling and natural affection among them.

"After all the parts but the head had been consumed, and the feast ended, the king's son knocked at the missionaries' door, (which was opened by Mr. Hunt,) and demanded why their windows were closed? Mr. Hunt told him to keep out the sight as well as the smell of the bodies that were cooking. The savage instantly rejoined, in the presence of the missionaries' wives, that if it happened again, he would knock them on the head and eat them.

"The missionaries were of the opinion that after these feasts, the chiefs become more ferocious, and are often very troublesome. . . . I know of no situation so trying as this for ladies to live in, particularly when pleasing and well-informed, as we found those at Somu-somu."

Charles Wilkes himself did not have much difficulty with the natives at that time, although he was presently to come upon his greatest personal tragedy at the small island of Malalo, on the westward side of the Fiji group. He had gone to one of the tiny islands near by to survey Malalo by triangulation and had finished his observations and was about to put off for the ship when he was told that three boats were in sight, coming down before the wind, with their flags at half-mast. He saw in them the bodies of his nephew, Midshipman Wilkes Henry, and Lieutenant Joseph A. Underwood, who had been killed by natives.

"The melancholy event," wrote Wilkes, "of which I became aware in its fullest extent by the return of the boats under Lieutenant Alden, was calculated to excite the most intense feelings that can agitate the mind of a man or of an officer. It took place just as—after weeks of intense anxiety for the safety of those under my command, exposed in open boats to the perils of the sea, and in small detachments to the insidious attacks of savages, instigated not merely by cupidity, but by the horrible instincts of cannibal appetite—I had myself closed the operations of the survey, and awaited only my junctions with the boats to be satisfied that all our perils were at an end. One of the victims was my own near relation, confided to my care by a widowed mother; I had therefore more than the ordinary degree of sorrow which the loss of promising and efficient officers must cause in the breast of every commander, to oppress me. The blood of the slain inevitably called for retribution, and the honor of our flag demanded that the outrage upon it should not remain unpunished. On the other hand, it was necessary, in order that any proceedings I should adopt should be such as would be capable of full vindication and meet the approval of the civilized world, that my action in the case should not appear to be instigated by mere vindictiveness, and should be calculated to serve, not as an incitement to retaliation upon further visitors, but as a salutary lesson, as well as to the actual perpetrators of the deed, as to the inhabitants of the whole group."

Wilkes learned that Underwood had gone on shore without sufficient arms, having left most of his muskets in the *Vincennes* against orders. A hostage had been taken into one of the landing boats. When the hostage jumped overboard a gun was fired at him, and the hostage's father, on shore, shouted that his son was killed. Underwood and Henry were on shore with some men from the ship, and in the fight that followed they both were killed. When the boats, which had been lying off shore, pushed in they found the two officers stripped of their clothes. Later they were buried on a sandy little island called Henry's Island.

Wilkes had already burned one village as punishment for theft, and he had arrested two murderers of American sailors. All the men on his ship were clamoring to go ashore and shoot up the island of Malalo, where the murder of his nephew and of Lieutenant Underwood had occurred.

Then Wilkes began preparations to even the score. There

were two towns, Sualib and Arro, at opposite sides of the island of Malalo. The first was the more important, and it was there that most of those who had taken part in the attack on the officers lived. Arro was destroyed and burned, and then the landing party went across the island, burning plantations by the way, until they reached Sualib. The village was surrounded by a ditch twelve feet wide and full of mud and water; also, there was a palisade of palm trunks united by a wickerwork fence ten feet high. Inside the palisade was another ditch. When the men outside retired into the fortress, having fired arrows, they waved their spears and shouted defiance. They had never been defeated. Wilkes notes with what dexterity the natives dodged at the flash of a gun. One had to see it to believe it. One gate was left unattacked, and, as the shore party poured volleys into the huts, the villagers streamed out, carrying their wounded. Then a rocket struck one of the thatched roofs, and the village began to burn. The natives did not do much harm with their muskets, for they put in a charge according to the size of the man they wanted to kill. A big man, a big charge of powder; a small man, not so much. The result was that their shooting was not very efficient. The bows and arrows were mostly used by the women. After an hour the whole town was burned, and men entered through the barricade with difficulty and found four bodies, " . . . among whom was that of a child, who had been seen during the conflagration, apparently deserted, and in a state of danger, from which our men would gladly have relieved it, had it been possible."

It was Wilkes's misfortune—or perhaps temperament—that he had as much fighting and punishment to deal out in the Pacific as almost all his predecessors put together. He did not seek trouble with the natives, but as a heritage from former visitors he found plenty of it. Only one man in his landing party was hit by a musket ball and only one severely wounded by an arrow.

Then occurred one of the most extraordinary scenes ever enforced in the South Seas. Peace had been offered by a woman holding a white cock in her arms, an emblem of peace, but her gift had been declined. Wilkes had learned that in the event of defeat it was usual for them to beg mercy of their enemies before the whole of the attacking party and that they never acknowledged themselves conquered unless this was done. So he sent word that the chiefs and people must come to a hill he designated and sue for pardon. The next day they came.

"The day was perfectly serene, and the island, which, but a few hours before, had been one of the loveliest spots in creation, was now entirely laid waste, disclosing the place of the massacre, the ruined town, and the devastated plantation. The eye wandered over the dreary waste to the beautiful expanse of waters beyond and around, with the loneliness of white sparkling reefs, until it rested, far in the distance, on the small green spot where we had performed the last rites to our murdered companions. A gentle breeze, which was blowing through the casuarina trees, gave out the moaning sound that is uttered by the pines of our own country, producing a feeling of depression inseparable from the occasion, and bringing vividly to my thoughts the sad impression which the melancholy and dreadful occurrence would bring upon those who were far away.

"Toward four o'clock, the sound of distant wailings was heard, which gradually grew nearer and nearer. At the same time the natives were seen passing over the hills toward us, giving an effect to the whole scene which will be long borne in my memory. They at length reached the foot of the hill, but would come no farther, until assured that their petition would be received. On receiving this assurance, they wound upward, and in a short time, about forty men appeared, crouching on their hands and knees, and occasionally stopping to make piteous moans and wailings. When within thirty feet of us, they stopped, and an old man, their leader, in the most piteous manner, begged pardon, supplicating forgiveness, and pledging that they would never do the like again to a white man. He said, that they acknowledged themselves conquered, and that the island belonged to us; that they were our slaves, and would do whatever I desired; that they had lost everything; that the two great chiefs of the island, and all their best warriors had been killed, all their provisions destroyed, and their houses burned. They acknowledged a loss of fifty-seven killed. . . .

"The above are all of the importance facts relative to this tragical affair, both to the natives and ourselves. I feel little disposed to cast blame anywhere, but it must be apparent that if the precautions directed in the orders given for the conduct of the officers on boat duty had been adhered to, this misfortune would not have occurred."

Many of Wilkes's officers, by his own account, thought that all those connected with the murders should have been put to death, and he says they were not satisfied. That is hard to believe, for it would be a rather bloodthirsty man and one who would ill fill a naval officer's uniform to ask for more punishment than Wilkes inflicted. He mentions that the people of Malalo were quite peaceful afterward, the most peaceful of all the Fiji group.

When Wilkes got home he found himself charged with murder and of acting in a cruel and merciless spirit. The crawling of the natives up the hill was cited as evidence of the latter charge. That was silly, since this was their way of acknowledging defeat. But even Wilkes admits that his action was "rather severe." It is not a pleasing picture, but, considering the position of Wilkes and what he accomplished, one cannot censure him too severely.

We do not need to dally with Wilkes much more, although some of his most famous work was done on the west coast of the United States and British Columbia. On his way there he put in at the port of Honolulu, and he remarks of Pearl Harbor, which is now the Pacific headquarters of the United States Navy, that it would hold a large fleet but that there would be little point in doing so. The Hawaiian Islands, then called Sandwich Islands (so named by Cook), were independent, and Wilkes did not think much of them.

"They have no port that is defensible against a strong naval force, and therefore their consequence will be comparatively small in a political point of view. No foreign power, in fact, could well hold them, without great expense and difficulty. . . . By these circumstances, the neutral position of this group I think is insured; and this is most desirable for its peace and happiness. . . .

"The power on which they must become dependent hereafter is that which is to be established in Oregon and California; and, adapted as they are to supply all the products of the tropics, they will become a valuable appendage to those states; but, I deem the idea entertained by many, who suppose they ever can become so powerful as to command those states, to be a mistake. So far as the consumption of a small amount of manufactures go, and the convenience of our whaling fleet, but no farther, they will be beneficial to the United States. . . . I am rather disposed to think that, in the progress of civilization in the South Seas, this group will be considered of less importance than it now appears, and instead of its being looked to as it now is, as a point of attraction, or a place wherein to obtain information and supplies, it will only be visited by whalers for recruiting. . . .

"Unfortunately for these islands, a fictitious importance has been ascribed to their geographical position, in the belief that much political ascendancy in the Pacific must accrue to the nation which may possess them; this state of opinion has been brought about by the exertions of the American missionaries, who have been the means of raising the natives so rapidly in the scale of civilization, and from whose success our countrymen have acquired much influence."

Wilkes was not quite so perspicacious as the missionaries; neither was he as good a businessman. Even in his day he found that missionaries bearing names that are now quite important in the islands were establishing plantations and businesses. He met some people named Cooke and Castle, who were zealous in their help for the natives as well as in other ways. The firm of Castle and Cooke is now better known for its shipping, banking, and agricultural interests than for its religious activities. But the odd thing about Wilkes's summary of Hawaii is that he failed so signally, as a naval officer, to estimate its strategic importance. Of course, in his day Japan was still an unknown and mysterious power, industry on the Pacific was largely in whaling, and there were no steamships. Railroads had not been built from the east coast to California, and he could hardly have foreseen the tremendous westward push of empire that was about to come in the United States. Nevertheless, giving Lieutenant Wilkes the most charitable understanding, there are few greater understatements of the future than he pins on the Hawaiian Islands. Those Hawaiians who have been clamoring for statehood and those Californians whose welfare has for years been connected with the sugar cane and pineapple fields of Hawaii will forgive Wilkes, but they may laugh heartily.

After leaving Hawaii, Wilkes set sail for the Columbia River, for little was then known about the northwest coast of North America. And there he lost another of his ships, the *Peacock*, which, as we have seen, had always been an unlucky vessel. Captain Hudson had been conducting a survey of island groups not touched by the *Vincennes* and was hurrying to rejoin Wilkes three months after he was due. The bar at the mouth of the Columbia River is one of the most dangerous on the coast. The strong current sweeping out and the heavy seas rolling in create a tremendous breaking surf, through which, in Wilkes's day, there was no definitely known channel. Hudson had some sketchy bearings for entering the river and decided to trust to them, and it is typical of Wilkes that he supports Hudson's judgment in attempting a passage through the bar when the weather was as favorable as could be hoped for and when speed in rejoining the expedition to aid in surveys on shore was essential.

But the *Peacock* struck and immediately started to pound heavily. The sea began to make up under a freshening wind, and in a short time the ship was smothered in breakers. It was impossible then to put a boat over, the cutter already having been smashed against the side while sounding. The light spars were sent down, and the shot hove overboard, and the ship was finally brought around with her head to the sea. As night came on, those on board had little hope that the ship would hold together until morning, but by some miracle she did, and after dawn the sea went down. A large canoe with some Indians in it came out to give what aid they could, and the boats were hoisted out and filled with as many men as seemed safe, the ship's charts, books, and papers being taken on the first trip.

On the second trip all the men except Captain Hudson, Lieutenant Walker, the boatswain, the carpenter, and thirty men went ashore. During the day the waves broke completely over the ship, and finally the masts were cut away, leaving nothing but a battered hulk pounding on the reef. It was impossible for those on shore to make another trip out to the ship, one boat being thrown end over end in an attempt. Hudson finally signaled to those on shore to recall the boats and to wait for a more favorable opportunity, although it did not seem possible that the ship would last long. It was not until late in the afternoon, after a day of intense anxiety, that boats managed to reach the ship and take off the remaining men, Captain Hudson being the last to leave. The next day there was nothing to be seen of the *Peacock* except the cap of her bowsprit, her timbers being strewn for miles along the coast.

But Wilkes was thankful to get his men back and purchased a brig to replace the *Peacock*. With his surveys along the coast we are not concerned, for many of them were overland, but he made the most thorough examination of the northwest coast conducted up to his time, continuing his careful observations of the natives and the resources of the country. His survey of the Columbia River, overlooked by Vancouver, was as complete as possible in the time at his disposal. And finally, after charting San Francisco Bay, he made sail for Honolulu again and went from there to the Philippines, little knowing that one day a fellow countryman and a naval officer would fight a famous naval battle under the guns of Cavite and that Manila would some day fly the American flag. He looked over the Sulu Sea, as he calls it, rather thoroughly and then put up his helm for Singapore, the Cape of Good Hope, and home, having been gone four years, a long voyage, even in whaling days.

And so we leave Charles Wilkes, our little known Captain Cook, whose expedition probably surveyed more islands in the Pacific than any other and who did an outstanding piece of work on the northwest coast. Only one tiny island in the Pacific bears his name. There may be two reasons for this. The expedition was long in getting under way, and the preparations were remarkably muddled. And when Wilkes, selected because of his energy, although a junior officer, was put in charge of it, the whole affair had become an object of ridicule. He had difficulties with some of his officers, as was natural on so protracted and dangerous a voyage, lost two of his ships, and on his return was court-martialed and was subjected to what he mildly terms "persecution." Certainly no able commander of a fruitful expedition was ever welcomed home with more ingratitude. Perhaps his own temperament may have been somewhat to blame. It appears, even from his own narrative, that he was a rigid disciplinarian and at the same time an impetuous and fiery spirit. He could not tolerate sluggishness or stupidity in the execution of his orders. But at the same time he seems to have been just and to have attempted to be impartial and even conciliatory and forgiving at times if the circumstances seemed so to dictate.

Sailing with Wilkes was no picnic; the dangerous waters into which he penetrated and his own stubborn insistence on carrying on in the face of possible disaster in order to fulfill his orders must have at times bred uneasiness, disquiet, and even criticism among his subordinates. However, that is something that the wise commander of such an expedition must always expect. Apparently Wilkes did understand and, after the expedition was over, forgave. Obviously, during a long voyage, he could not compromise on naval vessels with anything that might impair his authority. That he was acquitted on his court-martial and censured only slightly because of one act of punishment against treacherous natives is a fair indication of how unjust most of the charges against him were.

The other probable cause of Wilkes's obscurity, except to those particularly interested in the subject, is that his expedition was gone for nearly five years at a time when this country was pushing westward, when discoveries on the continent were leading those on the eastern seaboard to realize what an amazing country the United States was to be, when California was in the people's minds, although seemingly as far away as Japan, and when the whole forces of empire were expanding. Gold was about to be discovered in California, the slavery question was on everybody's lips, and twenty years after his return Wilkes was actively engaged in the Civil War. All these momentous happenings and the tension of the times served to minimize Wilkes's discoveries despite the controversy immediately following his return. But it is high time that somebody wrote his biography, for he should go down in our history as one who would probably have delighted the heart of Cook himself. He was an honest and meticulous explorer who defied storm, ice, disagreement, and even opposition, in trying to do what his government had ordered him to do.

The Opening of the Japanese Door

THERE have been few events more important to the modern world than the opening of Japan's ports to Western commerce in 1854, only eighty-six years ago. In such a short period of time, formerly insulated and isolated people have adopted with amazing rapidity the customs and machines of the Western world, have become a world power, and now not only compete with Europe and America commercially but are attempting to dominate eastern Asia and make themselves a force that must be reckoned with in all international affairs. This result was brought about by the United States, through Commodore M. C. Perry, but, although many know that Commodore Perry broke down the barriers of Japanese reserve, few know the story of his efforts or how illuminating a light they throw upon present conditions in the Pacific and Asia. The same difficulties that Perry met with in 1853 and 1854 exist today, and anyone who studies his attempts to cultivate the Japanese will find an astonishing parallel between his negotiations and those that have made relations difficult in recent years between the United States and Japan. The Nipponese mentality and psychology have not changed, and neither have those of the United States.

Perhaps, if Commodore Perry were alive today, he might wonder whether he had contributed so much to the peace and amity of nations as he had intended when he set sail. The qualities of inquisitiveness, adaptability, shrewdness, and hauteur that he immediately recognized in this island nation he would recognize in their descendants. The difficulties that our State Department have had with Japan would meet with an instant understanding. The able Commodore would wonder whether it had been worth while and whether it would not have been better to have left the wily Japanese to their self-imposed isolation. But, being a Yankee trader at heart and having as much desire for commercial gain to his own country as might be possible from a treaty with Japan, he might also shrug his shoulders and ask, "How could I have known?"

The conduct of Japan in her early relations with the outside world was so similar to her conduct in recent years that one cannot read the record without amazement. And the fault was not entirely on Japan's side. The Japanese were early taught to distrust Westerners, and that they still do, only eighty-some years later, is to be expected. Their early adventures in amity were not such as to excite their admiration or respect. And the memory of some of those events is still in the Japanese mind and may go far to explain why they react as they do at present. They are a proud if not arrogant people who inhabit a land that is as beautiful as any in the world. They have a culture that is ages old and a continuity of rule that no other country in the world can equal. They are artistic and have been civilized for centuries. They have never been conquered, and the only two attempts to lick them, those by Kubla Khan and, much later, by Russia, were decisively repulsed. Until they tackled

China, that old, old country, older than their own, which has absorbed so many conquerors, they thought they were invincible. They yield to only one form of persuasion, as Perry quickly perceived, that of force. They are hospitable, courteous to a fault, suspicious, and they believe that they are the chosen ones of the earth. And most of their fortunes as well as their misfortunes spring from these traits.

It was Marco Polo, that almost mythical adventurer, who first made known the existence of Japan. When he returned to Venice from his service under the Khan, he told of a great island off the coast of Cathay, known as Zipangu. It was this Zipangu that Columbus sought, and when he reached the West Indies he thought he had found it, not knowing that he had discovered another continent that made Zipangu seem tiny indeed and that was later to hold a people who did not find the people of Zipangu particularly easy to negotiate with but who did open it to the world.

However, it was the Portuguese who, first of all Europeans, set foot in Japan. Ferdinand Mendez Pinto, one of the great Portuguese navigators who built that country's remarkable power in the Atlantic and the Far East, arrived in Japan in either 1543 or 1545. The Japanese and Portuguese annals differ as to the date, but they are strikingly similar in content. Pinto was received with open arms, and, since the Japanese had not then acquired their suspicion of Occidentals, he and his men were permitted to go where they pleased and to trade freely. Arrangements were made to send a ship every year from Macao, the Portuguese settlement near Canton, or from Goa, in Malabar, to Japan for goods. But in 1549 the Portuguese, through a Japanese who had fled from his country to Goa and been converted to the Catholic faith, were persuaded not only that they would find trading profitable but that the Jesuit missionaries would find many converts. The first missionaries, headed by Francis Xavier, were all that such men should be, courageous, kind, understanding, and benevolent souls. But their successors were not. They proved arrogant, selfish, greedy, and incapable of inspiring respect. What is more, they apparently tried through their converts to stir up a revolt against the throne, a form of treason that is perhaps more abhorrent in Japan than in any other country on earth, for the Emperor is believed to be the lineal Son of Heaven, divine as well as secular ruler. That ended the Portuguese influence, and the missionaries were thrown out in 1637. The first contact with Europeans, who had been received with all friendliness, was disillusioning to the Japanese and has probably affected their attitude to the present time.

But before the Portuguese were sent away, the Dutch arrived in April, 1600. A fleet of five ships put into Nagasaki, which had been designated the port for foreigners—the Portuguese—to trade with. The Dutch were permitted to open a trading station, and when the Portuguese were expelled the Dutch remained. But their lot was not a happy one. They were confined on the little island of Dezima in Nagasaki harbor, and every Dutch ship that arrived was made to send ashore her guns and ammunition and was also searched. They were followed by spies when they went ashore, were not permitted to visit anyone except by express permission of the governor, and were subjected to endless humiliations. It is also charged that after the Portuguese left, a Dutch ship aided the Japanese in capturing a town in which were many Christians, the converts later being exterminated. But most of the Dutch captains put to sea when they heard of what was to happen and would have no part in it. However, the part that the Dutch played in Japan was an inglorious one, and their virtual imprisonment on their island and their submission to the Japanese for 200 years did not raise Europeans in the Japanese estimation.

The English had a happy beginning of trade with Japan, for the East India Company sent out a ship under command of Captain John Saris, which arrived at Japan in June, 1613. Saris was accustomed to the ways of the East, having sailed there before and established amicable relations, but the ventures of the company did not prove profitable, and they gave up the trade before the persecution of the Christians. When they tried to establish it again thirteen years later, they found that the Portuguese attempt at treason had made friendship with the Japanese impossible. Charles II of England had married a Portuguese princess, of Braganza, and, since the Dutch, hoping to keep all other Europeans out, had told this to the Japanese, the officials of the island kingdom believed that an alliance with Portugal, even a marriage, made the English enemies. So their later effort came to nothing. If it had succeeded, the history of the Far East might have been different. The British tried to take over the Dutch settlement after their defeat of Holland and their temporary acquisition of Java, an event that is now nearly forgotten.

Then came the Russians, and, if there is anything to suggest that nations persist in their ambitions through changing regimes, it is the relationship between Russia and Japan. The Russian-Japanese war, which gave Korea to Japan, was but an interlude. The flying fields of Vladivostok still menace Tokyo, and the Russian and Japanese armies face each other in Mongolia. It is no new-founded enmity. In the official account of the Perry expedition prepared by Francis L. Hawks and endorsed by Perry as authentic, printed by resolution of the United States Senate, there is this interesting observation:

"The efforts of Russia to obtain foothold in Japan commenced in the latter part of the last century [the eighteenth]. Her possessions in Asia, her seizure and occupation of some part of the Kurile island which belonged to Japan, and her small portion of territory in America, in the colony of Sitka (Alaska had not at that time been purchased), have placed her on every side of the Japanese Empire but the south. She has pursued her policy noiselessly; possibly meaning at the proper time to make her communications as complete as circumstances will allow between her Asiatic and American possessions. With Corea, Japan, and the Aleutian Islands, stretching over to the promontory of Alaska on our northwest coast, and with a strong point at Sitka, she might be in a situation to show the world that her plans of extension were by no means confined to the limits of the eastern hemisphere. With harbors on the coast of Eastern Asia and Western America, opening on a sea which must be the seat of an immense and lucrative commerce, she might aim to be a great maritime power, and to rule mistress of the Pacific. If she possesses Japan, she would have an abundance of harbors, unrivalled in the world for excellency, and with her resources, would control the commerce of the Pacific. It is not, therefore, to the interest of any part of the commercial world that Russia should ever own Japan; but Russia has, doubtless, seen the importance to her of its acquisition. If she aims at being a commercial nation, the possession of Japan would make her eminently so."

It must be remembered that Commodore Perry authorized this statement after he had been the special ambassador of the United States to arrange a treaty with Japan and that the Americans were specific in asking if a Russian mission, which reached Japan about the same time as their own, had been successful in its efforts, which it was not. It was also written into the treaty eventually that if any nation were granted privileges greater than those afforded the United States, they would automatically be embodied in the treaty. Also, some thirty years before this, the Russians had been exploring the Pacific, going as far south as the fringe of the Antarctic. Maybe these are some of the reasons why Seward bought Alaska. But it can easily be seen how far back the antipathy between Russia and Japan existed and why it did.

When, in 1804, the Emperor Alexander made an attempt to arrange a treaty with Japan, he was kept waiting until the following year for his answer. The Japanese then reminded Russia that their suggestions had been rejected ten years before, and the Japanese Emperor significantly said on the occasion of the renewed representations: "This proves that Russia has a strong inclination for Japan." In view of all that has happened since, it would seem that the Emperor was right, but since then the Japanese have had ambitions of their own, which do not set well on the stomachs of other nations than Russia. The inaccessible kingdom of Nippon has grown a few hydra heads, under the influence of Western culture. Perry started something.

It was against this background of deception, intrigue, suspicion, hatred, and misunderstanding that Commodore Perry sailed his ships. Not a promising outlook. No wonder that he spent many months searching for everything that might be known of Japan, of its history and its connection with other nations, its people and its customs. That he finally succeeded in breaking through the wall of distrust is due to the instinctive knowledge he gained of the country before he reached it and of his indomitable perseverance after he arrived. Just as the Japanese dealings with the United States find their counterpart in the early experiences of Perry, so does this country's present policy present the same firm demand for equal rights in Asia and the respect for treaties that Perry enforced on the Japanese. That the issue should have arisen again in its present form in China is one of those coincidences in history that show how difficult it is for any nation to interpret another's feelings by its own. The Japanese were undoubtedly badly treated before Perry arrived and have probably been unfairly dealt with since; but they also have been just as reluctant to yield anything. Perry's dealings with the commissioners might be a paraphrase of what American officials have been through in China.

This long introductory to Perry's expedition is necessary to show the hostility and distrust with which he was at first received and to make more impressive his achievement. To the average person Perry's journey was one of exploration or adventure. It was nothing of the sort. He did not take any civilian scientists with him, because his purpose was not primarily scientific; it was a commercial and diplomatic adventure. (The only civilian he took to Japan was Bayard Taylor, the American poet, who met the squadron in China and overcame Perry's reluctance to have a civilian on the voyage. Taylor's descriptions of the country were of great value.) The Dutch dominated Japanese trade, the British sought it, as did Russia and France, and the United States did not wish to be left out in the cold. California had recently been annexed after the Mexican war. It was the back door to the vast territory of the growing nation. Gold had been discovered there, and the rush westward was on. The United States promised to be one of the highways between Europe and the East; railroads were about to be built across the continent. There were those in this country who said that Japan had no right to remain an isolated kingdom, that, if necessary, force must be used to open her gates to commerce. The trader spirit was much in the ascendancy. It was the same motive that drove the sealers to the Antarctic and the whalers through the innumerable islands of the Pacific and that gave impetus to the great voyage of Wilkes. Curiosity and commerce as well as national prestige sailed together.

As usual, when an American expedition left port in those days, there was incompetency and delay. As with Wilkes, ships were not properly outfitted, there were jealousies and discords, and, finally, to save the national honor, Perry put out with only one ship of his proposed squadron, the *Mississippi*, hoping that his other vessels would eventually catch up with him. Of his voyage across the Atlantic, around the Cape of Good Hope, and through the Indian Ocean to the China Sea, it is not necessary to deal. It was the usual way to voyage to the East, running with the prevailing winds. When he arrived at Hong Kong, he found the sloops-of-war *Saratoga* and *Plymouth* and the store ship *Supply*. Much to his disappointment, the *Susquehanna* had gone on to Shanghai. The visit to the island of Lew Chew or to the Bonin Islands—to the latter of which Perry decided the British had no reasonable title—may be passed over, despite their interest, for what he had come for was to visit Japan.

Perry had transferred his flag to the *Susquehanna*, and on July 7, 1853, the steamer—for she was a paddle-wheel ship—steamed, with sails furled, into the bay of Yedo, much to the astonishment of the Japanese fishermen who saw a ship moving against the wind. The *Susquehanna* anchored off Uraga, on the west side of the bay, followed by the other ships. A gun was fired from a fort and a rocket sent up, and in a short time the ships were surrounded by guard boats. Perry would not permit them to come alongside, because he had heard of their custom of immediately boarding a ship or threatening it, and he had determined to be as exclusive as the Japanese. The tow lines of the guard boats were cast off, and when their crews attempted to climb aboard they were threatened with pikes, cutlasses, and pistols. So they quit. The guardboats were beautifully built vessels, with sharp bows, broad beams, and clean lines, and moved with remarkable speed. Their crews were powerful, half naked men, most of them bare headed, with shaved crowns. One boat came alongside and showed a message to the effect that the ships weigh anchor immediately and go away. When this was ignored, an interpreter said in Dutch that the vice-governor was in the boat and would like to communicate with the commodore, although the Japanese were told he was an admiral, since that was the only high rank they understood. Perry appointed his aid, Lieutenant Contee, to receive the vice-governor, and communication with Perry, who remained in his cabin, was only through Contee. It was asked why the governor himself had not come out to the ship, and it was said that the governor was forbidden by law to visit ships in the roadway. And Hawks continues:

"It was directed that the dignitary should be informed that the Commodore, who had been sent by his country on a friendly mission to Japan, had brought a letter from the President of the United States, addressed to the Emperor, and that he wished a suitable officer might be sent on board the ship to receive a copy of the same, in order that a day might be appointed for the Commodore formally to deliver the original. To this he replied that Nagasaki was the only place, according to the laws of Japan, for negotiating foreign business, and it would be necessary for the squadron to go there. In answer to this he was told that the Commodore had come purposely to Uraga because it was near to Yedo (Tokyo), and that he *should not go to Nagasaki;* that he expected the letter to be duly and properly received where he then was; that his intentions were perfectly friendly, but that he would allow of no indignity; and would not permit the guardboats which were collecting around the ships to remain where they were, and that if they were not immediately removed, the Commodore declared that he would disperse them by force. When this was interpreted to him, the functionary suddenly left his seat, went to the gangway, and gave an order which caused most of the boats to return to the shore; but a few of them still remaining in clusters, an armed boat was sent from the ship to warn them away by gestures, and at the same time to show their arms; this had the desired effect, as all of them disappeared, and nothing more was seen of them near the ships during the stay of the squadron. 'This,' said the Commodore, 'was the first important point gained.' The vice-governor shortly afterward took his leave, saying as he departed, that he had no authority to promise anything respecting the reception of the President's letter, but in the morning an officer of higher rank would come from the city, who might probably furnish some further information.

"The policy of the Commodore, it will be seen, was to assume a resolute attitude toward the Japanese government. He had determined, before reaching the coast, to carry out strictly this course in all his official relations, as he believed it the best to ensure a successful issue to the delicate mission with which he had been charged. He was resolved to adopt a course entirely contrary to that of all others who had hitherto visited Japan on a similar errand—to demand as a right, and not to solicit as a favor, those acts of courtesy which are due from one civilized nation to another; to allow of none of those petty annoyances which had been unsparingly visited upon those who had preceded him, and to disregard the acts as well as the threats of the authorities, if they in the least conflicted with his own sense of what was due to the dignity of the American flag.

"The question of landing by force was left to be decided by the development of succeeding events; it was, of course, the very last measure to be resorted to, and the last that was desired; but in order to be prepared for the worst the Commodore caused the ships constantly to be kept in perfect readiness, and the crews to be drilled as thoroughly as they are in time of active war. He was prepared, also, to meet the Japanese on their own ground, and exhibit toward them a little of their own exclusive policy; if they stood on their dignity and assumed superiority, that was a game at which he could play as well as they. It was well to let them know that other people had dignity also, which they knew how to protect, and that they did not acknowledge the Japanese to be their superiors. Hence he forbade the admission of a single Japanese on board any of the ships, except those officers who might have business with him; and the visits even of such were to be confined to the flagship, to which they were admitted only on the declaration of their rank and business. The Commodore, also, was well aware that the more exclusive he should make himself, and the more unyielding he might be in adhering to his declared intentions, the more respect these people of forms and ceremonies would be disposed to award him; therefore it was that he deliberately resolved to confer personally with no one but a functionary of the highest rank in the empire. He would have been ashamed, in the indulgence of a contemptible pride founded on mere official rank, to assume a superiority, and effect a dignity, too lofty to stoop to the level of men below him in station. As a man, he did not deem himself too elevated to hold communication with any of his brethren in the common heritage of humanity; but in Japan, as the representative of his country, and the accredited guardian of the honor of that flag which floated over him, he felt that it was well to teach the Japanese, in the mode most intelligible to them, by stately and dignified reserve, joined to perfect equity in all he asked or did, to respect the country from which he came, and to suspend for a time their accustomed arrogance and incivility toward strangers. The Japanese so well understood him that they learned the lesson at once. It was this feeling, and this only, which prompted him to refuse to see the vice-governor of Uraga, and to refer him to his aid for conference. He saw him often enough afterward, when matters had been arranged between the governments, on terms of friendship and equality. And we have been thus particular, not for the information of our countrymen, who know Commodore Perry, but for strangers who may read our story, and, without this word of explanation, misapprehend the character of the man. No man is more easily approachable by his fellow-men, or assumes less on account of the honorable position he fills in the service of his country."

Despite the stilted style of Mr. Hawks's explanation, it does serve to show the manner in which Perry approached his problem. Admiral Yarnell, recently in command of the China Squadron, who had to combat Japanese demands at the outbreak of the undeclared war in China, and Commander

Hughes, of the *Panay*, whose gunboat was bombed and sunk in the Yangtse, maintained that same unalterable position in defence of American rights that Perry had maintained in all his dealings with the Japanese leading up to the signing of the treaty. Hughes, however, did not fare so well as Perry, and he very nearly lost his life. The Japanese have a better armament now than they had in Perry's time.

The first night in Yedo Bay was to be remembered by those on the ships. The presence of these strange vessels in waters that were inviolate caused the liveliest consternation on shore. Beacon fires burned on the hills, and the tolling of a big bell lasted nearly all the night. A few boats lingered far from the ships but kept an anxious eye on them, although there was no attempt at interference. When the nine o'clock gun was fired from the flagship it caused quite a commotion on shore. Many of the fires were quickly extinguished. A stranger situation could hardly be imagined. The ships, many thousands of miles from home, were anchored off the shore of a country whose people were suspicious and hostile. That they were a warlike and brave race was well known, and their antipathy to foreign intrusion almost fanatic. So the guns were ready, the muskets stacked, and grapeshot and ball piled high. But the night went by peacefully.

Early the next morning the Governor, Keyamon Yezaimen, came out to the ship, richly attired in an embroidered silk robe, with borders of gold and silver. His presence flatly contradicted the statement of the vice-governor that the governor was forbidden by law to visit ships. The Governor told the Commodore's aids that it was impossible to receive the President's letter at Uraga and that even if that could be accomplished the answer must go to Nagasaki. He was told that such an arrangement would not be considered and that if the Japanese government did not appoint a proper person to receive the letters the Commodore would go on shore with a sufficient force and deliver them in person, "be the consequences what they might." So the Governor said he would send word to Yedo and ask for instructions but that it would take four days to obtain a reply. Since Yedo was only a few miles away, the Governor was informed that the Commodore would wait only three days. The Governor also protested against boats that were out surveying, on the ground that to do so was against Japanese laws and was told, perhaps a little high handedly, since the waters were Japanese, that the Americans had to obey American law, just as he, the Governor, had to obey Japanese law, and that the surveys would go on. So this point was also gained. The policy of firmness was bringing results. The Governor was also asked to use the same terms in speaking of the President of the United States as in speaking of the Emperor of Japan, which he afterwards did.

"It was found," says Hawks, "that by a diligent attention to the minutest and apparently most insignificant details of word and action, the desired impression was made on Japanese diplomacy; which, as a smooth surface requires one equally smooth to touch it at every point, can only be fully reached and met by the nicest adjustment of the most polished formality."

When a survey boat approached the shore at Uraga, a boat filled with soldiers put off to intercept it, and the officer in command had the crew rest on their oars and fix the caps on their carbines. They were then left alone. The next day which was Sunday, July 10, a number of Japanese, apparently of high rank, went alongside the flagship and requested permission to board her. When they said they had no business with the Commodore but merely wished to talk, they were politely told that by the Commodore's orders they could not be received. The next day the survey boats were sent higher up the bay, and the steamship *Mississippi* was ordered to accompany them. The purpose was to stimulate the authorities to action, and apparently it succeeded, for the Governor came aboard and said that probably the letters would be received on the next day and forwarded to Yedo. So the Governor was informed that if the matter was not arranged during the present visit the Commodore would return with a larger squadron next spring and that in the meantime he wanted to get as near Yedo as possible so as to find a safe anchorage. Perry was being a bit rough, but successfully so.

When the day for an answer arrived, July 12, the Governor came aboard again and said that a special building would be erected on shore in which to receive the Commodore and that a high personage appointed by the Emperor would be there to receive the letters from the President. But, he added, no answer could be given in the bay of Yedo; the Commodore would have to go to Nagasaki to receive the answer through the Dutch or Chinese superintendent. Aware of the lack of respect—contempt, Hawks calls it—in which the Japanese held the Dutch and the Chinese, Perry again replied that he would not go to Nagasaki and would receive no communication through the Dutch or Chinese. The Commodore's exact message was:

"He [the Commodore] has a letter from the President of the United States to deliver to the Emperor of Japan, or to his secretary of foreign affairs, and he will deliver the original to none other:—if this friendly letter of the President to the Emperor is not received and duly replied to, he will consider his country insulted, and will not hold himself accountable for the consequences."

That afternoon the Governor returned, and it was arranged that both the original and the copies of the letter would be transmitted at the same time, that they would be delivered to a representative of the Emperor, properly accredited, but that the representative of the Emperor would not be able to speak because Nagasaki and not Uraga was the proper place to receive communications from foreign governments. It was also stated that Commodore Perry would not wait to receive the Emperor's answer, since he suspected he might be kept waiting such a long time that it would be embarrassing but that he would return in a few months. Then the Governor and his interpreters had a few drinks of whisky and brandy, which they greatly relished, particularly when mixed with sugar, and had a very good time. The American officers, despite their annoyance at the petty hindrances put in their way, hindrances that are easily understood in view of Japan's former contact with the outside world, constantly commented on the courtesy and good breeding as well as education of their guests.

Despite the fact that Japan was an isolated kingdom, these Japanese officials understood Dutch and Chinese and knew much of the world. When shown the United States on a globe, they immediately pointed out Washington and New York and seemed equally familiar with kingdoms in Europe. They asked about American railroads, and, when they examined the ship's engine, showed by their comments that they had some understanding of its principles. They also wanted to know about the canal across the Isthmus of Panama, referring to the railroad then being built, since they had seen a canal but not a railroad.

On July 13 the Governor again came aboard bearing a message from the Emperor to Toda, Prince of Idzu, commanding him to receive the President's letter. To it was attached the Imperial seal, and it was treated with such reverence that the governor would permit no one to touch it. The next day the whole squadron moved down the bay nearer the building where the letters were to be delivered. The shore was gay with banners and screens of cloth bearing the Emperor's arms. On the beach were regiments of soldiers, and in the distance could be seen cavalry. The boats, bearing all the officers and sailors who could be released from the ships, started for the shore, and, when they were halfway, thirteen guns from the *Susquehanna* announced the departure of the Commodore.

Nearly 300 sailors and marines landed, with two bands, and drew up in lines along the shore. The officers formed a line on either side of the landing place, and as Commodore Perry stepped ashore they fell into place behind him. It was a most punctilious affair.

In the building, at one end, were Toda, Prince of Idzu, and Ido, Prince of Iwami, richly dressed and impassively silent and dignified. They rose from their seats when Commodore Perry entered, made a formal bow, and sat down again. A scarlet box at the upper end of the room had been prepared to receive the President's letter and the letter from the Commodore. Two page boys brought up the boxes containing the letters, followed by two big Negro members of the crew. At the scarlet box the Negroes took the letters from the boys, displayed the writing and seals, and then put them on the lid of the Japanese box. Not a word was said by anyone. Then the Governor of Uraga and his aide went up to the Prince of Iwami, and, prostrating themselves, received from him a roll of papers. This the Governor took to Commodore Perry, falling on his knees as he delivered it. It was the Imperial receipt for the letters. The receipt mentioned that the letters had been received at Uraga at the request of the Commodore but "in opposition to Japanese law," which was quite a concession. Then the Commodore rose, and the princes rose and remained standing until he left. Neither of them had said a word.

The ships later went up the bay a bit farther, despite the protests of the Japanese, and some of those in the surveying boats became so friendly with Japanese officials on government boats that they paid each other visits and smoked a few pipes of peace together before other government officers called off their own people. But the Americans were very favorably impressed with the kindliness and good nature of the Japanese. These two qualities, natural friendliness and official suspicion, were continually cropping up together.

Perry's first visit of eight days prepared the way for the treaty to be signed later. In the message to the Emperor, President Millard Fillmore pointed out that the progress of steam navigation was such that the two countries were being brought closer together and that they had many valuable things that might be exchanged to their mutual benefit. He asked that if the Emperor did not think it safe to abrogate the ancient laws against foreign trade, he try the experiment for five years. He also asked that whalers who might be wrecked upon the Japanese coast be treated with kindness and hospitality and returned as soon as possible to ships of their own country, for they had often been imprisoned and treated with cruelty. He also requested that a coaling port be set aside for American steamships.

When presents had been exchanged between the Governor and his officials and the Commodore's aides, care being taken that every Japanese gift be met by one of at least equivalent value, the ships sailed for Lew Chew and then for Hong Kong.

Before Commander Perry sailed back for Yedo early in 1854 he heard that the Emperor of Japan had died and was also told by the Governor General of the Netherlands East Indies that the Japanese had asked him to inform Commander Perry not to return at the time he had said he would, lest the people become upset. It would take a long time because of the Emperor's death, it was stated, to bring together the nobles of Japan to consider the American requests. Just another case of delay, thought Perry, inasmuch as the government would probably carry on.

Perry was also in a hurry because he had reason to suspect that the French and Russians were trying to get to Yedo first, which would have complicated his problem considerably. The French frigate *Constantine* went out under sealed orders from Macao, near Canton, and Admiral Pontiatine, of the Russian Navy, had just arrived at Shanghai from Nagasaki. Perry was waiting for the storeship *Lexington* with presents for the Japanese aboard, but he decided that, despite the winter storms, he would put off from Yedo immediately. He sailed from Hong Kong on the *Susquehanna* on Jan. 14, 1854, with the *Pawhatan, Mississippi,* and the storeships *Lexington* and *Southampton.* The *Macedonian* and *Supply* had gone on before, the *Plymouth* was at Shanghai and, with the *Saratoga,* had orders to join the fleet at Lew Chew. So this time he had a fleet of nine ships, quite an imposing force, and he arrived at Yedo Bay with seven ships on Feb. 11.

This time he anchored about twelve miles beyond Uraga and about twenty miles from Yedo, which was at the head of the bay. The usual incidents took place. Japanese officials came aboard and tried to persuade him to return to Uraga, saying that the Emperor had appointed Uraga—not Nagasaki this time—as the meeting place and that the meeting could be held nowhere else. They were told that the meeting would be on shore near the place where the ships were anchored, that it was a safer anchorage than Uraga, and that the Commodore would not return. If necessary, he would go up the bay to Yedo itself. Much politeness. Refreshments were served, and the Japanese left in the most cordial manner. The next day officials came off and said that the commissioners who would discuss the treaty would arrive in a few days and receive the Commodore at Kama-kura, which is near the present city of Yokohama. The day before they had been adamant in specifying Uraga. They said the Emperor had named both places, although Kama-kura had not been named the day before. However, they were told that Kama-kura was also an unsafe anchorage. The Americans then suggested that the Commodore go to Yedo, only to be told with great firmness that he could not be received at Yedo. The Japanese also asked if the Commodore had received a message through the Dutch and were told that there was no authority to speak on that subject. More delay. More demands that the squadron go back to Uraga, which was farther away from Yedo than

the anchorage. To this Commodore Perry replied that his
instructions were to proceed to Yedo for the Emperor's answer
to the President's letter. While he despatched an officer to
Uraga to make known his views, Perry moved his squadron
still farther up the bay to a point opposite the town of Yoku-
hama, as it was then spelled, within eight miles of Yedo, or
Tokyo. This settled the matter, and arrangements were made
for the conference at Yoku-hama for fear that the ships would
go still closer to the capital. As Perry reported to the Secretary
of State:

"I was convinced that if I receded in the least from the
position first assumed by me, it would be considered by the
Japanese an advantage gained; and finding that I could be
induced to change a predetermined intention in one instance
they might rely on prevailing on me, by dint of perseverance,
to waver in most other cases pending the negotiations;
therefore, it seemed to be the true policy to hold out at all
hazards, and rather to establish for myself a character for
unreasonable obstinacy, than that of a yielding disposition.
I knew that upon the impression thus formed by them would
in a measure hinge the tenor of our future negotiations; and
the sequel will show that I was right in my conclusions. Indeed, in conducting all my business with these very sagacious
and deceitful people, I have found it profitable to bring to
my aid the experience gained in former and by no means
limited intercourse with the inhabitants of strange lands,
civilized and barbarian; and this experience has admonished
me that, with people of forms, it is necessary either to set all
ceremony aside, or to out Herod Herod in assumed personal
consequence and ostentation. . . .

"It is probable that arrogance may be charged against me
for persisting as I did, and against the judgment of all about
me, in changing the place of conference, and thus compelling
four princes of the Empire to follow the squadron, and sub-
jecting the government to the trouble and expense of erecting

another building; but I was simply adhering to a course of policy determined on after mature reflection, and which had hitherto worked so well."

Perry was undoubtedly stubborn, and in this report he shows that he overcame the opposition of his advisers in the fleet. It was undoubtedly a one man expedition and probably succeeded for that reason.

In a short time a treaty house was erected on the shore, and Perry, with all the formality and ceremony at his command, went ashore. There he was welcomed by the five august commissioners, nobles of the highest rank, well dressed and of the most courteous and formal deportment. At the head of the commission was Hayashi Daigaku-no-kami, prince councilor, a man of about fifty-five, handsome, but grave and saturnine. Ido, Prince of Tsusima, was about fifty. The third was the Prince of Mima-saki, about forty, a jolly fellow, by all accounts. There were also Udono and Matsusaki Mitchi-taro. After a day of polite conversation and some discussion of the treaty, it was arranged to bring ashore the presents sent by the government of the United States to the Japanese. When it was mentioned that presents would be returned, the Japanese were told that all presents received would become the property of the United States government, and the Americans were gravely informed that such was the case in any presents received by Japanese officials. The list of presents is interesting:

For the Emperor

    5 Hall's rifles
    3 Maynard's muskets
   12 cavalry swords
    6 artillery swords
    1 carbine
   20 army pistols
      Boxes of tea
    1 box of books
    1 box dressing cases

1 box perfumery
1 barrel whisky
1 cask wine
  A quantity of cherry cordials
  Baskets of champagne
1 telescope

For the commissioners

1 box of tea
  Baskets of champagne
1 box chinaware
  A quantity of maraschino

And where these went is not indicated, although some are marked "for distribution":

   2 carbines, cartridge boxes and belts, containing
120 cartridges
 10 Hall's rifles
 11 cavalry swords
   1 carbine, cartridge box and belt, and 60 cartridges
   2 telegraph instruments
   3 Francis's lifeboats
   1 locomotive and tender, passenger car and rails, complete
   1 volume Audubon's *Quadrupeds*
   4 volumes Audubon's *Birds of America*
    Several clocks
 10 ship's beakers, containing 100 gallons whisky
   8 baskets Irish potatoes
   3 stoves
   1 box containing 11 pistols
   1 box perfumery
    A quantity of cherry cordials
    Boxes standard United States balances
    Boxes standard United States bushels
    Boxes standard United States gallon measures
    Boxes standard United States yards
   1 box coast charts
   4 bundles telegraph wires
   1 box gutta percha wires
   4 boxes batteries
   1 box machine paper
   1 box zinc plates

1 box insulators
1 box connecting apparatus
1 box machine weights
1 box acid
1 box seed
    Large quantity of agricultural instruments, etc.

It might be well to insert here the list of presents received by the Americans, although they were not presented until later. Nothing could better illustrate the commercial difference between the two countries.

For the government of the United States of America, from the Emperor
    1 gold lacquered writing apparatus
    1 gold lacquered paper box
    1 gold lacquered book case
    1 lacquered writing table
    1 censer of bronze (cow shape), supporting silver flower and stand
    1 set waiters
    1 flower holder and stand
    2 brasiers
    10 pieces fine red pongee
    10 pieces white pongee
    5 pieces flowered crepe
    5 pieces red dyed figured crepe

From Hayashi, first commissioner

1 lacquered writing apparatus
1 lacquered paper box
1 box of paper
1 box flowered note paper
5 boxes stamped note and letter paper
4 boxes assorted sea shells, 100 in each
1 box of branch coral and feather in solver
1 lacquered chow-chow box
1 box, set of three, lacquered goblets
7 boxes cups and spoons and goblet cut from conch shells

From Ido, second commissioner

2 boxes lacquered waiters
2 boxes containing 20 umbrellas
1 box 30 coir brooms

From Izawa, third commissioner

1 piece red pongee
1 piece white pongee
8 boxes, 13 dolls
1 box bamboo woven articles
2 boxes bamboo stands

From Udono, fourth commissioner

3 pieces striped crepe
2 boxes porcelain cups
1 box, ten jars of soy

From Matsusaki, fifth commissioner

3 boxes, porcelain goblets
1 box figured matting
35 bundles oak charcoal

From Abi, first Imperial councilor

14 pieces striped figured silk

From each of the other five Imperial councilors

10 pieces striped figured silk (taffeta)

From the Emperor to Commodore Perry

1 lacquered writing apparatus
1 lacquered paper box
3 pieces red pongee
2 pieces white pongee
2 pieces flowered crepe
3 pieces figured dyed crepe

From commissioners to Captain H. A. Adams

3 pieces plain red pongee
2 pieces dyed figured crepe
20 sets lacquered cups and covers

From commissioners to Mr. M. Perry, Mr. Portman, and Mr. S. W. Williams, each

2 pieces red pongee
2 pieces dyed figured crepe
10 sets lacquered cups and covers

From commissioners to Mr. Gay, Mr. Danby, Mr. Draper, Dr. Morrow,
and Mr. J. P. Williams

1 piece, red dyed figured crepe
10 sets lacquered cups and covers

From Emperor to the squadron

200 bundles of rice, each five Japanese pecks
300 chickens

When the American presents were put on shore and un-
crated, workmen put up the telegraph apparatus, which
astonished the Japanese, and also put up the miniature railroad train and its tracks on a level bit of ground. The circular
track of the little locomotive was big enough for it to travel
at about twenty miles an hour. It was so small that a child
could hardly ride in it, but the Japanese insisted on riding on
the roof of the car and went whirling around, hanging on as
best they could, with their robes flying in the breeze. It must
have been a sight worth seeing, and one might even venture
the dangerous thought that perhaps the train eventually
found its way to the Emperor's palace yard.

During this period of amicable intercourse, which apparently took place whenever the Japanese and Americans were
not talking business, the members of Perry's party tried to
learn something of the customs of the people. They were met,
however, with a studied reserve that defied inquiry, although
the Japanese were very inquisitive themselves. It was the only
point, aside from their incredible proclivity to evade any direct
negotiation, with which the Americans had difficulty. Perhaps
the two were somewhat allied. It is also amusing, considering
the delicacy of their paintings, to know that the Americans
thought the Japanese very poor artists. There are indications
in the Perry report that the Americans were not at all times
unconscious of a sense of superiority that they resented very
much in their hosts. And there is a certain tendency to accuse
the Japanese of mendacity at any time that they opposed what

Perry desired. It was probably a question of Greek meeting Greek, and it would be interesting to know just what caused the Japanese to accede to most of the Commodore's demands. Certainly it was not fear. It is probable that Japan was about to burst out of its swaddling clothes anyway, that the curiosity of the people as to the rest of the world had been aroused by what they had heard through the Dutch merchants, and that their national ambition to be an important part of the family of nations was beginning to ferment. It is hardly believable that Perry got all he wanted merely because he insisted upon it. If the Japanese had been determined to remain insular, they could have done so.

Whatever the influences brought to bear upon the Japanese, the negotiations went on until a treaty was concluded that satisfied both parties. This arranged that the port of Simoda, in the principality of Idzu, and the port of Hakodadi, in the principality of Matsmai, be granted as ports for the reception of American ships, where they should be supplied with whatever Japan could furnish them. It was also provided that when crews of wrecked ships came ashore in Japan they should be taken to these ports and turned over to their own countrymen, and it was specified that they should not be restricted, as were the Dutch and Chinese at Nagasaki. Consular agents might also be appointed after the expiration of eighteen months, although this was a provision to which the Japanese strenuously objected and to which they were won over only when it was pointed out to them that it would be as advantageous for Japan as for the United States. This treaty was signed by the President of the United States and unanimously ratified by the Senate.

And so Japan opened its doors to the Occident and acquired its superficial Western culture. It may be worth noting in this respect that members of the expedition observed that:

"In the practical and mechanical arts, the Japanese show great dexterity; and when the rudeness of their tools and their

imperfect knowledge of machinery are considered, the per-
fection of their manual skill appears marvellous. Their handi-
craftsmen are as expert as any in the world, and with a freer
development of the inventive powers of the people, the
Japanese would not remain long behind the most successful
manufacturing nations. Their curiosity to learn the results of
the material progress of other people, and their readiness in
adapting them to their own uses, would soon, under a less
exclusive policy of government, which isolates them from
national communion, raise them to a level with the most
favored countries. Once possessed of the acquisition of the
past and present of the civilized world, the Japanese would
enter as powerful competitors in the race for mechanical
success in the future."

That was only a little more than eighty years ago. Again
it may be remarked, Commodore Perry started something.

The Last Pacific Frontier

MOST of our story has been laid in the South Seas, from the Horn up the coast of South America, across the ocean, through the myriad islands that dot the Pacific so thickly that, as the eye wanders across a chart, one wonders how a ship ever made a passage there without running aground, across the trade routes from the Horn to Canton and from Acapulco to Manila. There was romance there, if one wishes to look at disaster, suffering, battle, and sudden death as such, as well as riches and fame and discovery. But the last treasure coast of the Pacific was the northwest coast of North America, the last Pacific frontier.

There was reason for this. After a ship rounded the Horn, it hit the trade winds or drifted in the doldrums or perhaps struck a sharp and terrific hurricane. But in the North Pacific, along the coast from what is now northern California to Alaska and the Aleutians and up into Bering Strait, there were fog and cold and ice and biting weather that made scurvy ridden sailors even weaker than they could have been in the warm southern latitudes. But men went there, for they were drawn by the same motives that sent them south and west, the allure of unknown lands, of possible passages across a continent of wilderness, of rich skins for sale in the Eastern market, and of gold. The whole history of the Pacific is summed up on the northwest coast, all its desperate seeking for the unknown, all its greed, all its daring.

This search for geographical discoveries and riches and the development of commerce have made the northwest coast the scene of some of the greatest sea adventures on all that mighty ocean that Balboa glimpsed from his mountain peak. And it has witnessed, as perhaps no other coast, the growth of oceancrossing vessels, from the great Manila galleons that wallowed along far offshore to the better ships of Cook and Wilkes and Gray and Vancouver, to the California clippers, the fastest and most beautiful sailing craft ever built by man, and to the wide winged clipper planes that now put out from San Francisco for their six day passage to Hong Kong, their motors roaring, their cockpits filled with instruments that would have made the ancient navigators giddy, and their fuselages filled with passengers drowsing in comfortable chairs. How a luckless captain, running down the coast in a galleon filled with pieces of eight, silk, tea, scurvy, and vermin, would have stared if he could have seen one of those vast birds pass over him faster than the wind of the typhoon.

The early voyages to the northwest coast were, as usual, the union of desires for discovery and profit. The Spaniards and the Dutch and the English had found gold in the South Seas, and it was being perceived that this great ocean presented more opportunity for profit to the daring than any other ocean in the world. And there were fabulous tales about it. The early map makers delighted in putting on paper lands that they said must exist, passages through America in which they had faith, continents to the south, and open oceans to the north that they knew must exist to keep the earth from turning over. All navigators had heard of the Strait of Anian, just as they had heard of the Strait named after Juan de Fuca, that imaginative sailor who gave his name to the majestic opening to Vancouver. There was a northeast passage; there was a Gamaland to the north, between Asia and America; there were countless hopes and beliefs and absurdities, scientifically supported, concerning the seas off the northwest coast.

Peter the Great of Russia had heard of Gamaland. This ambitious ruler, who had worked in the shipyards at Amsterdam, started that Russian invasion of the Pacific that was finally checked by the Japanese, which explains why to this day the Japanese do not like the Russians, either commercially or politically. He had in his service, as he lay dying, a man named Vitus Bering, a Dane, after whom Bering Strait is named. Peter told Bering to cross Siberia, build ships, explore the Arctic coast, and learn what lay between Asia and America. And, although Bering was primarily a discoverer, it was due to the skins he found that Russia stretched eastward until she nearly commanded the fur industry along the northwest coast and then annexed Alaska.

Bering's task was one that would have daunted most men. He was forty-four, in the prime of his life, and, having fallen into disfavor, was living in Finland, from which he was recalled. His instructions were very simple. They were to cross Siberia to Kamchatka, build boats, and sail east until he found something new. He did just that. It took him three years to cross from the west coast of Europe to the east coast of Asia. He had to cross a wilderness, carry with him all his food and supplies, except what he could get en route, and he even used dog sleds at times. Two of his lieutenants followed his trail by the dead horses they found along the way. He had built a ship to get from the mainland to Kamchatka, even before he built the two ships in which he sailed from the west. He had little iron, and the ships were partly tied together, or wooden pegs were used to hold their planking. But all this he did, and on July 9, 1728, he sailed from Kamchatka with forty-four men and three lieutenants.

Bering's voyage was successful because the great seaman was left to his own devices. He left his mark all along the coast, and, as a result of his two voyages, the islands and points of eastern Asia and the Aleutians are dotted with names that he gave to them. The track of this Russian expedition and the one following may not be on the maps, but the names of Bering and his men still mark its passage. There is none who would change them. Bering sailed past St. Lawrence Island and along the coast to where the shore turned back to the northwestward at 67 degrees and 18 minutes and proved to him that there was no connection between Asia and America.

This was his greatest discovery, although he did not realize it, and his claims were ridiculed for years later. He did not find Gamaland. He almost reached America, but fog hid it from his view. All Bering returned with was the knowledge that Asia did not extend to America, and, if he could only have known, that would have been quite enough. But there must be land he thought somewhere there to the east because of the driftwood of strange trees, the seaweed, and the birds. He was laughed at when he returned to St. Petersburg, but he obtained command of a second expedition in 1730.

His second voyage was one of the most disastrous that ever went north, equaled perhaps by that of the American naval officer De Long, who went through the strait discovered by Bering to find death on the Siberian shore. Russia's ambitions in the Arctic have always been on a lavish scale, and when Bering put forth again he was accompanied by a group of scientists and other wise men who would have confounded any explorer, even if he had authority. But poor Bering, being a Dane, was this time put under the authority of a council of savants who would decide what he should do and who could veto his decisions. It was an impossible position for a commander of such a dangerous venture. There is something strangely reminiscent of Bering's troubles in the difficulties Soviet army commanders have, in finding themselves saddled with Bolshevik commissars, without whose approval they can do nothing. Bering's commissars, who believed in Gamaland, brought disaster to him, as they probably did to the Red Army in Finland. (As a matter of fact, as one learns of Perry's experiences in Japan with the government officials and of Bering's trials with his Russian advisers, modern history takes on a rather moth-eaten appearance. These things have happened before.)

On June 4, 1741, Bering set out in the *St. Peter*, accompanied by the *St. Paul*, from the Bay of Avacha on the east coast of Kamchatka. It was eight years since the expedition had left St. Petersburg, and it had cost $200,000, which was a lot of money even before Admiral Byrd began exploring. One of Bering's group was Louis la Croyére d'Isle, member of the family of a famous map maker who showed Gamaland on his maps. So Gamaland must be found, if only to save the family reputation. Bering knew it did not exist, and so did Chirikoff, commander of the *St. Paul*, his first assistant. But hunt Gamaland they must; so they yielded to the council and sailed south southeast.

Out of the north came fog and storm, and the ships were driven apart, not to meet again. The *St. Paul* returned home, but not the *St. Peter*. After searching for a time for the *St. Paul*, Bering turned northward, constantly harried by the council, and after a time raised high mountains that were certainly not Kamchatka. This was an unknown continent, and Bering knew he was in unknown seas. Icebergs floated about; on shore were ferns and flowers. The ship put into an island to fill her water casks; the scientists went ashore under the valiant naturalist, Stella, but when the dark fog came rolling down on them and the wind sprang up Bering ordered the ship to sea, this time without consulting his officers. They were 2,000 miles from home and had provisions for only three months. Bering knew that the better part of wisdom was to head for home while there was time and to try again.

But the coast fooled them. It did not trend north, as it should have, but south. Instead of cruising along a coast that would have taken them across Bering Strait to St. Lawrence Island and back to land with which they were familiar, the coast trended to the south. They did not know it, but they were coasting along the Alaskan peninsula and the Aleutian Islands. The sailors became sick with scurvy. On Aug. 30 there were only twenty-five casks of water left; provisions were running low. One sailor, Shumagin, died as he was being taken ashore to an island where it was thought rest and strength might be found, and his name is on that island to this day.

They found only brackish water and a few antiscorbutic plants. Fire was seen through the fog, and the rumbling of voices was heard in the storm. A few Indians were seen, but they fled. They put to sea and ran into a storm, so that the ship had to flee before it. The sailors were exhausted from disease. The ship was coated with ice and hoar frost, vapor rose from the sea, and the cries of walruses and seals came through the mist. It must have seemed to the despairing sailors like something out of Dante's *Inferno*. They were lost and hopeless. A sight of the sun was impossible.

Then they saw land that they hoped at first might be Kamchatka but that turned out to be two islands. On one of them the ship was driven ashore, and it is called Bering Island. There they dug holes in the dirt and made huts of tarpaulins and stuffed the cracks with the furs of an animal they found, a queer animal that seemed part beaver and part seal. It was a sea otter. They were halfway between the Aleutians and Kamchatka, but they did not know that. They did not know where they were. The clever savants who had got Bering into this fix were quarreling; the others were just desperate. They killed what creatures they could and ate their flesh and used their skins for coverings and for making tents. Their only other food was grease and moldy flour. Bering was brought ashore, for it had begun to snow, and placed in a sand pit under a tent. It was not very cold but so wet that everything rotted.

Poor Bering never left his sand pit. He became weaker and weaker and finally begged to have the sand that blew from the sides left over him because it made him warmer. And there, on Dec. 8, 1741, over sixty years of age, worn with suffering and broken in heart because of the disasters that he knew were avoidable, racked with scurvy, he died. He was buried on a hillside with others and a Greek cross placed above his grave. He was a great discoverer, one of the least known, although his name will always be on the maps above the strait that he found separated Asia from America.

Eventually the men who were left built a boat from the timbers of the *St. Peter* and made their way to Kamchatka. And with them they took several hundred skins of the sea otter. It had a black fur that showed a silvery gray when rubbed, and it was worth from $40 to $1,000 in the China market, according to the number and quality of skins available. They yielded a fortune to the survivors.

It was fifty years after Bering that Captain Cook, hunting for the northeast passage, traded with the natives around Nootka and Cook's inlet for sea otter skins of inferior quality. Since Cook spent a long time hunting for a way through America to the east, vindicating Bering's decision that there was no land connection between Asia and America and then going back to the Sandwich Islands, most of the skins were spoiled when Cook's ships reached Canton. And yet the half rotted part of what they returned with brought the sum of $10,000. As one of Cook's officers tells it, his commander having been killed in the Sandwich Islands:

"A brisk trade had been carrying on with the Chinese for

the sea-otter skins which had every day been rising in their value. One of our seamen sold his stock alone for eight hundred dollars; and a few prime skins, which were clean and had been well-preserved, were sold for one hundred and twenty each. The whole amount of the value in specie and goods that was got for the furs in both ships, I am confident did not fall short of £2,000. sterling; and it was generally supposed that at least two-thirds of the quantity we had got from the Americans were spoiled and worn out, or had been given away and otherwise disposed of in Kamchatka. The rage with which our seamen were possessed to return to Cook's River, and by another cargo of skins to make their fortunes at one time, was not far short of mutiny."

And well it might have been, for these skins brought back by the men of Bering and Cook—both commanders being dead, strangely enough—started a new fur trade. The Russians had been busy in the northern islands for some time and were destined to spread eastward, at first obtaining their loot with the most callous cruelty to the natives.

But news of the wealth brought back by Cook's men also reached New England. The Hudson's Bay Company was at this time stretching across Canada, and the call for sea otter skins acted very much as later did the discovery of gold in California. A little group of canny Bostonians decided that it would be a very wise thing to send out some ships to Alaska and the Aleutians while there were still some sea otters left. So they outfitted two ships, with only one of which we are concerned, the *Columbia*, Captain Robert Gray. Gray started out on the *Lady Washington*, a much smaller ship than the *Columbia*, but he was so much more daring and successful than Captain Kendrick of the *Columbia* that he took over the larger vessel when they reached the Pacific coast. How this was done is not clear, but apparently Kendrick was perfectly willing to relinquish the leadership of this dangerous adventure to the younger man.

Gray is little known to Americans, even to Bostonians. He was a Rhode Islander who had served in the Revolutionary Navy. Fifty thousand dollars were invested in the ships by Charles Bulfinch and five associates. In the fall of 1787 the ships left Boston, rounded the Horn, and while Kendrick in the *Columbia* had to stop for repairs Gray kept on going. He met the English Captain Meares, who had been up the Strait of Fuca, which Cook had decided did not exist, and which later Gray sailed up for fifty miles. After a few trifling adventures he sailed for Canton in the *Columbia*, having taken her over from Kendrick and sold his skins. He reached Boston on Aug. 11, 1790, the first American ship to sail around the world, on a voyage of almost 50,000 miles.

The sea otter had not sold well at Canton, because the market was glutted; so Gray was sent back in the *Columbia* to try again. He apparently got plenty of sea otter, for there was no report of disappointment as the result of this voyage. Kendrick was sent to China in the *Lady Washington* with furs, and Gray prepared to winter south of Nootka. Here he built a small vessel, the *Adventure*, to collect skins for the *Columbia*, the *Adventure* being the second ship built on this coast and the first American ship built on the Pacific.

When he turned south in the spring of 1792, he met Captain George Vancouver, the famous English navigator, who had been persuaded that there was no River of the West, as the Spaniards had reported. Vancouver went on to do his thorough job of surveying, but Gray went back to Cape Disappointment, where he was sure the river entered the sea, if it existed. He found a bar where the waters of the river met the sea waves with a roar like thunder and was sure that he had found what he sought. Waiting for a favorable wind, he drove at what looked like a channel and made his way into what is the Columbia River. When he sailed out again, he went north to get more skins, sold the little *Adventure* for seventy-five otter skins, and pointed for China on Oct. 3.

He had 3,000 otter skins below decks and 15,000 other pelts. A good businessman and hunter, Gray, and also one of the great little known American navigators and explorers. When the Columbia is seen, think of the ship captain out of Boston, one of those who commanded more than 100 American ships that visited the northwest coast before 1812.

Most of these ships were hunting the seal and sea otter for the Russian-American Fur Company, and they ranged all the way up the California coast to Alaska. One of their favorite places of sail was the then sleepy Spanish town of San Francisco, which had been discovered by an overland expedition from down the coast. It was not an important port, for Monterey was the official port for the colony, but its seals made it important for a time. It seems impossible now to the visitor who watches a few seals bark on the rocks in front of the Cliff House, but there was a time in 1810 when an American ship took 73,000 seals off the Farallone Islands. Sea otters were so common that they were caught in the bay, the Russians following them in canoes into the inner harbor. This period did not last long, for the seals and otters were almost exterminated, and the Russians were finally overwhelmed by the Indians at Sitka and so discouraged that they were glad to sell Alaska to the United States eventually for $7,000,000. Now they possess two seal islands in the north, on one of which Bering died—all that is left of their once great east Pacific empire in which they challenged Spain, England, and the United States and in one year took out pelts worth the amount paid for Alaska. They didn't know there was gold there.

But it was gold that brought the next great rush of ships to the northwest coast and brought the California clippers, those magnificent sailing ships. At this time American ships were all over the Pacific. There were whalers on every whaling ground in the great sea, hundreds of them, and sealers in the far southern islands, and tea and opium ships that made fast voyages to Canton. But the California clippers, built to meet an immediate necessity, beat them all. There had been clippers before, of course, schooners and brigs of unusual design that plied in the Atlantic trade and to China, but when the gold rush hit California there was a demand for a new type of ship that could carry sail, make time, and handle a cargo that often paid for the ship in one voyage.

It was in 1846 that California was taken over by the Union after the Mexican War, and it was in 1848 that Sutter discovered gold in Sacramento Valley. San Francisco, up to that time, had been visited by sealers and whalers and had a small trade in hides, tallow, and horns. From Apr. 1, 1847, to April in 1848, two ships and nine whalers sailed in through the Golden Gate. But in 1849, 775 ships cleared from Atlantic ports for San Francisco. One sailed from Cleveland, Ohio, via the St. Lawrence. Many of them did not arrive, but in that year 91,405 passengers landed in San Francisco from all over the world. It was the greatest gold rush in history.

The effect on Pacific shipping was devastating as well as stimulating. Ships were abandoned as soon as they reached port; their sails were left unfurled; they were anchored so that they drifted together and fouled; and some even went up on the beach, where they were turned into living quarters for the homeless people ashore. Officers and crews vanished for the gold fields, fighting to be the first ashore. The ships were turned into hospitals, hotels, prisons, storeships, and many of them just rotted. The hull of one was used as the basement for a hotel, and years later bottles of champagne were dug out of the hold in perfect condition. Captains paid seamen from $125 to $200 a month to get a ship out of harbor. Shades of the Seamans Union!

Provisions and other supplies went to tremendous figures. Beef, pork, and flour brought from $40 to $60 a barrel; tea, coffee, and sugar, $4 a pound; spirits, $10 to $40 a quart, with other things in proportion. What did it matter when there was no other food and miners came into town to pour gold dust for supplies out of their pouches? Freight rates, naturally, jumped to fabulous figures. The steamships that were connected with Atlantic shipping across the Isthmus of Panama could not handle anything but passengers, mail, and light freight; so all supplies had to be shipped around the Horn. Some ships received as much as $60 a ton for cargo, and, since sail was then faster than steam, it was natural that men who wished to make a quick profit, who did not know how long the rush would last, should turn to sail. And out of this demand, between 1850 and 1860, arose the clippers whose records even now make many a steamship look like a shabby traveler.

The clipper ship had originated in the Atlantic trade and had been a slow evolution in a period when American ships were the fastest things afloat. They went to England and to China, and their slim lines and their captains' habits of carrying canvas in all sorts of weather had made them the envy of other nations. Nearly all the famous California clippers, about 160 of them, were built between 1850 and 1854. Nearly all of them were launched along the New England coast. After leaving California, they returned in ballast around the Horn or took on tea in China for London or New York.

Those who know the harbor front of New York now would not believe that in the California clipper days ships were being constructed all along the East River front, with all kinds of sailmakers' lofts and chandlers' shops to supply them. The smell of new timber, tar, and hemp filled the air. People used to go down to see the ships built and listen to the hammer of sledges, mauls, and corking mallets. The American people knew their ships in those days; they were bred in the tradition of the sea, with a rich maritime history about them, a history filled with tales of adventure and exploration and quick voyages by hard-riding skippers. The ships were well rigged and well outfitted. Experienced sailors of that day were given better working conditions and better pay on American ships than on any others. However, the clippers were often manned in part by mere adventurers bound for the gold rush, and they were not treated so well. A description of getting one of those ships to sea with a half drunken crew, does not read politely.

The peculiarity of the clippers lay in their tall masts and their slim, sharp lines, which enabled them to make fast and regular passages. They could reach for the wind aloft better than the older types of ship, they could be coaxed with a wisp of air, and, in a gale and heavy seaway, they were wet, but they kept going. They might bury their bows in a high sea, but they slid through it as the bluff-bowed ships never could do. And they had the hardest-driving captains the world had ever known. Any time a clipper ship captain reefed his topsails it was blowing more than an ordinary gale. They often carried on with royals and studding sails when ships of other nations were under reefed topsails. But many of the best of them never lost a yard in doing so. The skippers did not sleep much; some of them seldom did more than change their clothes and caught cat naps between watches during all the bad weather.

Thirty-one California clippers were launched during 1851, and all the large shipyards were represented. Perhaps one of the most famous of these ships was the *Flying Cloud*, built by Donald McKay. She was a beautiful ship, of 1,783 tons register, 225 feet long, 40 feet 8 inches in the beam, and drew 21½ feet. Her mainyard was 82 feet and her mainmast 88 feet in length. She was commanded by Captain Josiah Perkins Creesy—and if that isn't a Yankee skipper name, nominate one—who was born at Marblehead in 1814. She once made a run on the voyage around the Horn to California of 374 miles in twenty-four hours, the fastest day's run under steam or sail that had been made up to that time, exceeding by 42 miles the best day's run made by a mail steamship on the Atlantic.

In 1851 the first clipper to arrive from New York at San Francisco in less than 110 days was the *Seaman*. She did it in 107 days. The second to arrive was the *Surprise*, which wandered in 96 days from New York. She had sailed 16,308 miles since leaving New York and had reefed topsails only twice. Not that it didn't blow. Her cargo filled a manifest twenty-five feet long, and her freight brought $78,000, about what she cost to build.

One of the great ocean races to California shows what these great clipper ships could do. The *Raven*, the *Typhoon*, and the *Sea Witch* sailed from New York for California in 1851 within a few days of each other, from Aug. 1 to Aug. 6. The *Sea Witch* kept her lead at the equator, crossing on Aug. 30, and was followed closely the next day by the other two ships. Off Cape St. Rogue they stood away for a dash of 3,000 miles and at 50 degrees south took in their studding sail booms and skysail yards, put extra lashings on the boats, spare spars and skylights for the thrash around the Horn. With reefed topsails, taking in sail and letting it out, they kept within sight of each other in one of the best ocean races ever known. The *Sea Witch* and the *Raven* were ahead, driving through the heavy seas, making tack for tack, carrying all the sail they could bear, and the *Typhoon* was not far behind. The *Sea Witch* and the *Raven* rounded the Horn side by side, with the other ship only twenty-four hours behind. From there to the equator the *Sea Witch* tore through the water, and crossed the equator two days ahead of the *Raven* and four days ahead of the *Typhoon*. But then sail power did its part, and the *Typhoon* headed the *Sea Witch* on the trip to port, and the *Raven* also headed her for the first time. The *Typhoon* went through the Golden Gate on Nov. 18th, 106 days from Sandy Hook; the *Raven*, on the nineteenth, 105 days from Sandy Hook; and the *Sea Witch*, on Nov. 20, 110 days from Sandy Hook. But the *Sea Witch* was then five years old; she had been strained and had lost some speed through absorbing water, as all wooden ships of that period did.

There was another race in 1853 in which the *Flying Fish* made the trip in ninety-two days and the *John Gilpin* in ninety-three days, a race of 15,000 miles, in which the difference of time was only twenty-four hours, or a difference of six seconds a mile over the entire distance. What would Drake or Cook or Dampier have given for a ship of that caliber!

These California clippers lasted until 1860 and overlapped the era of steam, for steam came to the Pacific before these clippers, strange as it may seem. The coming of steam was before the Mexican War, before gold was discovered in California. But it was many years before steam established superiority over sail. It was only thirty years after the great Russian-American Fur Company collapsed while the Pacific was still the happy hunting ground of sealers and whalers, that the paddle-wheel steamship of wooden construction puffed its way around through the Straits of Magellan to revolutionize Pacific transport.

It came about in this way. William Wheelwright, of Newburyport, Massachusetts, was a ship captain who was appointed United States Consul at Valparaiso. Communications on the west coast of South America were not very good, and Wheelwright started a shipping company. In 1835 he decided to put steamers—which had been found practical in the Atlantic—on a run between South American ports. Two wooden paddle-wheel steamers, the *Chili* and *Peru*, of about 700 tons, 198 feet long and 50 feet over the paddle boxes, were built in England and came through the Straits of Magellan in 1840. These were not the first steamships in the Pacific; a smaller steamer, the *Telica*, had been tried on the coast in 1825 but proved a failure, the owner blowing up himself and the ship. But the two new steamships belonging to the Pacific Steam Navigation Company were the first successful vessels ever to move under steam power on Magellan's ocean. The coaling difficulties were serious, and Wheelwright had to open his own mines. But he weathered the storm and finally had a bimonthly service from Valparaiso to Panama, where there was a connection across the Isthmus with Atlantic steamships.

When, in 1855, the Panama Railway was opened across the Isthmus, the business of the company was greatly increased.

The annexation of California stimulated the idea of trade by sea with the Pacific coast. In 1848 a contract was made with the United States government to carry mails to Panama and then from Panama to San Francisco. This steamship company, organized by C. H. Aspinwall on the Pacific side, was the beginning of the Pacific Mail Line. The first steamer, the *California*, sailed from New York in 1848. She was also a wooden paddle-wheel steamer, and she was welcomed at San Francisco with wild excitement, the first steamer ever to puff its way through the Golden Gate. She was followed by the *Pacific* and the *Oregon*, the latter built in 1845. They made good passages around Cape Horn, which is to be marveled at when one imagines the buffetings their paddles must have had in that tempestuous sea. These two lines representing the Law and Aspinwall interests amalgamated in the Pacific Mail Company, which for years was the dominating steamship line in the Pacific. In the gold rush decade, the line carried 175,000 passengers and brought back gold worth $200,000,000.

Now there are steamships running from the east coast to Panama and New Zealand and Japan and the East Indies. When they first puffed their smoke over the Pacific, the ocean was filled with sailing ships, clippers, and whalers and sealers. But now they have the great ocean to themselves. Even the steam schooners from the lumber camps on the northwest coast are not so important as these vessels that leisurely leave their docks and steam out into what was once an unknown ocean over tracks that their captains know so thoroughly that they do not worry about their ships except in a storm. Steam has vanquished sail; the clippers are gone, but the graceful passenger ships and the lumbering freighters carry on the work that the Manila galleons began.

But there is another chapter in this conquest of the northwest Pacific, perhaps the most dramatic of all. That is the flight of the clipper planes from San Francisco to China. For the world has moved so fast since the days of Wilkes and Cook and Vancouver, and they were not so long ago, that now men spurn the waves and take to the air in craft that weigh more than some of Magellan's tiny ships. It is odd that the widest ocean in the world should have been the first to be spanned by commercial aircraft, but so it is. Perhaps the reason lies in that name Pacific. It was a testing station for flights over its more stormy brother, the Atlantic. The air above its waves has borne most of these roaring ships safely, although two have been lost, and when an airplane is lost at sea it is lost even more thoroughly than one of the wooden ships of the early explorers. But day by day and month by month, the passage becomes more sure, and, where Magellan took months to cross the Pacific, the deep-throated clippers cross it in five days.

There were many years of preparation for these flights. The little company that had a tiny hop across water from Havana to Key West, ninety miles, has grown until it almost encircles South America, flies the Pacific, and carries people to Europe in not much more than a day. It was built up with instruments such as the early navigators never dreamed of. What would Magellan have thought of a gyrocompass, a radio direction finder, an octant instead of his astrolabe, a thing on his ear that would give him information as to weather ahead and direction? Magellan, seeking blindly, was glad, when a drop of rain fell on his canvas, that he could catch it for drinking water. What would he have thought of 4,000 to 5,000 horsepower driving him through the air at a rate of more than 150 miles an hour? How would he have enjoyed a Thermos jug of warm coffee or iced tea, of soup, or a whole dinner kept warm for his convenience? What would he have made of the bridge of a flying clipper, with its engineering panels, its controls, its constant checks against a wrong course, of its calm captains at a wheel that they seldom touch because a mechanical device holds their ship steady for them? When one thinks of that hard-bitten navigator with his rotten water tanks, his maggoty food, his sick and disheartened crew after three months at sea, the clipper ships come into a new perspective as a measure of man's progress.

It was not so long ago that that first flight was made, only Nov. 22, 1935. The captain was one who should also go down in history with the pioneers of the Pacific, Captain Eddie Musick. Musick was an unobtrusive sort of person. He was the first chief pilot Pan American Airways ever had, when that ninety mile hop between Havana and Key West represented their entire route. He was a good pilot, and he grew with the needs of the company. He mastered all the intricate instruments needed for flying; he became a master mariner of the air, the first.

Musick took the first plane across the Pacific; the big wings hummed their way to Honolulu, to Midway Island, to Wake Island, to Guam, to Manila, and there the great craft came down on what is one of the finest bays in the world. It was the last conquest of the great ocean.

Musick died, flying near Samoa, on a new route that was to be opened to New Zealand from San Francisco, when an explosion blew his ship to bits. It was to have been his last flight.

And now let us take our leave of them, these great-hearted adventurers, these men who can look the unknown in the face and stare it down, these buccaneers and pirates, these hard-trading and hard-fighting Spaniards and Dutchmen and English, these explorers who sought the impossible and in seeking it found something even more worth while. They had their faults, all of them, but they had the inner instinct that makes men do great deeds. They suffered greatly and often came back empty handed. Some brought back things that were of great price and words of new places that moved nations. They had their faults, but who has not? And so to them all, gentlemen adventurers, hail and farewell.

Index